Richard and Bookey Peek are professional safari guides. After an idyllic childhood in the Bvumba mountains and ten years spent travelling the world, Bookey became a lawyer, a profession she was only too happy to leave for a life in the bush. She was a winner of the prestigious Africa Geographic Travel Writer of the Year competition in 2003.

Richard Peek was born in Zimbabwe and raised on a farm in Mashonaland. He spent fourteen years in the Department of National Parks and Wildlife Management as a game ranger and then as an ecologist, after obtaining a degree in zoology. He later became curator of mammals at the National Museum of Natural History. Winner of two Agfa photographic awards, Richard has published his work in magazines, calendars, travel brochures and publications such as the *Handbook of Birds of the World*.

For the incomparable Mausi
And for Dad, who always told us to
"press on – regardless"
And did just that.
With all my love

Wild Honey

Every day is a fresh beginning,
Listen my soul to the glad refrain.
And in spite of old sorrows
And older sinning,
Troubles forecasted
And possible pain,
Take heart with the day and begin again.

Susan Coolidge

Wild Honey

More Stories from an African Wildlife Sanctuary

BOOKEY PEEK

with photographs and illustrations by
RICHARD PEEK

Published in the United Kingdom in 2009 by Max Press,
an imprint of Little Books Ltd, London W11 3QW

10 9 8 7 6 5 4 3 2 1

A CIP catalogue record for this book is available from the British
Library.

ISBN 13 978 1 906251 20 8

Printed in the UK by CPI Bookmarque, Croydon, CR0 4TD

Foreword

They say everyone has a book in them, but the real test is if they can sustain the effort and produce a second. Bookey Peek's first book, a cracker called *All The Way Home: Stories from an African Wildlife Sanctuary*, described with wit and emotion the joys and traumas of raising an orphan warthog at Stone Hills, the Peeks' game sanctuary in the Matobo Hills of Zimbabwe. In the sequel, *Wild Honey*, she focuses on an even more challenging subject: the honey badger. An almost mythical creature in Africa, this flatheaded, pocket-sized dynamo with attitude has the square-jawed bearing of a pit bull and a reputation to match. But that is only half the story. The Peeks dig beneath the surface to try and discover the true nature of the honey badger by raising an orphaned cub, and in so doing offer us a unique insight into the character and individuality of these much-maligned animals.

A feeling of attachment to both wild and domestic animals is part of what makes us human. In *Wild Honey*, Bookey Peek explores this connection on many levels: the fact that Africa is the ancestral home of all human beings; the rich tapestry of cultures that connects Africans to their roots and to the earth; and that every animal is an individual, over and above the indelible attributes that define each species. In a quest for certainties, science tries to analyse every aspect of an animal's behaviour, but the results – however fascinating – are only part of the story. By contrast, Bookey Peek illustrates perfectly the fact that the beauty of nature is in the beholding of it, and that its wild inhabitants are uniquely formed for their place in nature. They are complete. And however much we think we know, there is always something new to be gleaned from the natural world.

The view from the Peek's bedroom window is achingly beautiful: giant slabs of granite set against rich green forest with open grassland dotted with giraffes and impalas, all capturing the essence of being on safari. The view might be perfect, but this is Zimbabwe, a land that has been torn apart by violence and land invasions, where hunger and sky rocketing inflation are the norm. In *Wild Honey*, Bookey Peek deftly weaves together all the elements that made her first book such a resounding success: love and loss, the allure of life in the African bush, the joy of nurturing an orphan wild animal back to health and freedom and the harsh reality of living through the seemingly endless troubles facing the country. Running through the whole tale are the humour, stubbornness and stoicism needed to survive in a place called 'home', a home that can be taken away from you at any moment.

You have to love Africa – to have lived and breathed it – to write like this. *Wild Honey* is irresistible, in turn heart-rending, funny and revealing, and will strike a chord with all who love Africa, its people and its wildlife. I panicked every time I mislaid my copy (everyone else wanted to read it too), eager to find out what new mischief the Peeks' young honey badger was up to, or whether the family would have to abandon their beautiful home in the Matobo Hills in the wake of the chaos that is Zimbabwe today.

Richard Peeks's charming photographs and illustrations, accompanying the text, provoke a fascinating insight into life at Stone Hills and its wild inhabitants. If reading this book doesn't leave you wanting to take a safari to Africa, then nothing will.

Jonathan Scott

Malalangwe Lodge

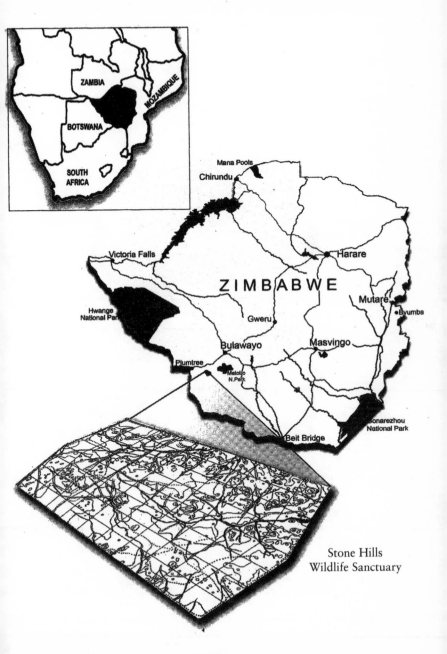

Stone Hills
Wildlife Sanctuary

Chapter One

If a man does not keep pace with his companions perhaps it is because he hears a different drummer. Let him step to the music which he hears. THOREAU

Watching my husband at the head of the dinner table, thoughtfully combing his beard with a fork, once again reminded me how crucial it was for our son David to have some contact with normality before it was too late.

When he was too young to protest, I'd encouraged him to play with other children who visited our safari lodge in Zimbabwe's Matobo Hills. It was only during his first year at school in Bulawayo, an hour away from home, that David made his feelings quite clear by placing a sign on his bedroom door reading: *Only Peepul who belive animals can talk can enter.*

And to reinforce the message for those who missed it the first time, there was another scrap of paper underneath it on which he had written: *Bugga off!*

He was, I am afraid to say, a chip off the old block.

Those who choose to live in the bush usually do so

1

because they want to get as far away from other people as possible, so it's not surprising that some of the most brilliant safari guides, like my husband, march to a different beat when it comes to socialising.

Before plunging into the hospitality industry, we should have listened more carefully to those in the know, like the owner of a well-known lodge in the Zambezi valley. We were having dinner under a magnificent Natal mahogany, watching the moon come up, while a herd of elephants splashed in the river below us.

I told her how much I envied her. 'Oh, yes, it's a wonderful life,' she said. 'But you can't do this job unless you really like people.'

Well, we didn't. Individuals, of course, but not the faceless masses. Even Parkinson and the Dalai Lama can't possibly like *everyone*. It wouldn't be healthy. In any case, I was referring to life on the banks of the Zambezi, not to the guests, nor to the booking agents on whom we relied to give us business.

One of the lady agents who came for the weekend on a 'famil' (as we old hands called it) complained that our waiter had produced the same pink dip before dinner for two nights running. To which I replied that she must have been mistaken, because I clearly recalled seeing green spots in it by the second night. It was incredible. In a world faced with the melting of polar ice-caps and the sixth great extinction, the fate of our safari lodge hung in the balance over the colour of a cottage cheese dip. She went on to make the quite correct but rather mystifying observation that the toilet seats wouldn't stay up.

Our lodge-keeping days were littered with final straws, like the large lady squeezed like bratwurst into black lycra shorts who asked to meet our warthog piglet,

Poombi. We followed her as she flip-flopped down the drive, her thighs swishing.

Rich nudged me. 'Forget the matches, we could light the barbeque with the sparks,' he said in a loud whisper. I grimaced, but there was no point in protesting – Rich has a habit of making the most appropriate remarks at the most inopportune moments.

We found our piglet tucking into a pile of vegetables in our front garden, and the lady bent down to have a better look.

'Oh my!' she snorted through a haze of cigarette smoke, 'Aren't you a funny-looking thing?'

Luckily for her, Poombi had a mouthful of cabbage at the time and couldn't respond in kind.

Worse than that, I've heard warthogs described as a 'disgrace to nature', when the truth is that they are an evolutionary triumph, perfectly adapted for a life in the African savannah – unlike the lady in lycra, who was suited for little else but pushing a trolley around a supermarket.

Dealing with people is an art that doesn't come naturally to everyone, particularly those like my husband who have spent years in the bush – often alone for weeks or months at a time. This sort of life breeds eccentrics, of whom there is no better example than Jeff Stutchbury, a bearded reincarnation of the famous British hunter/naturalist, Frederick Courtney Selous, who trekked north across the Limpopo in 1872 in search of adventure.

My enduring memory of Jeff is sitting in a dry riverbed and listening to him and my father singing *Happy Birthday* to me in the Matusadona National Park on the shores of Lake Kariba. Dad was employed by a hotel chain at the time, and he'd been sent to give a report on the lodge that Jeff and his wife Veronica were opening on one of the islands. We'd become stuck in deep sand without a radio or a weapon, and when it was obvious that we couldn't dig ourselves out, we celebrated my 25th with a few warm cokes, listening to the lions roaring nearby and to Jeff's tall hunting tales from all over Africa. It was the night of the half moon, so we decided to walk the fifteen kilometres back to the boat. 'But what about lions or elephants?' we asked Jeff nervously.

'That's no problem,' said he, 'we'll sing.'

So every time we heard a crashing in the bush, or just for the hell of it, in case lions were lurking, we would break into a loud rendition of *It's a long way to Tipperary*. We did an awful lot of singing that night.

Once, when Jeff was guiding at the Hwange Safari Lodge, he strolled across to the swimming pool to alert the guests to a herd of elephants drinking at the pan in front of the hotel. To his amazement, most of them continued lying on their sunbeds, ignoring him completely. He couldn't believe his eyes.

The next moment, he was striding around the pool, snatching paperbacks from the hands of the astonished guests and flinging them into the water.

'What the bloody hell are you doing in Africa! Look at those elephants, for God's sake!'

Jeff got away with it because he couldn't have given a damn either way, but I doubt if that level of eccentricity would be tolerated today, when the things that sell a lodge are the *nouvelle cuisine* and the fluffy towels – and luxury seems to be more valued than the experience itself.

David and Poombi had been childhood companions, and it was very important that she, too, learn to mix with her own kind. When she was a year old, and much to her indignation, we fenced off a well-appointed antbear hole some distance from the lodge, and she began to spend her nights there, and her days patrolling the river with her devoted keeper, Abel Ncube, until she finally became independent.

But there was no escape for us from the paralysing boredom of munching our way through the same old dishes and listening to the same old music night after night. Far from being inspiring, even Pavarotti belting out *Nessun Dorma* only served to remind us that we too weren't getting enough sleep.

There were bright spots. Anita and Giles, a couple of English doctors, gave us a thrilling couple of days. They were already arguing in the minibus on the way from the airport to the lodge, and by lunchtime he was puce with anger and she was in tears. Everyone politely tried to look the other way but this became impossible when all twenty of us were sitting at the table while the couple screeched at each other over the egg mayonnaise.

Suddenly, the husband rounded on me.

'Well, what do *you* think?' he demanded.

'Umm, er ... about what?' I asked him, looking wildly around for some help from the other guests. They all sat in silence staring at their plates or out of the window.

'About this stupid cow refusing to send our kids to public school! Just because she went to a grammar school, she reckons they have to do the same. It's bloody ridiculous.'

'You're the one who's stupid!' Anita yelled from the other end of the table. 'Why can't you take a turn looking after the kids? I'm as qualified as you are and I don't see why I have to be the only one to sacrifice my career.'

I quickly realised that this was a reality show, years

ahead of its time. A host was needed, someone to turn an ugly scene into entertainment.

I took a deep breath. 'Well, in my opinion...'

'We don't want your opinion,' snapped Anita. 'This is a private matter!' Her husband pointed his knife at her in the general direction of the jugular. As a trainee surgeon, he knew what he was doing.

'It's not private any more, the way you're carrying on. I want to know what other people think.'

Suddenly the whole table was talking at once. Order was needed.

I tapped the side of my glass with a teaspoon.

'One at a time. Let's hear what Shelley has to say.'

The American lady on my right agreed with Anita. Children were much better off in a state school, where they would have to mix with 'all sorts'.

Not so, said Peter, the South African lawyer. Private education gave you far better opportunities. And then there was the old boy network, still the best way of finding a job.

I moved along the table, giving everyone a couple of minutes on the air. When they'd all had their say, Jimmy, the soccer player from one of the better known English teams, piped up.

'Ow many children 'ave you got, then?'

The couple looked at him as if he was crazy.

'None of course!' said Anita, 'We're on honeymoon!'

Surprisingly, the pink dip lady never sent us any more clients – and I thought she had a sense of humour. Actually, it didn't pay to be flippant with the agents because almost all our bookings came through them. I remember the night our very first agent visited the lodge, when my only help in the kitchen was Major, who had some experience in herding cattle but absolutely none with Beef Wellington, the main course for the night. I had been training him, which wasn't much help, as there is only so much you can do with a boiled egg. Still, after hours of poring over the books, I thought I'd picked the right dish – I had a roll of ready-made pastry, and all I had to do was to cook the fillet for fifteen minutes or so and at some stage wrap the pastry around it.

While Rich plied the agent with stories and strong drink, I popped the meat in the oven, re-read the recipe and set the alarm clock.

'Now, Major,' I said. 'You chop up the potatoes and boil them. Right?'

He nodded. I had another look at the book. 'Then when the clock goes, the meat comes out of the oven and *phumulas* – rests.' I made a soothing gesture over the kitchen table as if I were settling a baby in a cot.

'No problem, madam.'

I rushed off for a quick shower and change. No doubt about it, despite my own shortcomings, I was a pretty good teacher. Perhaps this lodge lark wouldn't be so terrifying after all.

Fifteen minutes later, I was back. The potatoes were boiling away nicely but I couldn't find the cook. Ten minutes passed.

'Major!' I yelled, forgetting that the agent was within earshot. 'Where the hell are you?'

Major emerged from the back of the storerooms rubbing his eyes.

'What do you think you're doing?'

'I've been sleeping,' he said indignantly. 'You told me to *phumula*, so I did.'

I let out an anguished yelp and leaped down the stairs

into the kitchen. The meat dish was nowhere to be seen. I flung open the oven door and pulled out something shrivelled and black – a pot scraping from a cannibal's Christmas party. With dinner five minutes away, there was no plan to be made. But I did discover that you can get away with a lot if you dim the lights, turn up the music, cover your disasters with six inches of pastry, and stun your guests with your non-stop scintillating chatter.

In Southern Africa, the ability to improvise, to rely on your own ingenuity is known as 'making a plan', and both Rich and my brother David became experts at it during their years in the Department of National Parks and Wildlife Management. Dumped somewhere in the bush for weeks at a time without any back-up, they simply had no option – if they didn't do the job, no one else would.

We were sitting on the roadside one hot afternoon some two hundred kilometres away from home, when my father made a memorable remark.

'If I was stuck on a desert island with appendicitis, I'd only want one person anywhere near me.'

We all knew whom he meant. Rich's head appeared from under the bonnet of our ailing Land Rover. 'It's the accelerator cable,' he said. 'It's snapped.'

He stared at the engine reflectively for a few moments (which is very different from merely gawping helplessly, as the rest of us would have done), went around to the back of the vehicle and reappeared with a thick length of string. Having attached this to the cable, he fed the string under the bonnet of the engine and operated the accelerator through the open car window. Simple.

Brother David has always had a particularly relaxed

attitude to life's little hiccups. When his camp at Rukomechi was inundated by the floodwaters of the Zambezi, he made himself a raft, and having loaded up his remaining possessions, stretched out comfortably with his book on the *Power of Positive Thinking* as he floated off down the river.

His tendency to dream, however, sometimes led him into a spot of trouble, like the time during Zimbabwe's bush war when he was asked to take the South African Minister of Tourism on a river cruise at the Victoria Falls. They cracked a few beers, my brother and the Minister, and both were in a fine mood as they sped home in the glow of the setting sun to the sound of hippos honking and the river's roar as it plunged over the lip of the Falls.

When he approached the ramp, David very expertly headed the boat straight on to the trailer parked in the water and attached to the back of his Land Rover. But just as the two men were getting to their feet, the boat began slipping backwards.

'Yoiks!' yelled the Minister, and tumbled over the side.

He was still flailing about, imagining monstrous crocodiles cruising around in the murky waters below him, when the Land Rover slid past and slowly began to sink in a cloud of bubbles. David hauled him out of the water and up on to the ramp.

'My god, man,' said the Minister, staring at the water, his head festooned with Kariba weed, 'What are you going to do now?'

'I forgot the damn handbrake,' said my brother. 'But don't worry, I did the same thing two weeks ago.'

Why Parks HQ continued to give David the delicate task of entertaining the political hierarchy is still a mystery to the rest of his family. On another occasion during the bush war, he was tasked with taking the Rhodesian President and his entourage for a day's fishing on the Kyle dam. 'V.I.P.s,' warned his Provincial Warden. 'Just make sure everything goes smoothly.'

It was a perfect morning, and by lunchtime the President had pulled in a couple of good-sized bass. David moored at a little island, but no sooner had he laid out the checked tablecloth and unpacked the picnic hamper when the President announced that he was feeling unwell, and asked to be taken back to shore.

Leaving everyone else to get on with their lunch, my brother helped his most important guest into the front of the boat and pulled the starting cord, quite forgetting that he had left it in gear. The engine fired up and the boat surged forward – not into the open water, but straight up the bank and into the middle of the picnic party. David shot over the stern and the President landed on his back in the bottom of the boat.

So, as you can appreciate, from necessity, my brother became more expert than most at making the proverbial plan.

Rich is a master of on-the-spot improvisation. Once, I watched him and Scout Jabulani Khanye peering into a lilac-breasted roller's nest inside a tree. It was too dark to see anything, so Rich whipped out his knife, angled one side to the sun and beamed enough light into the hole for them to count three white eggs.

Running a safari lodge in the bush regularly taxes my husband's ingenuity. Nothing motivates one more quickly than twenty people about to arrive for dinner when the gas has run out. Or there's no water in the taps, and the lights are down.

Fortunately, we have a back-up solution for most of

these problems. Each cottage has its own brick bush boiler. A fire heats up the water in a central conical flue insulated with sand, and this provides hot water for at least twelve hours. Other than the fancy stuff, cooking can be done on our wood stove, and Rich has built two huge water storage tanks on Dibe Hill behind the lodge so there's something in reserve if the borehole engine packs up (which didn't pacify the lady who found bits of disintegrating rat in her tooth mug).

And then there's the generator, for many years the darkest of all my *bêtes noires*. First, we had the Lister, 1928, dark green, slow but utterly dependable.

My brain is like the old generator, I confided to my diary in a melancholy moment, *it switches on a few lights but can't manage them all. Still, Rich is very fond of it in a nostalgic sort of way. I hope he feels the same about me.*

As we became busier, the demands on the Lister grew too much, and Rich upgraded to a monstrous contraption that squatted belligerently on the floor of the generator room, and roared like a fleet of tractors. Rich could fire it up on his own, but I had to ask Obadiah, our waiter, to crank the wheel, faster and faster, till his eyes nearly popped out with the effort. And then, when he was almost airborne, I would pull the handles towards me with an expert flick of the wrists, and the ghastly thing would explode into life. But turning it off was far worse, at least from a psychological point of view.

Eleven pm – Rich is away and the last guests have finally gone to bed, taking my umbrella with them. They've ordered tea at 5 am and a game drive, whatever the weather, because it is their last day in Africa. The wind screams through the gap in the sliding doors and the blast sends me reeling when I step outside. I start to run but halfway down the drive, I almost collide with a couple of eland cows who thunder off into the dark. Now I'm past the house and down the hill, drenched, flashing the torch from one side of the track to the other to make sure that the eland bull isn't waiting in ambush for me. He nearly got Rich last week. The head-splitting roar from the generator room gets louder and louder, like a Tyrannosaurus Rex straining at the end of his chain. All I want to do is run away, but right now I'm the only person in the world who can stop this monster. It's an inferno inside the little room. I take a lunge at the handles, push them away from me, and it dies, instantly, without a fight. Silence comes rushing in, but far from being a relief, the sudden emptiness is terrifying. Now is the moment that someone steps out of the darkness and sticks a spear in my back. I leap out of the generator room and tear up the hill towards the house.

Rather ironically, our least welcome guests were the ones who were really enjoying themselves. They didn't want to go to bed any more than we wanted to leave them with the run of the bar. But we had a special plan for them. At around 10.30, I would jangle the pantry keys importantly and slip out via the kitchen, and Rich would follow me a few minutes later, muttering something about fuel for the generator. This would leave Rupert, our first trainee guide, whose social skills made my husband look like an honours graduate from the Dale Carnegie Institute. He spoke rarely, and looked so forbidding on game drives that the guests were frightened to ask him any questions in case they looked foolish. Occasionally, he'd unnerve them even more by bursting into maniacal laughter for no apparent reason. Rupert would take up a position slumped in a chair opposite our laggardly guests and stare at them fixedly with a haunted expression. It was all over in five minutes. They would prattle on trying to pretend that they hadn't noticed, but they soon lost their nerve, and when we heard the generator sputtering into silence, we'd know that our protégé had done it again.

We often thought of making a movie – *Fawlty Safaris*. Rich was a natural for Basil and I'd been practising being Sybil for years, minus the cigarettes and the blue rinse. Rupert would appear occasionally to provide an original touch of horror, and our string of guides and hostesses had given us heaps of potential material. Rich's idea was to have two guides – one the tall, bronzed denizen of the African bush with sawn-off sleeves and gigantic biceps, and the other a white and weedy individual who wore spectacles and had a propensity for bird-watching.

Naturally, Tarzan would pull the ladies, but somehow he would always end up falling out of his tree, while his counterpart, who was enormously knowledgeable and competent beneath his puny exterior, won the day. If MGM feels like making an offer, we are ready.

We battled on for four years before handing over the running of the lodge to a safari company who promptly forgot to pay the rent. But even the protracted legal battle was worth it for the pleasure of having dinner with the family alone – in our own house.

Very, very rarely, people revisited the lodge, probably because they had forgotten they had been there before. This was always a particular strain as presumably they had actually enjoyed themselves the first time and were now expecting a similar experience.

I made the first blunder by failing to recognise the

Williams family when I met them off the plane at Bulawayo airport, and I was desperately hoping that Rich's memory was better than mine. It was.

'Well, if it's not the Williamses!' he exclaimed as he met them on the stairs of the lodge.

'What in God's name are you doing here? We thought we'd got rid of you the first time!'

Chapter Two

Our son looked very handsome on his first day of boarding school, but far from happy. He could tolerate the red blazer, grey shirt and flannels and even the tie, but the clumpy black lace-ups were torture for a boy who was used to running barefoot in the bush. He was as relieved as I was that our two years of school by correspondence were over – but he'd miss Nandi, our Labrador, snoring at his feet, and the vervet monkeys who sat on our kitchen window sill, watching us struggling with infant number and the adventures of Janet and John. Number was overwhelming for both of us, but since English was my subject, I didn't bother much with the instructions. As soon as David had learned the alphabet, I assumed that he would be able to get stuck straight into *Winnie the Pooh*. Instead, thanks to my idiocy, he had to relearn the whole process in our second year. Time and immense patience were required, the natural attributes of any decent parent.

'Mo-th-er sh-i-ts on the ch-air,' David read out, as I stood behind him, making tortured faces and wringing my hands in a parody of strangulation.

He didn't miss a trick. 'Look, Dad, I can read!' he shouted, holding his book at arm's length and squinting at it myopically, just like Mum.

I wish I had spoken to some of the neighbours during those lonely, guilt-stricken years. If I'd known that Chappie Rosenfels used to chuck his books out of the window when Betty was called to the phone, I would have felt a lot better. In those days, they still had a daily half an hour of school on the air, which Betty loved. She would turn around to see how the children were enjoying it, to find that Chappie had his eyes shut and his fingers in his ears.

Betty's husband, Ernest, heard her yelling one morning.

'You'll never get through to them that way,' he admonished her, 'you should have more patience.'

'Right!' she said, handing him the book. 'You have a go.'

Five minutes later, she heard a loud smack and a yell, and Ernest stormed out of the schoolroom, never to return.

Old Boetie Rosenfels, grandfather of the clan, didn't hold much with education. Many a time, when Pam was preparing for the day's lessons, Boetie would drive up to the house to look for young Max.

'Hey, Maxie,' he would say, 'can you write your own name yet?'

'Yes, oupa, I can.'

'Well, that's OK then. Come along with me and we'll dip the cattle.'

And the last Pam would see of her son for the day was the dust of their departing vehicle.

I found the daily transformation from mum to schoolmarm almost impossible, but one mother I knew had the answer. After breakfast, she would dress her child in a uniform, pack his satchel, kiss him goodbye and send him around the house a couple of times on his bicycle. When he returned to the front door, there she would be standing in a new set of clothes with her books under her arm.

'Good morning, Sam,' she would greet her pupil briskly.

'Good morning, Mrs Grant,' he would reply, and off they would go for a productive morning in the schoolroom.

They say that the first seven years of a child's life are the most formative. I had sleepless nights worrying about what David had absorbed from his socially challenged parents and if this could ever be eradicated. Perhaps hypnosis was the answer, but then there was the danger that he might forget about us altogether.

But irrepressible nature triumphed over nurture. Other than an inability to sit still in the classroom and a tendency to lose his shoes, our son fitted in to school life amazingly well.

Strangely enough, with Poombi (the dumb animal), nurture initially had the upper hand. Scornful about others of her kind, she was quite content to wander about with Abel, her keeper, and spend the nights alone in her antbear hole. Only when her hormones sparked into life did she begin to appreciate the charm of warts and tusks and testes, falling headlong into a relationship with sexy old Harald, one of the better-endowed hogs on the farm.

But in the world of warthogs, real men don't hang around to change the nappies. Poombi was alone when she gave birth to her first litter of two in mid-October, hidden amongst some thickly wooded koppies and far

17

away from home. Nature immediately took over. She kept her piglets hidden away in the den for the first week or so before bringing them out on little excursions, but never far from safety. Gruntabel and Squeak were around ten days old when I saw them for the first time, playing at the base of a koppie while their mother grazed peacefully close by.

There followed one of the most extraordinary experiences of my life. Poombi had been living wild for over a year, she had no further need of us, especially now. And yet it seemed as important to her as it was to me that I be accepted into her new family. Instead of following her natural instincts and running away, she called the piglets and brought them close to me for a proper introduction. In sharing that moment of joy, another, much stronger bond had been forged between us. You can't explain it, you only know that something has happened at a far deeper level than words could ever describe.

As totally self-centred beings we have made endless discoveries about the human brain and its activity under stimulus. A neurosurgeon can tell if you are musically gifted, a mathematical genius, or even a pathological liar. But apart from eating them, we have made only one startling discovery about the brain of the pig. Taking into account the size of the animal, it is the biggest among the ungulates – the hoofed mammals – and that's saying something. If we had exposed Poombi to a bit of culture and a brain scan, we might have found that she preferred Beethoven to Mozart, but now we could only guess what was going on in that clever head of hers.

But surely, you might argue, a pig is a pig is a pig? Once you've met one, you've pretty much exhausted their possibilities. Not so. Although, like humans, they've got a lot in common with each other, each pig is an individual. This isn't anthropomorphism: personality has as much evolutionary relevance as any physical characteristic. Bold pigs protect their families better than timid ones, careful pigs make better mothers. Saucy sows get out there and find their man. And pragmatic pigs live in the present and don't waste time, as we do, in pointless speculation about the future. Poombi was always aware of the threat of leopard, cheetah and other potential predators, and even when she was apparently deeply asleep during her afternoon siestas, she would leap up at the slightest sound or sign of danger. But that's as far as it went. She took precautions, but she didn't lose any sleep over life's uncertainties, and nor did the heeby-jeebies spoil her appetite. It's called keeping things in perspective, and I found I wasn't very good at it.

Only a few kilometres away from Stone Hills, war veterans were tossing bottle tops in a crude form of lottery for ownership of local farms. Since 2000, land invaders had spread like locusts throughout the country, creating chaos for people, agriculture and wildlife. It might be a week, a month, sometime, never – we didn't know, but we were always waiting for the radio call announcing strangers at the gate, or for the sound of an unfamiliar vehicle in the driveway.

Why drive yourself crazy with anticipation? I kept asking myself. We had been living with uncertainty for years, but against the odds, we were still here, watching the sun rise over the same hills, day after day. Nothing on Stone Hills had really changed, but pushing that constant, nagging anxiety to the back of our minds was like trying to squeeze a bullfrog into a matchbox. It just wouldn't go. How I envied my philosophical pig.

Having spent that first, magical afternoon with Poombi's family, I brought mine to meet hers on the following day. And, just as I expected, she welcomed the two other people who had been so important in her early life as an orphaned piglet.

Gruntabel and Squeak wanted to play and they homed in on a delighted David, who was only too happy to join them. As he sat in the late afternoon sunshine, the piglets crept up to take a quick nibble at his fingers and toes, then scooted away like a couple of naughty bell-ringers on a suburban street. When they weren't chasing each other, they played a special game in a shallow hole where they practised rapid entrances and exits, headfirst and then in reverse. Being the smaller of the two, Squeak wasn't always successful, and we would see her head popping up and down like a piston until she finally made it to the top.

At dusk, we began walking back to the vehicle and the family followed us. While David practised his long jump in the sand, the piglets bounced around him for the sheer joy of being alive.

Time out is an essential for all new mothers. Our eland begin giving birth shortly before the onset of the rains and the mother hides her baby away for a few days before bringing it out to join the nursery. Here, it will be supervised by another female, often a youngster, whose job it is to keep the babies together and steer them out of trouble. Meanwhile, mother wanders away with her friends, strolling back occasionally to give the baby a feed.

The female giraffe is relaxed to the point of negligence. Her birthing style may have something to do with the fact that her brain is a long way from her vulva, for the calf arrives in this world with a bang from which it probably never recovers. After its five-foot dive from the womb straight on to its head, its mother mooches off to browse, leaving it to struggle up on legs and feet that are clearly designed with economy in mind. It will grow into them of course, but in the meantime, the calf must learn to walk in a pair of outsize gumboots. When it finally reaches her for its first feed, its mother looks down with mild surprise. Heavens above, you can hear her saying, where on earth did you come from? Things never improve: if the calf tries to suckle while she is eating or simply not in the mood, she ignores it and walks on, even when it's tangled up in her legs.

As a migratory animal, the wildebeest is used to giving birth on the move with one eye open for predators. Within six minutes or even less, her tiny calf is on its feet, and after its first drink, running by its mother's side. Our herds are sedentary on Stone Hills, and the calves soon band together to play – exploding out of the grass like popcorn from a pan. No bother at all.

But warthogs have none of the benefits of communal living. For a week or so after the piglets are born, the female spends most of her time in the den with them, venturing out occasionally for a quick bite and a drink. Although Poombi took to motherhood as well as the next pig, she did make one mistake. The rains hadn't yet begun, and since the nursery area was almost a kilometre from water, she had to leave the babies for a good hour or so every day. To ensure that they didn't try and follow her, she would turn around at the entrance to the den and direct a few long, deep sniffs at her offspring, then amble off happily for a bit of 'me' time. If I was there, she left me in charge and I think she must have liked the arrangement, for often the quick drink would turn into a few hours away, until I began to worry about the babies dehydrating. But just as I thought that she'd gone for good, I'd see her trotting casually through the trees, stopping for the odd mouthful. A few yards away from the hole, she would give a low grunt, and with much scuffling and squeaking, the piglets would come tumbling out for their long-awaited drink.

When Gruntabel and Squeak were nine months old, horny Harald turned up to woo their mother once again. I found them all at the boma near the compound, hoovering up marula nuts and crunching them loudly between their back molars like a bunch of kids with a bag of boiled sweets. We all love them, but to extract the tiny but delicious nut inside, you have to place the dried marula on a flat rock and bash it to bits with a heavy stone. Fearsome Aggie, the laundry lady, took it upon herself to show David the right way to deal with them and how to winkle out the nut, but the lesson came to an abrupt end when her over-zealous pupil forgot that she was still holding the marula, and brought his stone down heavily on her index finger.

After watching Poombi and family's effortless performance, we were always careful not to put our hands too far into her mouth in case she forgot that this was part of a greeting and sheared off a finger for a quick snack.

Up to now, Poombi had always been careful to keep the piglets well away from any adult males, including Harald, but today all this had changed. He'd hardly been an exemplary father, but nonetheless he was welcomed by his offspring, who didn't seem at all bothered by his lack of interest in their welfare. After Poombi had greeted me, I moved away to watch them at a distance. A warthog of any size is formidable, but a male constructed along the lines of a Sherman tank with a built-in armoury and testicles the size of soccer balls should always be avoided, particularly when he has no fear of you whatsoever.

As Gruntabel was rooting away in the dust, his father moved up close and put his nose on the very same spot. Instead of giving ground as I thought he would, Grunt threw a tantrum, stamping his feet with rage and squealing into Harald's face. The old hog didn't move an inch; he stood there with his head down until his son had recovered himself, and then the two of them carried on rooting together as if nothing had happened. Quite possibly, like any scheming male, he was trying to ingratiate himself with Poombi by being nice to her kids, because half an hour later, he lay down and invited them to groom him.

It was an amazing sight. Squeak nibbled up and down his tummy, and under his leg, which he lifted obligingly for her, while Grunt tried to lever his father's enormous bulk over on to his other side. As Harald lay there like a basking hippopotamus, little Squeak clambered right over him and began chewing at one of his enormous warts. I'm not sure if Poombi even noticed, but in my opinion, Harald deserved to get lucky after that performance.

From a very early age, humans start to develop mental maps; if we didn't, we'd get lost going to the loo. As an extreme example, if you examined the brain of a London cab-driver, you would probably find a condensed version of the A–Z bulging from his frontal lobe. A warthog, too, carries very detailed maps in her head, but for her, it's not just a question of finding her way around, she must remember the location of dozens of homes and what makes one more suitable than the next on any particular day. Caves, for instance, are cooler than antbear holes in summer, but may be less easily defended; and the piglets' den must be safe from flooding as they are invariably born in the rainy season. The again, ideal homes for single girls won't fit a growing family, nor the series of boyfriends who provide the entertainment around May or June every year, and so on.

Poombi never dithered about anything. She always seemed to know exactly where she was going and where she would finish up at the end of the day. It wasn't random wandering that took her to the fruiting trees, or the best grass or the mud wallow at lunchtime before the family siesta, it was simply good planning.

I envied my pig her unerring sense of direction because most of mine is by association. I remember places by their landmarks, the shape of a koppie perhaps, or some incident that has occurred there in the past. Hongwe-Tekwana, the balancing rocks we can see from our bedroom window, resembles a family of baboons contemplating the sunrise from one side and a pig in a bonnet with a baby on her back from the other. The sun doesn't help me at all; if it's behind my right shoulder when I start out, it's bound to be straight ahead of me when I'm trying to get home again, so I ignore it. Admittedly, I did get lost for hours among the hills when we first came to the farm, but gradually it all became familiar. It works – until I have to give someone else directions. Rich and each of the scouts carry a map of the farm around with them, a small laminated card covered with squiggly contours for the koppies, dark lines for the rivers and dotted ones for the roads. It's divided into grid squares so that when the scouts call in with a report, they will say 'leopard kill at D5/80' and Rich will know exactly where to go. Lucky old him.

My husband, too, adores his gadgets. He has a GPS in the vehicle that he fiddles with for hours on long journeys, even when we've been on the same trip hundreds of times before. I can't understand it. Why doesn't he just turn left at the signpost?

Before we acknowledged our differences, we decided to map out the eighty-odd Bushman rock art sites on the farm. We began discussing it in the bathroom as the three-year-old David splashed about in the water with his rubber ducks.

The conversation went something like this:

'Have you seen the one with the people walking on all fours?' I ask.

'No,' says my husband. 'Where is it?'

I gesture towards the bedroom window. 'Down there. You see that rock shaped like a tooth sticking up behind the very green tree?'

'What rock? There are hundreds of the bloody things and it's the middle of summer, all the trees are green, for pity's sake!'

'Don't shout at me! I'm not a magician: I can't tell what tree it is from a kilometre away.'

'I'm not shouting, I simply want to know whether you mean north, south, east or west. Here, find it on the map.'

'I don't need your stupid map. Remember where we found the Pittosporum in flower in the summer of '94? You can't forget that.'

'No.'

'Of course you do, we were together!'

Then it's Rich's turn to give me directions.

'This is easy.' He positions his body between two imaginary koppies. 'We have Dibe on my left and the rocks immediately to its south.' He jabs his finger in the air. 'Head west towards the boundary...'

'Which boundary?'

'I told you, the western boundary.'

'You mean Julius's boundary?'

'Yes! Now, take the path between the koppies, cross the river and across the quartz ridge, past the large kirkia. The painting is immediately in front of you, facing north-east. You can't miss it.'

Silence.

'I don't know what you're talking about. You're not making it clear.'

My husband starts to choke. 'You're not listening to me! You *never* listen...'

That's it, war has been declared. I open my mouth to scream abuse, but suddenly there's a swirl of water and our child is standing up in the bath, looking very stern indeed. 'Stop it!' he shouts. Just in time. We still don't have a map of the Bushman paintings.

Actually, I don't know why I insist on denigrating myself – it was only because of my feeling about a certain place that we rediscovered the *Erythrophysa transvaalensis*, the red balloon tree, on the banks of the Matanje River.

I found it on my first visit to the farm, long before it was ours. Rich was away, so one of his friends from his National Parks days, James Perry, showed me around. I stopped to look at a francolin, and noticed a strange multi-stemmed tree growing among the rocks, its swollen fruits a rich red with a waxy sheen.

'What do you reckon this is?' I called to James.

He gasped. 'Good God! It's the red balloon tree. I've only ever seen it growing in the Transvaal and even there it's a rarity.'

He fetched his tree book from the vehicle and flipped through it. On the distribution map, he put his finger on an arrow pointing to a tiny dot south of Bulawayo. Only one wild specimen of the red balloon had ever been found in Zimbabwe, until today.

We were still living in Bulawayo when I wanted to show Rich my discovery, so we called James to ask him to describe its location. But it wasn't where it should have been, and for months afterwards, I explored that part of the river – up and down the koppies, scrambling over rocks and through dense undergrowth – with no success. Then one day, about two years later, I woke up in the morning and felt absolutely positive that I was going to be lucky. For a change, I wasn't going to follow anybody else's directions: I was going to listen to my instincts.

Having parked the Land Rover at the river, I walked another kilometre or so downstream from where we had been searching. I went very slowly, constantly listening and looking – trying to get a feel for the place. And where the trees gave way to a small clearing between the koppies, I stopped. It wasn't there today, but I felt I could almost see the francolin on the rocks in front of me. As if drawn by a magnet, I moved back into the woodland shadows and looked up – and there it was, our elusive tree, covered in wintry brown balloons.

What fascinated me was that a similar game of hide and seek had been played after the *Erythrophysa* was first made known to science in the 1930s. An engineer in charge of building a dam in the Rustenberg district had noticed the shiny black beads worn by the local women as necklaces and they had shown him the tree. But soon after sending a sample to the Botanical Research Institute, he left the area. After eight years of searching, two frustrated botanists finally rediscovered it – hiding on the slope behind the dam wall. The mystery is how the tree got to Zimbabwe. Did the Matabele women bring the seeds in as beads in the 1830s, or did some come up from the south stuck to a pioneer's wagon wheel?

When we looked more carefully, we found around eighty red balloons in the same area, close to the Matanje river. But despite their numbers, they still have a habit of disappearing. One blistering October morning, I decided to take a short cut with a party of elderly tree boffins, and spent four hours searching for the site I could usually find in my sleep. In the end, I was alone when I located it, and had to make the return trip rescuing dehydrated octogenarians on the verge of expiry and helping them back to the vehicle.

Chapter Three

'Rain, rain go away,' we chant in the classroom, 'come again another day!' The white man has been in Zimbabwe for over a hundred years, and we still teach our children the nursery rhymes that are so apt for the old country, but so utterly unsuited to the new.

We long for rain, we pray for it in our churches, and come November we talk of nothing else. We get bent necks from peering at the sky. Will the crops grow this year? Will the animals have enough to eat? Will the rain fill our dams and flood our rivers?

Izulu liyana, say the Matabele people, the rain has come – words as sweet as the sound of birdsong after the first storm. *Their* children wouldn't dare to tell the rain to go away.

December 10: Another scorching day. No clouds break the dazzling sapphire sky, no cool green grass beneath the trees, only their shadows stretched out like skeletons in the dust. I wake every morning before dawn, and in that sombre early light, the same portents appear: no wind, no cloud, no hope.

Nothing escapes the glitter of the sun's all-seeing eye. The leaves droop and sag, the grasses wither and turn blue. Countless millions of harvester termites are foraging in the vleis, cutting grass for storage in their underground tunnels, and filling the air with the snap, crackle and pop of a gigantic bowl of Rice Crispies.

The birds are silent but, bloody-minded as ever, the red-winged starlings refuse to be defeated. From dawn to dusk, they swoop past with beakfuls of food for their nestlings in the chimney: though sometimes I see them open-mouthed and panting at the bird bath below my window.

But the silky acacia at the garden fence is in cahoots with the enemy. As one exuberant flowering ends, so another begins, the fluffy white heads massed against the fierce blue sky, nodding their approval.

The Matabele pray for rain in natural shrines like Njelele, on the southern fringes of Matobo Hills; so revered a place that people flock to the annual ceremonies from as far afield as South Africa and Namibia. Rain dances are conducted by the priests and priestesses of the ancient cult of Mwali, or Mlimu as he came to be known when the headquarters of the cult moved to the Matobo from Great Zimbabwe over five hundred years ago.

Mlimu is primarily the god of rain, but he keeps a strict eye on the morality of his flock, who must placate him with gifts and offerings. In keeping with tradition, they sacrifice black oxen to their god at Njelele, and leave rapoko beer overnight outside the cave for his pleasure, which, our head scout Mafira Chanyungunya assures me, has inevitably been drunk by the next morning.

Njelele is not on the tourist map: its sheer walls rising for a hundred feet or so are concealed by vegetation and unremarkable in an endless vista of rugged granite outcrops. Its custodians were expert ventriloquists, traditionally from the local Kalanga tribe, who acted as Mlimu's mouthpiece by addressing his supplicants through rocks, trees and even from deep within the earth.

When Mzilikazi and his Matabele army fled north from Shaka Zula in the 1830s and subjugated the Kalanga, they wisely adopted the Mlimu cult, well aware of the dangers of upsetting such an important deity. The king himself would send black oxen and maidens with beer to the annual ceremonies. This respect for the religion of their new subjects seems to have paid dividends, for in time the Kalanga merged quite peaceably with their conquerors, calling themselves Matabele and even adopting the language.

The Matabele had their own remedies for drought. If he heard that it was raining elsewhere, the king would send two or three of his men to the place with instructions to step in the mud. It is said that when they returned home and wiped their sandals clean, the rain would fall. The king himself was a powerful rainmaker, but when he held his ceremonies, the whites living in the area were forbidden from hanging out their clothes to dry, as this was believed to drive the clouds away.

Soon after we bought the farm in 1989, and when we were still living in Bulawayo, Julius Rosenfels, one of our neighbours, phoned.

'You know the rain rock on Stone Hills?' he asked. We didn't.

'Well, I've just had a delegation here asking if they can move it on to our place. Is that OK?'

Yes, we told him, that would be fine. Whatever the rock was, if the people wanted it moved, we couldn't see a problem.

'I'll take my tractor over, then, to give them a hand,' said Julius.

The lodge and house were still under construction when we received his next call six months later.

'Change of plan,' he told us, 'All hell's broken loose here – the police are even involved, wanting to know who gave us authority to move the rock. Apparently, the custodian has received orders from above to get it back to your place immediately.'

So back it came, and in early October each year its custodian, Emily Sibanda, brings a little group of *gogos* (grandmothers or elderly ladies) and young girls to the farm in order to prepare the rock and sweep the area around it for the dance. For the next seven days, rapoko beer is brewed in readiness, and the celebrants sometimes dance and play their drums, not only for practice, but to warn the departed ancestors that the ceremony is about to take place.

Our rain rock, also called Njelele, is an enormous slab of granite uplifted from the shrine in the Matobo decades ago and brought to the farm by ox wagon. It's around two metres in diameter, with a slightly concave top that would make a magnificent birdbath. When I first met Emily's predecessor, Entombana, I asked her why they had moved the rock away from Stone Hills to Julius's farm.

'We were frightened of your wild animals,' she told me, 'and we thought that you might not allow us on to the land.'

Then, in a dream, she heard the voice of Mlimu, telling her that he was angered by the removal of the rock and instructing her to restore it to its rightful place.

In areas where there are no koppies, the people may choose a tree under which to hold the ceremony. At Scout Khanye's home near Victoria Falls, they dance under a great baobab that must have seen the seasons come and go for hundreds, if not thousands, of years.

It's mid-morning on a sultry day when the little procession files through our gate – five dancers, three male musicians beating their drums, eight children and a tiny, skinny gogo skipping along behind them on grasshopper legs. 'Yoi, yoi, yoi, yoi, Tombela!' she ululates as she goes. Tombela was the first keeper of the Njelele shrine and one of the most sacred Kalanga spirits, believed to be very close to God. In the same way that Christians communicate with the supreme deity through the medium of Jesus Christ, in African tradition the living request the *amadlozi*, their departed ancestors, to intercede with Him on their behalf.

Having removed their shoes, the celebrants approach the rock on their knees through a narrow gap between two boulders. Today, they will call on the ancestors for rain and also honour their dead. One of the drummers is a young Tonga man from the Binga area.

'He shouldn't really be here,' says Scout Khanye, sitting with his arms around his knees. 'He doesn't play properly, but they couldn't find anyone else.'

Despite his young age, Khanye is a keen student of local history and traditions. 'People are forgetting their traditions,' he says sadly. 'Everything is confused these days.'

Another of the musicians is wild-eyed and gaunt, his

skin stretched over his bony face as tightly as the hide on his drum. He bunches his fingers to peck softly at it, gradually changing to a stronger beat as he thumps it with his palm: first with open fingers, then with closed. I can feel the deep, rhythmic throb vibrating right through my body. And suddenly I'm transported to the land of King Solomon's Mines (and wasn't that Zimbabwe?) watching the witch Gagool struggle under the weight of the rock that crushed her, as storm clouds fly across the face of the moon.

When the drums speak, their ageless stories belong to Africa alone. In the early 1900s, a Mrs Mea Broderick and her husband were sent to open a mission station at Bonda, close to Zimbabwe's border with Mozambique. Mea had been brought up on a remote farm and was an accomplished linguist in a number of African languages. As a midwife, she brought many a baby into the world, gaining the trust and friendship of the local people. Music and language are first cousins, and Mea learned to interpret the different rhythms of the drums as they echoed through the mountains surrounding the mission. Her husband was away one night when she was woken to a new sound, a beat that was slow and sinister, one that she had never heard before, nor ever wanted to again. Something evil was afoot, and she felt it her duty to investigate.

Daubing herself with black, and taking a terrified girl with her, she made her way to the kraal from whence the drumming came. They hid in the rocks and looked down at a scene that would haunt her forever. 'There was a big fire burning round which a large group of people knelt in silence while the drums boomed their menacing rhythm,'

Mea's husband wrote after her death. 'Grotesque figures entered the circle, dancing and singing as they drew nearer and nearer the kneeling figures. Suddenly one of the dancers sprang on to a member of the circle and speared him or her … it was impossible to see who was the attacker or the attacked as the fire was immediately stamped out. The atmosphere was so intense that Mea was almost paralysed with fear.'

The drums of death, she called them, and for a long time she kept what she had seen a secret, even from her husband. Many years later, when they had been transferred elsewhere in the country, she heard once more the ominous drumbeats of death in the middle of the night. A single shot rang out, followed by silence. The next morning, Mr Broderick found an African man sitting in his office. His would-be assassins had fired into the side of his hut, but luckily he was forewarned and had moved his bed away from its usual position by the wall.

Today, the rain dancers, *amahosana*, all of whom are spirit mediums, are dressed in black and white, the colours of worship. Evelyn and Bicte wear headbands of black and white beads and, as director of the proceedings, Emily has a bright blue duk on her head and a shawl of the same colour over her broad shoulders, for it is the sky god whose favours she seeks. The others fall back, and Elitte Tombigaysi Kambo enters the stage with an earthenware gourd on her head filled with frothy rapoko beer. She asks for the blessing of the spirits as she slowly pours the creamy brown liquid into the centre of the rock. Each dancer approaches in turn, dropping to their knees and bending over to drink with their hands behind their backs. 'They must drink as the animals do,' whispers Mafira, who is acting as our interpreter.

Now, the women are bending down to fit the *amahlwayi* to their ankles – the strings of oval grey cocoons of mopane moths filled with tiny stones that rattle as they stamp their feet. They straighten up. They are ready. A gust of wind blows the last of the dead leaves from a large mukwa tree, a bulbul calls from the top of a koppie, and then Emily's strong voice is heard, singing alone. One by one she is joined by other voices, and now we hear the drums roll in and the swish and rattle of the *amahlwayi* as the dancers shuffle forward, then backward, in a line; Bicte waves a wildebeest tail over her head and the others push their arms out in front of them as if they are driving evil spirits away.

Although I am lost in the primal beat of these drums, their rhythm is foreign to me, and I know that I could never dance to it. And yet these women are immediately responsive: when the drums speak, their bodies instantly melt into synchrony. I wonder what makes our natural rhythms so different? Perhaps it has something to do with the cadence of language – if I could speak Sindebele properly, I might begin to understand their music.

Suddenly, four of the dancers step back. Simangaliso Ndebele has fallen to the ground. It must be the heat, I think, they have danced continuously for an hour or more without a break or a drink. But she hasn't collapsed. Twice, she rolls head over heels, then lies in the dust, trembling, while the other women gather to dance and sing around her.

'Her father died this year,' Mafira tells us. 'They are calling his spirit to ask him if the rains will come.'

And Khanye whispers: 'When a spirit medium goes into a trance, her clothes don't move.'

But I notice that when she goes head over heels,

Simangaliso keeps her skirt tucked carefully around her legs. Ten minutes later, the other women help her to her feet and lead her to the rock for a sip of beer.

The tiny gogo holds up her hands, she wants to dance too. A younger woman removes her *amahlwayi*, and comes to wrap them around the old woman's legs. She curtseys, and gogo rewards her with a wide toothless smile: seventy, eighty, a hundred – like an old tortoise, she could be any age. But there is nothing of the tortoise about her dancing, the others move back to give her the stage, and she skips and hops and twirls, to the delight of her audience.

The children are bored with sitting quietly and watching. A boy, maybe eight years old, jumps up and starts to gyrate for Rich's camera. He drops down again self-consciously and everybody giggles at him. A pale-skinned little girl in a yellow dress pushes a tok-tokkie beetle along with a stick, flips it over and finally buries it in the sand. They have walked maybe five or six kilometres in the heat of the morning and sat here without food or water for two hours or more without complaint.

Whistles may not be used in the dance – they are the wind that drives away the rain, but the drums are the thunder that heralds the approach of the storm. Slowly the dancers begin to retire, their faces glistening with sweat, until all that is left is the steady pulse of the drums, singing out to the hills. Finally, Gladys Mabechu comes forward with a gourd full of water drawn from a river or a well. This is the *umphungo*, and if it is left behind or broken before time, the ceremony may not take place. Gladys stops by the rock and suddenly spins around and throws the gourd over her shoulder. It smashes on the ground, water flies into the air. *Izulu liyana*! And unbelievably – it has worked.

The sky has gradually darkened through the afternoon. Earlier I heard Wonder Issah, the handyman, telling Rich in sepulchral tones that the 'clouds appear to be gathering in the firmament', and sure enough, the far hills are now veiled in a light mist of rain.

A perfect rainbow glows in a shaft of sunlight – *umcilo wamakosikazi,* the Matabele call it, the Queen's ribbon. Just as she can deflect her husband's anger with kind words, so the rainbow keeps the wrath of the storm at bay and brings gentle rain to the land. She is the queen of all things peaceful.

Today is particularly poignant: we are sitting in a mixed group watching a ceremony from the old times, unconnected to the chaos and destruction around us. In a few short years, Zimbabwe has been transformed from the 'bread basket of Africa' into one of the poorest nations in the world, thanks largely to the violent government-sponsored invasions of agricultural land by veterans of our bush war, which culminated in independence some twenty years previously.

Scout Big Boy Ndebele is talking and laughing with Khanye in that easy way of his. He lives in the southern Matobo close to Njelele, and although Europeans are generally forbidden to visit the shrine, he thinks that he can organise a visit for us. Mafira tells me that Big Boy's brother is the chief war veteran in the Kezi district. I raise my eyebrows.

'Yes, I know, it's crazy,' says Mafira.

Who is the enemy? Our staff have been with us for years, they are smiling, friendly, hard-working, and yet we hardly know them. Courteous old Shepherd, with four teeth left in his head, has been given a plot of land on the next-door property. The farmer was running three hundred head of cattle on it, but now he's been evicted, and the land has been designated as a 'village': home for at least fifty families.

I am reminded of the story of an English judge sent to India during the days of the Raj. After a year, he wrote to a friend: 'I am discovering a lot about India.'

Ten years on, he wasn't quite so sure, commenting: 'I find there is a lot to learn about India.'

And finally, at the end of his professional career: 'I have reached the conclusion,' he wrote, 'that I know nothing at all about India.'

A white man's Africa and a black man's – and yet today we are united by this ancient ceremony.

It is all over, we drive the dancers back home in two vehicles. I have the children in mine, I can hear their oohs and ahhs as we pass impala, tsessebe and a herd of sable antelope on the way to the gate. Rich is ahead with the adults: they are still singing in the back to the music of the drums, they don't want to let it go. We off-load them with bags of mealie meal, sugar and beans. Little gogo can't make it on her own. Willing arms lift her down, still yodelling and smiling.

'*Siyabonga*,' we call to each other, shaking hands. Thank you! For we have all taken something away with us today.

Rich remembers the drums from his childhood. The workers on his father's farm were mostly Malawian, of the Yao tribe, and they would smear their bodies with ash and spring out of the darkness in great masks of nodding chicken feathers that covered their heads and faces, the strips of cloth around their waists representing the traditional monkey tails. On Saturday nights, the beer would flow and the Yaos would dance, two at a time, squaring up to each other like a pair of fighting cocks, then dropping into a crouch and kicking up the dust with their feet. Mesmerised by the sound, Rich would leave his bed and creep down to the compound to watch, and still today the sound of drums draws him back to the dancers leaping and spinning in the firelight – half bird, half man – lost in a haze of alcohol and the rhythmic thump of the drums.

Rich was braver than I was. When I was a child, I'd lie tucked up in bed, warm and safe, listening to the distant throb of Zuze's tomtom. He was head chef by day, and high priest of the Apostolics on Saturday nights in the heart of the verdant Bvumba mountains, where my father ran the country hotel called Leopard Rock just a few miles from the Mozambique border. At well over six feet and with a roar like a lion, Zuze was terrifying enough when he was in the kitchen. I couldn't imagine what he was like when he and his followers were calling up the spirits in the dead of night, all adorned in ghostly white robes. His services didn't seem to have much in common with the ones I attended on those long Sunday mornings, where you knelt for hours on a wooden pew, head bent, murmuring Amens and surreptitiously checking your watch. Zuze's version sounded much more exciting.

I asked Khanye to tell me more about the drums.

'There is a particular beat for every stage,' he said. 'One when the rain dancers approach, another for the dances, and a third when they leave the rock. Then there's a different rhythm for the *inqhuzu*, a celebration like a wedding or a party where people wear the *amahlwayi* on their legs and dance, and another one again for the *mande* ceremony, when the *nyangas* go into a trance in order to heal.'

'Have you ever heard the drums of death?'

He nodded. 'But not quite like your story!'

'A tribe called the Nambiya come from my area in the north-west of Zimbabwe. They are related to the Kalanga people and they have their own ceremony for bringing the spirit of the deceased home to his family a year after death. For six days, young girls and boys learn the songs, and the boys beat drums, while the elders go through the stages of brewing beer.

'The person who put the deceased into the grave is known as the hyena man. At midnight on the seventh day, he goes into a makeshift hut and fills a bucket with beer. Then he runs through the back of the hut with it, whooping like a hyena, and the men and young boys chase him. The first ones to find him are considered to be very lucky and clever. The beer is shared between everyone and the singing and dancing goes on all night. Sometimes four or more groups of drummers will sit some distance apart, each beating a small drum with special sticks and a big one with their hands, but all in harmony. Women are forbidden to beat the drums and it's very unlucky to look inside them.'

'And how do they bring the spirit home?' I asked.

'The relatives bring soil from the grave and give it to the person in whom the spirit of the deceased now rests. The elders decide who this should be – sometimes it is even a very young person. The chosen one takes on the position of the deceased and is the only person who can communicate with his or her spirit.'

At last, the rains have come: *Inkosi ithabile*, the king is happy. And in nature, timing is everything. They may last for a week or a few months, no one can predict. So when those first drops hit the ground, everybody must be primed for instant action: dressed in their best and ready to roll.

One bitterly cold winter's night in 1968, when Rich was doing a six-month army stint, he camped next to another young soldier who liked to brew up a couple of cups of tea before bed. When he woke in the small hours, it was far too cold to wander away from his snug bivvy, so he relieved himself close by. He woke at dawn to find a cross between a mottled green balloon and a dinner plate glaring into his face. Science dreams up some strange names, but to call the giant bullfrog with his bulging eyes and mouth like a gin-trap *Pyxicephalus* must have required a real flight of fancy. Or a magic well. This poor fellow might have been underground for years, wrapped in his water-retentive cocoon, dreaming whatever *Pyxicephali* dream, and waiting for the rain to fall; and now here he was, alone in a bleak, unwelcoming world, thanks to some idiotic human who had chosen to pee precisely on his parade.

Like amphibious Rip van Winkles, all sorts of modern developments have passed the bullfrog by, and if the early rains are generous, we see dozens of their flattened bodies on the roads. Small talk is for little frogs – he lets fly with his resounding baritone whoo-oop, then gets on with the serious job of fighting and fornicating (in his fashion), sometimes tossing his rivals into the air and seriously wounding them. Strangely enough, though, he is a model parent. It's he and not the female who fusses over his swarm of tadpoles, and if they become marooned when the water is drying up, the bullfrog turns engineer and quickly constructs a channel that will lead his brood to another pool.

The morning after the dance, we wake to the deep

resonant tattoo of the ground hornbills as they march slowly through the vlei below the house. The grasses are alight in the early sunshine, their heads heavy with sparkling raindrops, and the thatch is dark and wet. Crusty old Mlimu must be enjoying himself, because it looks as if he's popped a bottle of Dom Pérignon all over the farm.

Chapter Four

It's impossible to raise a warthog and not fall in love with her. But like most wild animals, once they are grown up, you can't share your house with them. One of you has to move. To start with, all pigs are incurable gluttons. When Poombi was only a few months old, she learned to ambush the waiters on their way to the dining room, and when her nose was buried in a chicken pie or covered with chocolate mousse, any defensive tactics were met by a short (short because she didn't want to stop eating) but meaningful rush at the legs and a piercing squeal.

What to do? People we knew who ran a lodge on the fringes of the Hwange National Park were loathe to lock up their beloved but totally destructive pig, so they decided to banish him. Having driven thirty kilometres to what appeared to be the ideal location, they left him there, alone and vulnerable. Which is a bit like dumping a pygmy in the middle of Piccadilly Circus. For his whole life, that pig had been learning to survive in one particular place, developing an intimate knowledge of his surroundings. No wonder he was home by the next morning.

As many Zimbabweans and other unfortunate people around the world can attest, moving home or, even worse, moving country, especially if this is forced upon you, is one of the most stressful events of one's life. Adjustment takes time, often years, and sometimes it never happens at all. No matter who or what we are, security is our familiar environment, our own place, where we are known and accepted. It's a slow process, until that wonderful day when someone greets you by your first name in the supermarket, or gives you a call – just for a chat. Or waves at you from across the street. At last you are building a network, just as Poombi did when she moved from the comfort of our sofa to the antbear hole on the banks of the Matanje River. By the time she became independent at eighteen months, she knew every inch of her new home range, and although she sneered at them behind their backs, she was on nodding terms with the other warthogs in the area (or hoi polloi as she preferred to call them). I often followed her and her current family on their daily excursions, and I know that their route was never a random choice. Whether drinking at the river or feasting on fallen fruit, wallowing in a favourite patch of oily black mud, followed by a delicious back rub on that perfectly placed tree stump, Poombi had decided in advance exactly where she would go and where the family would be spending the night. Naturally. What sort of mother, human or otherwise, heads off for the day with her triplets without a firm plan of action? Or arrives at the supermarket without a list, or at least a good idea of what she needs to buy?

Fortunately, because Stone Hills is ours and we make the rules, we could gradually rehabilitate Poombi to a life in the bush while continually monitoring her progress.

And when she finally succumbed to Harald's charms, she made sure she brought him home to meet the family.

New mothers are a touchy lot, and no one more so than the warthog, who won't hesitate to use her tusks to carve up anyone threatening her litter. I once saw a truly remarkable photograph of a female warthog squaring up to a martial eagle. The eagle had raked her face, and its leg was raised with talons extended. When both bird and pig had gone, the photographer discovered that the eagle had been mantling over a dead piglet. So we were always very respectful of Poombi's privacy at those sensitive times, and even after we had located her nursery, we kept our distance until we could see that she was ready to receive us.

In a good year, light rains in October bring on the first flush of fresh, tender leaves, sprinkling the lifeless vleis with patches of new grass. And after the first storms a month or so later, the koppies stand out like islands afloat in a sea of green. Very prudently, Poombi gave birth to Luciano, Placido and Maria, her second litter, in mid-November in an antbear hole near the eland boma, close to water and rich grass. Rich named the operatic trio, a bit pretentiously I thought, considering my christening efforts of the previous year. When the rains began in earnest, Poombi moved them to a cave almost a kilometre away where they would be better protected from the weather.

I often sat for hours on the rock facing the nursery while she wandered off on one of her regular walkabouts. She couldn't have expected the piglets to stay still and quiet for such a long time; and nor did they. Within an hour or so, they would pile out of the den and start bouncing around like clockwork toys. I arrived there at nine o'clock one morning to find them lying in a tightly layered heap, as oblivious of the perils around them as a club sandwich. At first Luciano and Placido lay nose to tail with Maria balanced rather precariously on the top, and I hoped they might have done this on purpose so as to keep watch at both ends; but a little while later, they were fast asleep again, their heads towards the den and three little bums facing the world. I scolded them, and they ignored me. The shadow of a raptor swept over them, a squirrel panicked and scooted past inches away, dassies (animals a bit like outsize guinea pigs, though in fact related to the elephant and the dugong) called in alarm. The piglets slept through it all.

When their mother arrived, grunting softly, the porcine pyramid collapsed as they scrambled for safety. But when they realised who it was, they ran back to sniff her nose in greeting, and nibble at her tusks. At last, it was lunchtime for three little pigs. Poombi flopped down with a loud sigh, lifted her back leg and let them have it.

When her third litter, Charlie, Sophie and Danny (the Dahlings) were only two months old, she lost them. I found her grazing at the compound, her face grey with mud, all alone and utterly unperturbed. I searched for ten minutes or so, until Poombi suddenly woke up to the fact that her family had disappeared. She trotted off towards the nursery area, nose to the ground like a bloodhound, grunting and squeaking alternately. Her slow trot became faster as she began to panic and I ran after her, just as concerned as she was. The den was empty. She took off through the trees to the cave where the piglets had been born, but they weren't there either.

One imagines that for every mother, nothing can be more nightmarish than losing your child. What would she do now? Poombi did what comes naturally to pigs in a quandary – she stopped for a snack. As if I had mislaid David in the middle of Oxford Street and decided to halt my frantic search for a quick cuppa and a slice of cake. Now revitalised, she took off again in another direction and suddenly the Dahlings came bursting out of a bush, and off they all trotted as if nothing had happened, leaving me weak with relief.

But far be it from me to take my pig to task on her relaxed style of parenting. Compared to the bushpig, she is a model mother. The bushpig female couldn't care less about child rearing, and except for suckling the babies (a job she can hardly avoid), she takes no further interest in their welfare, leaving that job up to the dominant boar of the sounder.

Poombi's next move was to another koppie in a rather gloomy spot under some trees, directly opposite a large, gently sloping rock where the bundles of thatching grass are stored at the end of winter. I was sitting with my back against a tree one early afternoon, calling her softly and hoping I wasn't interrupting her siesta. She came almost immediately, followed by the piglets, and they had nearly reached me when a tremendous panic broke out among the baboons foraging about fifty yards away. Poombi spun around, but the piglets were ahead of her and I heard three loud thumps as they dived back into their hole.

Turning my head, I saw an adult male cheetah walking very casually past the bundles of grass a few yards away, harassed from a safe distance by two yelling baboons. Once he was out of sight, I ran to the top of the koppie, hoping to catch another glimpse of him, but he had slipped into the undergrowth and was gone. It was thrilling, like every encounter with the big cats that are always around us but so seldom seen. What dignity he had shown as he strolled regally amongst the rowdy mob, ignoring their jeers and insults.

Generally, Poombi kept her piglets reasonably close to a familiar hole, but when she moved them between homes they became particularly vulnerable. Warthogs, especially piglets, are heavily preyed upon, but an adult female is no pushover. We once watched a documentary showing a family of giant forest hogs coming down to drink at a waterhole, oblivious of the presence of a leopard hiding in the grass. As the cat leapt out at a piglet, its enraged mother charged straight into the attack, hit the leopard in the chest and sent it flying clean into the air.

Apart from two-legged predators outside our boundaries, cheetah and leopard are the greatest threat to our warthogs. The Matobo Hills are the ideal habitat for leopard, but only in the last decade or so have cheetah become relatively common in the area. And the irony of it is that the cattle ranchers, who don't want them within a hundred miles of their stock, have, by providing ideal living conditions, quite unintentionally invited them in.

Cheetahs are timid creatures and in purely wildlife areas like National Parks, they can't compete with the lions and hyenas, who regularly steal their food and kill their cubs. But ranchers won't tolerate predators on their land: there are no lions left in our area and, under pressure, hyenas have become more and more elusive and cunning.

So there are oceans of grass and scattered woodlands available to the cheetah, with little competition: perfect hunting grounds for a cat that specialises in the high-speed chase. Unfortunately, though, other than in wildlife sanctuaries like Stone Hills, the easiest and most available prey is the rancher's calves. And, unless he can be persuaded otherwise, war is declared, with the cheetah inevitably on the losing side.

Landowners all over the world are a conservative bunch who don't welcome change, as Laurie Marker of Namibia's Cheetah Conservation Fund discovered in the early 1990s when she did a survey among the farming community. Ninety per cent of Namibia's wild cheetah live on agricultural land, so if they were to survive, the ranchers had to be won over. There followed an incredible success story, thanks to Laurie's charisma and determination. By working closely with them in a non-confrontational way, Laurie showed ranchers that a harmonious relationship with the cheetah was possible. Often only minor changes needed to be made, such as keeping their calves in protected camps and monitoring them on a daily basis, or putting a donkey with a foal in the kraal, as the mare will protect both the calves and her offspring. Particularly effective has been Laurie's introduction of Anatolian Shepherd dogs, which bond with the herd and will guard them devotedly.

The Marwell Trust has taken up the cheetah conservation challenge in Zimbabwe, and that's how we became involved with Dr Netty Purchase, their cheetah project coordinator. We first met this charming, very feminine girl with the long blonde ponytail when we hosted the Oxford University's lion conference at the lodge.

I was hoping that the delegates, all leaders in their field, would be discussing something intelligible like behaviour, but instead they were using computer modelling to determine the status and sustainability of lions in Africa, and as a non-scientist I couldn't understand a word of it.

On the first day, when the flip chart was covered in figures and strange symbols and everyone was talking at once, a quiet voice was heard at the back, saying something that sounded like 'rubbish'. With that, Netty handed the baby to her husband Duncan, marched up to the front and took over the proceedings.

Following Laurie Marker's lead, Netty decided to write a textbook on cheetahs. When she had finished the first draft, she asked us if she could base herself at the lodge to do a pilot survey in the local schools. Once we saw the book, we knew we could help, and after working on it together for a year or so, and the usual interminable delays that attend any publication, a beautifully illustrated *Living with Cheetahs* was distributed to every primary school in Matabeleland.

Our local Marula school has a copy, and every week Khanye cycles up the Mangwe Road, armed with a bag of sweets, to give the older children a lesson in conservation. Sugar is an unknown luxury these days, so the sweets provide incentive, but the kids respond wonderfully to Khanye's relaxed approach and his infectious, breathy laugh (which always reminds us of Frank Spencer in *Some Mothers Do 'ave 'em*). When Khanye is busy, I show them wildlife videos and I have ninety or so kids crowded around the television, all vying for the front row. The collective gasp when they see a chimpanzee for the first time, or a great white shark hunting a seal, makes it all the more worthwhile.

At a time when everyone is hungry, anxious and disillusioned, we don't expect miracles. But every child that cares can make a difference and maybe little Trymore Ndlovu in the front row, hanging on to Khanye's every word, will one day, in more enlightened times, become the

Director of National Parks and Wildlife Management. We will do well to remember the words inscribed on the Grzimek's memorial at the edge of the Ngorongoro Crater: *It is better to light a candle than to curse the darkness.*

Cheetahs are specially protected – only fifty may be hunted a year with a special permit, though many more are killed illegally. But it's a different matter with leopard. 'Oh, there are plenty of them about' is the attitude, and I fell into the same trap when I wrote the first brochures for the lodge. 'The Matobo Hills,' I wrote airily and in complete ignorance, 'has one of the largest populations of leopard in the world.' It sounded impressive and, like everyone else, I thought it was probably true, but my statements weren't based on fact, any more than Zimbabwe's annual hunting quota of 500, the highest in Africa for one of its smallest countries, was the consequence of any meaningful research. The truth is that the figure was nothing but a thumb-suck. The quota was set years ago as part of a pan-African study, but the numbers were never justified by fieldwork or any hard scientific evidence.[1]

Feral dogs are always a threat to our animals, so when Mafira came on the radio late one August morning to report that the scouts had heard barking on our boundary with Marshlands, Rich leapt into his vehicle and went to investigate, taking Mafira and two other scouts with him. But it wasn't a couple of starving dogs baying up a kudu; a cacophony of hysterical yapping was coming from a place deep within the crowded koppies of the Pundamuka valley. Rich parked the vehicle some distance away and walked in under cover. To his utter disbelief, sixteen dogs, with a strong resemblance to English foxhounds, were scrambling over the rocks, watched by a group of seven men, three of them armed with hunting rifles.

Rich strode towards them, boiling with fury. 'What the bloody hell are you doing here?'

A young white man dressed in khaki appeared from behind the rocks, looking very alarmed at the sudden appearance of this bearded reincarnation of Noah, apparently consumed by the wrath of God.

'It's OK, it's OK, man,' he said, waving his arms. 'We didn't know it was your land.'

'Didn't know? What sort of crap is that? You've just climbed over twenty strands of my game fence. If you don't get out, I'll shoot every last dog and you too!'

'We-e-ll, we've got a bit of a problem,' stammered the young man, 'You see there's a-a wounded leopard down that crevice, and we're trying to get it out.'

There's no need to repeat Rich's response. The enormity of the situation warranted a far more creative use of language than any dictionary could provide, and my husband gave it his all. The hunting party had wounded a leopard at least two days before on an adjacent property. Apart from the awful trauma to the animal, they hadn't reported the incident to the police, or to National Parks, as they are required to by law, and nor had they informed us, or any of their other neighbours.

Every year stories do the rounds of people being ambushed and attacked by wounded leopards. Daily our scouts patrol the Pundamuka valley, armed with nothing more than knobkerries. And Rich was off to town the next morning to pick up a group of English schoolchildren for an environmental awareness course at our bush school. Their camp was less than a kilometre away from the leopard's hideout.

'And who do *they* belong to?' demanded Rich, pointing

at the dogs. A burly, bearded man stepped forward. 'I've brought them up from South Africa. They're coon hounds, we breed them specially for leopard hunting.'

'Do you have permission to do this?'

'Sure.'

Under the circumstances, there was no point in driving everyone away, until the cat was finally put out of its misery and the danger removed. While the hunters tried to smoke him out with bundles of lighted grass, Rich drove back to the house and contacted the safari operator who had been responsible for phoning the authorities, but hadn't bothered to do so.

He had just finished a lengthy and very heated call when Mafira was on the radio.

'They've left,' he told Rich, who was by now almost speechless. 'They say the leopard will go back on to Marshlands and they'll hunt it tomorrow morning.'

Of course, this was merely guesswork; the leopard was just as likely to take refuge on Dibe Hill behind the house than to go back to where he was shot. No one could possibly predict what his movements would be. But fortunately for the hunters, he did return, and after a few shots rang out at ten o'clock the following morning, the débâcle was finally over.

Of all the big cats, none is more secretive or adaptable than the leopard. And this has been the reason for its success. For years, one wily old fellow lived at the Hillside Dams, right in the middle of suburban Bulawayo. No one suspected he was there, until the neighbourhood dogs began mysteriously disappearing.

Unless we are alerted by drag marks across the road or the smell of a carcass, most kills on Stone Hills go undetected, as leopards like to hide their prey among the rocks. One morning, Ruthie came to report that there was a dead adult impala by cottage number 3. We'd hosted an outing of the Matobo Society the day before, and the visitors had sat on the grass by the swimming pool having their lunch. A few hours after they left, and when darkness had fallen, a leopard chased an impala to the same spot, killed it and dragged it up against the stone-clad walls of the cottage. If Rich ever needed reassurance that his efforts to make the lodge blend in with the surroundings had succeeded, this was it. Having eaten a bit of the back quarters, the leopard was scared away by the staff passing by a few feet from his meal, so he left it, and we were pretty sure that, with all the disturbance, he wouldn't come back.

We were wrong. He hid up on Dibe Hill for the day, and after dinner, he came in to feed. And on the third night, he dragged the carcass behind the kitchen and finished it there.

Rather surprisingly, dassies are their favourite fare in the Matobo Hills, but as consummate opportunists, leopards will naturally kill anything else if the occasion arises, including calves. Cattle ranchers have always hunted, poisoned and trapped problem leopards, but they never managed to make any real dent in the population of this nocturnal and incredibly evasive cat.

So, for years, the leopard had the upper hand, until safari hunting became popular, and it made better economic sense for the rancher to sell his leopard rather than drape its skin over the back of his sofa.

Traditionally, hunters hang bait and sit up in wait for their prey, which is hardly sporting, but not always successful, as the wily old males soon learn to mistrust impalas that have mysteriously climbed halfway up a tree. And once upon a more ethical time, the foreign hunter who had failed to bag his leopard one year was content to come back to Africa year after year, to try again. No longer. In this age of instant gratification, many a modern hunter treats his safari like an on-line shopping spree. And the best way for a safari operator to provide a leopard off the shelf, so to speak, is to hunt it with a trained pack of dogs, a method so successful that one operator advertised 'leopard guaranteed' in the safari magazines. Billed as 'the most exciting hunt on earth today', hunting leopard and sometimes cheetah with dogs has become more and more popular. With a dozen or so pairs of eyes, ears and noses glued to his tracks, and the hunter and his entourage panting behind, even the most cunning old cat doesn't have a hope in hell once he is treed or trapped in a cave. And as leopards become scarcer, hunting them with hounds is the quickest and most efficient way of killing them.

Within a few weeks of opening the lodge in 1993, our guests were entertained to an all-night serenade by two leopard males in pursuit of a female in oestrus all around the cottages. When the older of the two disappeared a couple of years later, another male soon took his place, using Stone Hills as part of a far larger home range, and regularly popping in on his females to check if any of them were in the mood. Large males are now a rarity. If they do visit, they stay for a while, then they are gone for good, more often than not destined for a trophy room in Texas or Madrid.

The leopard is losing ground fast. You can almost sympathise with the rancher who wants to see an end to the old male that regularly kills his calves, but there is no justification in hunting leopards down purely for the sake of the almighty dollar, without regard to the effect on their numbers, their social structure or their future.

Overkill is only the start of the problem. Hunters want trophies, the Big Cats, so they target breeding males. And once he's at the taxidermist having a pair of glass eyes fitted, the next mature male to take over his territory is likely to kill the offspring of the resident females. They don't belong to him, and his only concern is to leave his genetic mark on the population as quickly as possible. Another downside of taking out too many breeding males is that where the youngsters would normally be driven far away to establish their own home ranges, there is now nothing to stop them from staying near home and interbreeding with family members. Add to all this the loss of leopard habitat and their natural prey through land invasions, and you have a pretty bleak picture for the future of this exquisite cat.

Leopards don't have a champion like Laurie Marker, but, along with other concerned people, we keep on pushing for change, and there are moves afoot to get the research underway, re-evaluate the quota, and ban hunting with hounds. But for now, the fate of the leopard is confined to committees, meetings, proposals – and we still know almost nothing about this magnificent symbol of wild places, the lord of the night, who may soon disappear altogether if we don't stop talking and do something about it.

[1] In 2007, this figure was reduced to 250, which is still likely to be far too high in the light of land invasions and the resulting loss of habitat and prey.

Chapter Five

I'm drifting slowly over a coral reef among a school of brilliantly coloured fish. As I float towards the surface, the deep underwater silence is broken by a faint sound. A bird is calling; it's a kurrichane thrush with a song so sweet it belongs among the roses in an English garden. I wiggle my toes but it's too early to open my eyes. During the night, we opened the curtains to air the room, and now the sun is streaming through the window. I turn and drape an arm over Rich's shoulders, but he doesn't stir.

Then suddenly, feet are pounding through the house, and the bedroom door flies open. 'Mum! Dad!' David is shouting. 'Somebody's been shot. Come to the radio!'

We fall out of bed, run to the base station in the lounge and turn up the volume. In seconds, the dream has become a nightmare.

Two sunny days ago, a group of boys from the orchestra of Scotch College, Melbourne, were playing Elgar and Beethoven on the lodge veranda. David lay above them with his head over the edge of a little balcony. From up there, the hills seem to stretch away forever – and how I wish they did. I sat to one side of the musicians, looking out over an undulating patchwork of green flecked with gold, the first sign of approaching winter. Some of the neighbouring farmers and their families were gathered on the lawn below us. As the strains of *Chanson du Matin*, Elgar's 'Song of Morning', surged over the farm and away into the blue, David suddenly noticed a friend, looked up to wave and bumped his head on the wooden railings. And having given the offending bar a good kick, our little redhead marched off scowling. It was the first time I had seen anyone smile that morning.

A farmer from Mashonaland had been killed a few days before, as part of a campaign of terror aimed initially at white farmers and later at their employees. Ron, Dee and Emma Hartley were visiting us for the weekend. Dee is a pharmacist and she was helping us to treat Grunt, who was partially paralysed. He had hit the boma fence when Poombi chased him, protecting her new litter. We laid him on a deep bed of straw in a hut at the compound and with great difficulty Rich managed to slide a needle into a vein in his ear and put up a drip. That afternoon, we sat on the banks of the Mathole river until the sun went down, watching the children play in its clear running water. David found a baby terrapin, the size of a fifty-cent piece, and they made a little dam for him, along with some water boatmen that whizzed about weaving crazy shadows on the sand. We could hardly believe that somewhere not far beyond such beauty and serenity, sinister forces were threatening to rip our world apart.

What if? we asked each other, what if this spreads westwards? Or was the campaign aimed only at Mashonaland, headquarters of the ruling party for whom

Matabeleland was almost a foreign country?

The radio message has given us the answer. The voices on the air are all of people we know. An hour or so ago, a farmer from Nyamandlovu, north-west of Bulawayo, called a friend in town to say that his house was surrounded and that he had been shot in the foot. Then the phone went dead. A friend from Figtree has put his plane in the air and as he circles the farm, others are going in by road, and an ambulance is on its way. But they can't get near the farmhouse. They are stopped by a roadblock manned by armed policemem who assure them that 'everything is under control'

The pilot reports that fifteen to twenty vehicles are parked at the farmhouse. People are lying in the garden, but he can't make out what they are doing. 'There's smoke,' he says, 'it looks as though the place is on fire.'

At around ten o'clock, he's back on the radio. The vehicles are leaving, and he follows them from the air as they roar off towards Bulawayo.

Members of Support Unit arrive and are the first to go in, but they are too late, for the farmer is dead – slumped out of the bathroom window with gunshot wounds to his head and body. It is no coincidence that today is the twentieth anniversary of Zimbabwe's independence.

The pilot follows the vehicles until he loses them in the traffic. He warns that they may be heading in this direction, so a group of farmers take up positions off the road concealed in the grass, ready to radio back if the assassins pass by.

Somehow, in moments of crisis, time slows down. Instead of panicking, we sit on the veranda and have a cup of tea. Outwardly nothing around us has changed, the dog is asleep under the table, the rock pigeons are preparing a nest in the chimney – it's an ordinary day, but suddenly we are being called on to make some extraordinary decisions. We can hear our neighbours debating whether to stay or go; it seems that most of them have opted to stay. Like Rich, they are armed, and feel less vulnerable in familiar surroundings rather than out on the road facing an unknown threat.

Rich hands me the .38 special Rossi revolver, and I strap it around my waist, much to David's excitement and admiration. We feel like actors on a film set, somewhere in the Wild West. Any minute, someone will shout 'cut!' and we'll be back to normal.

David's reactions are all-important. We tell him there has been trouble, but assure him that it's nowhere near us. We may have to go to town for a while, but not for long. He seems to accept that, and for the rest of the day, he plays happily with Ruthie in his room while she packs up his special things.

Two weeks before, I had been sitting in the office when Neville Rosenfels's voice came over the radio, calling all stations, to report that a gang of around 200 people were outside his house. They stood at his gate, ululating and chanting slogans, demanding that he leave his land. When he went to speak to them, he realised that only five or six were war veterans; the rest were locals they had picked up along the way – even a few of his workers' wives. After five hours or so, when everyone was bored and tired, they dispersed.

It was a warning. We packed up our most precious possessions, Rich's photographs and my diaries, and took them into Bulawayo. Since then, I had been compiling an emergency list in case of evacuation: passports, the basket of keys, radios, weapons and licences, tools, sleeping bags. These are important, but not irreplaceable. Not like the animals we would have to abandon.

Although we fully intend to stay, we have to be ready to leave in case the situation changes, so we begin packing. I find I am speaking and moving very slowly, or does it just feel like that? The phone begins to ring, friends from town are calling, concerned, asking us what we are going to do and making offers of accommodation. We cut them short: we're fine, we tell them, we're probably going to stay but we have to be prepared to go; we'll let you know. Please don't phone again, we may not have much time.

Rich pulls his weapons and ammunition out of the gun safe; he makes sure the radios are charged, packs his camera equipment. I gather up our essential paperwork – thank God it's all there, passports, birth certificates, I.D.s, gun licences – documents that rule your life, and prove you actually exist. They are especially valuable in Zimbabwe, because if they are lost, chances are you will spend another ten years trying to replace them. Luckily, we have few treasures around the house, and little of sentimental value. By choice, I've travelled for much of my life, become used to carrying all my possessions in one bag. But now we have been on Stone Hills for ten years, the longest I have lived anywhere, and leaving it is no easy task. What we lack in knick-knacks we make up for in books, hundreds of them, almost all devoted to Africa's wildlife. We carry them in armfuls to our walk-in safe and pile them up on the floor. We've been told it will withstand fire for around six hours.

David appears from the bedroom carrying three soft toys. 'Leppie, Lion and Warthog want to come too,' he reminds me. 'Are we taking Nandi with us?'

'Of course,' I tell him. 'I've already packed Nandi's dish, her bed and her lead.'

She isn't our immediate concern, the other animals are. Gruntabel is showing no improvement although he's been on the drip for three days. Geraldine, the secretary bird with the injured leg, will never fly again, but she's eating well and we've been hoping she'll at least have some quality of life, free to wander around the garden. Neither of them can come with us, but nor can we leave them behind.

The spotted eagle owl injured by a car still can't fly and probably never will. He is at least moveable, though, so we put him in a box and load him in the vehicle.

While we are packing, Johnson and Mafira cut a hole in the bushbucks' fence and then move away. Mary is always looking for the chance to explore and she's through it in five minutes, but the others stay behind, too timid to venture out. Mary often slips out of the gate and wanders around the garden, peering through the windows of the house, taking a sniff at the owls and saying hello to Nandi. Nothing I do will lure her back, not even her favourite bowl of tea with milk and sugar, until she is quite ready to return. Now she comes around to the front veranda and waits for me, her dark trusting eyes wide with anxiety. She knows something is wrong. I don't trust myself to have a long conversation with her, so I smooth her warm, russet coat and tickle inside her ear, trying to be reassuring, then leave her with a large pile of vegetables and tell her to be careful. Of all our animals, they are the most at risk from leopard – every other bushbuck on Stone Hills has disappeared, so for safety, Mary and her family live in a large enclosure around our house known as Buckingham Palace. Now there is no option, they will have to take their chances outside. Apart from vandalising property, farm invaders have been maiming or killing dogs, horses and other domestic animals around the homesteads. Nothing can be left for them.

The radio is turned up to full volume and we jump every time it goes. More and more of our neighbours are deciding to move to town. There is no news from the farmers on the road, the convoy has not come our way, and the plane is no longer in the air. We wonder if the assassins have taken another route.

White farmers are the target, so for the time being all our local workers opt to remain on the farm, and some others too. Khanye comes from Victoria Falls, but he decides to stay and will sleep at the lodges with keys, vehicle and radio at his disposal. We will call him twice a day, morning and evening. Mafira and the other Shonas, Manicas and Tongas are to come with us to town. Some will go home for a while, others will wait with us for a few days. At any sign of trouble, the staff who stay behind will hide their belongings in the bush and meet Rich at a pre-arranged place much further down the main road.

I'm suddenly bent double with stabbing pains in my stomach. I try some deep breathing but it doesn't help, so I lie down for ten minutes: ten wasted minutes when I should be packing. I curl up in pain on the bed and think about Poombi and her Dahlings, now five months old. She might be anywhere on the farm. What will she think when she comes to the house and finds it empty? What will happen if we can never come home again? How long will they take to find and kill her, or will she run from familiar places, knowing that something is wrong?

Rich comes in to check on me, his brown eyes full of love and concern. No one ever needs to remind me why I need a man, *this* man, in my life. I may not say as much when it's his day in town and he's left my shopping list on the dining room table. Again. Or when I find a set of irreplaceable title deeds in the rubbish basket, along with every other scrap of paper on his desk. These are trivial matters (I say in kindly retrospect), for when the chips are down, I trust Rich more than any other person on earth. The greater the emergency, the calmer and more in control he is. He thinks through his hands – whether he is taking a thorn out of David's foot, loading a weapon or fiddling in the guts of a tractor, his touch is sure and confident. A few years before, we had done a First Aid course together for our guides' licences. I was standing in the reception of our Bulawayo office the morning after we had written the exam when there was a sudden squeal of brakes, a sickening pause, and the crunch of colliding metal. I ran to the gate; one vehicle had smashed into the side of another, and the driver was slumped over the wheel.

St John's Ambulance service had taught us well: deal with the breathing, the bleeding and then the bones – the three Bs, in that order. But my priorities were different. Absolutely in control of the situation, I ran inside and yelled 'Rich!' Then took myself off to the telephone to raise the police and the ambulance; not the mucky stuff, I agree, but still a challenging task in Zimbabwe.

The pain subsides and I carry on packing, filling old stockfeed bags and wondering how much we can fit into the back of the vehicles. What do we really need and what can we do without? At last, they are full, not another thing can be crammed in. At four o'clock Anthony, lodge manager, arrives at the house – he is packed and ready, if we need to go. But we are loathe to leave. We are standing on the lawn talking when we hear one neighbour speaking to another on the radio. 'We're at the turnoff,' she says.

'Are you going to be much longer?' Rich cuts into the conversation to ask if any farmers are staying but nobody is. Now we will have to go too. If we stay and there's trouble, help will be far away, and other people will be putting their lives at risk for us. The sun is starting to sink and now a decision has been made, we begin to move more quickly, conscious that we have to be away by dark and off the main road. The gang might be waiting in ambush, or planning to attack at night.

Wonder Issah, handyman, goes first and we hear the rattle of the tractor and trailer as he heads for the gate. Just as we are about to leave, he arrives back at the house to tell us that the trailer has broken. Zimoyo, Anthony's assistant, drives his Land Rover on ahead. It's very slow and we want him to get a headstart before dark.

We begin locking doors, cupboards, shutting windows, a million things churning around in our heads, worrying what we might have forgotten to do or take. Rich has put Venture, the African goshawk, in her box; she is loaded. We must make a decision about Millie, the tiny duiker fawn found in someone's mealie patch and ours to rehabilitate. We could leave her in the bush, but she is so small and vulnerable, she probably won't survive. So we wrap her in a blanket and Solomon sits with her on his lap in the back of the green Hiace that I will be driving. We know a family in Bulawayo who keep duikers in their garden; it's better than abandoning her. Ruthie climbs into the back with them, and David squeezes between her and Solomon. Nandi sits in a corner in the back of the Land Cruiser, next to Francis Samunyanga. He will go back to Inyanga in the Eastern Districts on the other side of the country and await the all-clear.

We are ready to leave. Khanye stands by the vehicles,

a bunch of keys in his hand. I'm trying not to think. I start up the engine so I can't hear Rich go back to the garden – Geraldine and Gruntabel, after everything we had done to keep them alive. He returns to the vehicles without looking at me and climbs into the back of the Land Cruiser, next to Brutus, Anthony's excitable ridgeback. He is wagging his stump of a tail, but Nandi sits opposite him with her ears drooping. I can see the whites of her eyes. She doesn't like this sort of adventure.

Another voice on the radio. Graham Robertson has just passed the Marula store where a rowdy bunch of people are chanting and dancing. It could turn nasty, so we had better hurry. We are the last farmers left in the district.

Khanye steps back as Anthony starts the Landcruiser, laden to the hilt, sitting right down on its wheels. When they reach the bottom of the hill behind the house, we start up after them.

'Goodbye, Khanye! Don't forget to keep putting cubes out for the buck. And food for the rats. We'll call you tonight. Be careful!'

From the minute we leave the house, I start looking for Poombi and her family. I hope they are not near the road because I don't want her to see us leaving. If she had been alone, we could have darted her and moved her into town, but where? It would have taken weeks to build a proper enclosure, and then what? A life of pent-up misery? In any case, it was ridiculous even to speculate on that. Poombi had a family and we couldn't move them all. She had to stay.

Dusk. Dibe dam lies still as a mirror fired with the blood-red colours of the sunset. On the other side of the water, seven kudu file slowly down for their evening drink. They are the girls who come to the house at the start of winter asking for food. They are too trusting, too gentle. Run away! I want to shout at them. But they will go nowhere. In any case, they are trapped by the fence we have built to protect them.

We find Zimoyo at the turn-off to the compound. His eyes are huge and terrified. He can't work the lights in Anthony's vehicle. Now he'll be travelling in our convoy, slowing us all down so we won't make town before dark. It is imperative that we leave quietly, not attracting any attention to ourselves. David has armed himself with his catapult and a bagful of stones, Rich sits at the back next to a salivating Brutus. He has an ammo belt slung around his neck, the loaded shotgun propped up between his legs. With the long grey beard and the hat over his eyes, he is the old man of Africa, the patriarch in his wagon, with a bag of biltong and a bible, taking on the heathen hordes. I should have been wearing my bonnet.

Scout Billiard Mudenda is at the gate. I have told David to stay down on the floor but as we pass through, up pops his head. 'Bye, Bye, Billiard,' he shouts, 'we're evacuating!'

What an exciting day. He gets down on the floor again with Leppie by his side and keeps chatting. 'Where are we now? What's happening? Has dad shot anyone yet?'

We are trying to go quietly, pass by the store in the dark, not coming to anyone's attention. But Brutus begins to bark, loudly, hysterically. Saliva hangs in bubbly silver ribbons from his mouth. Anthony leans out of the window and slaps him, which makes him worse. Rich is toying with his shotgun. The more Brutus barks, the closer Rich sits to him. He elbows him in the ribs, until the dog is halfway out of the vehicle, still hollering. We go through Marula like a travelling circus. Not many people are left there now, but they can't miss the Peeks in convoy, heading for Bulawayo. Leaving home, maybe forever, and yet there's something thrilling about all this, as if we are in the middle of an adventure story, living it outside of ourselves, watching it on the movies. But the adventure ends in Bulawayo. Sue and Alan Bryant live in our house but they keep a room for us. Just in case. We have phoned them to say the day has come. I leave Rich at the gate and go on with Millie to her new home. Thank goodness the Jardines can take her. As I hand over the little bundle in the blanket, I want to ask if we can have her back one day, all being well. But I don't; I can't do that. I must just be thankful that she is safe.

We wake early the next morning in our little room, the three of us with the dog between the beds, to the sound of the early morning traffic, house sparrows and crows. Surrounded by boxes, stockfeed bags – chaos. What next? David sleeps on, Leppie's head beside him on the pillow. Yesterday, in the midst of the action, it seemed unreal and we were insulated by shock and disbelief. Now it is all too true. Nandi looks up at me and gives a long, shuddering sigh. Some of our staff catch buses home, all over the country; others, like Mafira, head scout, choose to stay; he wants to get back to the farm. We call Khanye, thank God the phone is working, and he tells us that everything is quiet. He hasn't seen the bushbuck but he's picked up their spoor around the lodge.

White farmers have poured into Bulawayo from all the outlying districts. Like us, they are camping with their families and pets somewhere in town, confused and indecisive. Some livestock farmers have refused to leave their land, dairy cows must be milked, chickens must be fed. How vulnerable they must feel.

Twenty-four hours in town are enough for Rich. There has been no more bad news, so he decides to go back and organise things properly. Mafira goes with him. I'm frightened for them, but I want to go too. I can't, of course, I must stay with David, and we wander around the garden listening to the doves calling: 'What'll we do? What'll we do?' Funny, I've never heard them saying that before.

Rich posts scouts on the koppie overlooking the main gate, which is now permanently locked. At any sign of trouble, they will radio Mafira at the main house. All the staff will then have time to run and hide in the bush, making their way to a rendezvous with Rich twenty kilometres towards town on the main road. Mafira has handled weapons in his National Parks days. Rich leaves him with the short-barrelled .303, the jungle carbine.

Now I can go shopping, go to the hairdresser and see friends. All the things I never have time for on my rushed visits into town. But I'm not interested in doing any of them. I long for the silence, the sound of the wind through the crack in the sliding doors, the noise of monkeys scampering on the thatched roof, sharing our toast with the bushbuck through the dining room window. All the things that make home the most wonderful place in the world.

Chapter Six

The world was a safer place in 1968, the year my father bought me a one-way ticket on the SS *Vaal* from Cape Town to Southampton. With a secretarial diploma tucked in my bag and my miniskirts at fingertip length, I was ready to take up my first job as junior secretary at the Charter Consolidated Company in London. Six months later, I was reading *The Times* at my desk instead of typing, when an item in the small ads caught my eye: 'London to Katmandu overland: one hundred pounds'. And not long after, I wrote to my parents telling them that I would shortly be boarding an eleven-seater bus heading for Nepal; they could write to me post restante in Istanbul, Tehran, Kabul, Lahore, Calcutta and finally Katmandu, but after that I could be anywhere. No need to worry, I'd be in touch some time.

If my son did that to me today, I'd be on the phone immediately, offering him all sorts of unwelcome advice, taking out travel insurance and insisting on contact every few days. But forty years ago long-distance calls to Africa were unheard of. My parents replied along the lines of:

'That's nice, dear, but don't forget your jumper'. And off I went.

To finance my wanderings I earned sixty rupees a day at the film studios in Bombay at the very start of Bollywood. The Indians liked my long blonde hair, and on one occasion they filmed me climbing alone up a flight of stairs to join a crowd at a cocktail party, where we all toasted each other with glasses of surgical spirit – an unexpected brush with stardom.

I found a kitten at rush hour on Hong Kong Island about to step into the traffic, and took him to work at the Radio Corporation of America where he played on my typewriter for the day. He lived with me for a year in a flat in Happy Valley, overlooking the racecourse, and when I left to travel through South East Asia my flatmates adopted him. From East Timor, I flew to Australia. There I took a variety of jobs, the most ill-chosen being a two-week stint on a prawn trawler, where I upset a lot of bottlenose dolphins in the Torres Straits by endlessly vomiting over the side of the boat.

What are you looking for? people asked me on my trips home. What's wrong with your own country? Nothing at all, I would assure them. I loved it, and with the naivety of youth, I believed that it would never change. Safe and predictable, Rhodesia would always be waiting for me.

It was easy to dream as a child growing up among the Bvumba mountains in the Eastern Highlands. For ten years, my father managed the Leopard Rock hotel with its breathtaking views across the Burma valley and into the remote and mysterious mountains of Mozambique, and while my mother played golf and arranged the flowers I spent happy days exploring the countryside with my donkey. I dreamed of travelling the world alone, wandering from one exotic place to the next – taking only my memories away but leaving nothing of myself behind.

Nikos Kazantzakis, author of *Zorba the Greek*, wrote: 'I hope nothing, I fear nothing, I am free.' His words in Greek are engraved on a stone among a mass of flowers at his Cretan memorial. He could have written them for me.

It was when I was stuck in the airless offices of the shipping company in Athens after an idyllic summer drifting around the Greek islands that I decided to get serious about my life. Every temperamental Greek I met seemed to be a doctor or a lawyer – and I came to the belated conclusion that if I wanted to escape from the typewriter, I had better follow suit and get some sort of degree. Despite my dodgy A level results, I was given a place in the law department of the University of Rhodesia as a mature student. No one could have been keener. Having worked (well, sort of) for the past six years, the prospect of spending the next three quite legitimately immersed in books was absolutely thrilling. *Lawyer*, I kept whispering to myself, imagining how impressed people would be when I qualified. On the first day, I proudly took myself off to the students' union, and stopped dead at one of the tables. There sat Richard Peek, a colleague of my brother David's from National Parks, at twenty-seven even more of a mature student than I was and far less qualified to be there, in my opinion, having failed his O levels three times. My first thought was that the university must be pretty desperate for mature students, but this was quickly followed by delight in meeting my old friend. In fact, Rich had earned his place at the university. Having attended a course on ecology organised by National Parks, his dissertation was so well researched and presented that he was offered a place on a BSc degree course, majoring in zoology. So there we were. Rich had already been married for a year, and I was deeply involved with a Greek basketball star. We would be buddies for the next three years but nothing more.

In 1974, home was no longer the secure haven of my childhood. After nearly two decades of savage fighting, the Portuguese colonists were about to be ousted from Mozambique, and in Rhodesia, the bush war that culminated in an independent Zimbabwe was at its height. Many of the young men I studied with were hardened combatants, having already spent a year in the army after finishing school.

Concerned about the future, I crammed for English law exams after completing my degree and managed, by coercing kind-hearted friends, to get a place as an articled clerk in a London law firm specialising in entertainment. The young Michael Douglas sometimes passed by my door in those two dreary years, and I had one memorable afternoon with Albert Finney teaching him how to speak with a South African accent. Weekends I spent alone at the Natural History Museum, or wandering around the London Zoo, feeling as trapped as the animals pacing their cages and itching to be away and on the move again. The minute I had completed my final exams and before I received the results, I left for Australia, where I practised law for as long as I could stand it. I was, I thought, a citizen of the world.

When we finally got together back in Zimbabwe in 1984, Rich knew all about my wanderlust, but he reckoned he knew how to cure it. He brought home a Labrador puppy, who was later joined by a Rottweiler and a feral tabby cat we rescued from the industrial sites. We bought a house and in 1987, breaking all the promises I had made to myself, we were married – in the garden. I wore a cotton dress patterned with parrots and toucans, and threw my pink high heels into the flowerbed the minute we had signed the register. The sleeping bag was stashed at the back of a cupboard full of crisp new linen and, until the novelty wore off, we drank tea from cups with matching saucers. A strange feeling was creeping over me – not claustrophobia, as I would have expected, but contentment.

Then my husband fixed me forever. At the age of 40, I became pregnant with David, and the following year, we moved to Stone Hills, 6,500 acres among the boulder-strewn hills of the Matobo. One journey had ended, but in creating a wildlife sanctuary from a degraded cattle ranch another far more satisfying one had begun: a journey that often took me no further than our front veranda, with David in my arms, looking out over the wild grey hills and windswept valleys that now set the limits of our lives. As the magic of Stone Hills seeped into us, its rhythms became our own. It was as though the rest of the world had ceased to exist.

The first time we drove on to the farm together, we meandered down a dirt track for four kilometres before pulling up at a gate under a couple of marula trees. Thinking that this was the boundary, I jumped out of the car and began tucking into the fallen yellow fruit (I've left them alone since then; the next morning my face, lips and cheeks were covered in crimson blotches and swollen to twice the size). Rich looked at his map. 'This is only a paddock gate. Let's carry on a bit.'

We followed the track for another four kilometres as

it wound through jumbled granite koppies, their boulders piled up in glorious disarray like toys in a giant's playground. It was unbelievable. This time we weren't visitors to the National Park, hurrying to make it out of the gate by six o'clock, we were actually going to belong to this place, wake up every morning to the sound of its birds, see the moon rise over its hills. But even then, we had no inkling of what the land would come to mean to us, how uprooted we would feel when we left it for a week, and later even for a day. For, over time, Stone Hills was to become a world in itself, a little community to which we all belonged, people and animals alike.

In the beginning, the rock dassies wouldn't come near the house, and if we passed too close to them, there would be a warning screech or a whistle and they would all dive for the shelter of the rocks. But it wasn't long before I was chasing them around the garden every winter, trying to stop them from stealing the bushbucks' cubes. The boss of the robber gang was old Scar Chops, and towards the end of one very dry year we could see that his life of plunder was ending. We didn't know his age, but as the drought dragged on through October and November, the old dassie became more and more emaciated. Now he was so venerable, I felt rather disrespectful calling him Scar Chops, so, to polish up his image a bit, I renamed him D'Arcy. We were finishing lunch one afternoon when D'Arcy's tufted, balding head appeared at the top of the steps. We froze, and Nandi lunged at him with a loud growl, but instead of running away, the dassie hopped up the last step and retreated under a cupboard. I ground up some cubes and left them close to him. He ate them and came back the next day for a bit more of the same, plus a banana. In the afternoons, when the house was quiet, we would find him on the mantelshelf over the fireplace or crouched on the low wall of the dining room, nibbling at the maidenhair fern. He needed help and he knew where to find it.

I was on the phone one afternoon when he suddenly keeled over in the grass on the other side of the window.

'Rich,' I shouted, 'poor old D'Arcy's dead!'

I rushed outside to retrieve the body and two glassy eyes stared up at me, and blinked slowly. The dassie raised his head, got to his feet and tottered off. He must have done that four or five times before he finally took up permanent residence on our front veranda. Too weak to stand, he leaned up against the wall, accepting bits of cake from our afternoon tea.

I couldn't find him one morning, but I knew where he'd be – hunched up in a dark corner of the empty firehose box, still on the veranda, waiting to die. It was a useless gesture, but I put food and water in with him, expecting to find him gone the following day. But he was still alive, very quiet and still. He died peacefully the following night under the protection of the very creatures he should have feared the most.

Funny how it's the small things that break your heart.

Our farm is aptly named: we are surrounded by hills of stone. From the veranda, we recognise every familiar contour of these ancient koppies, rising like castles from the morning mist or glowing in the soft light of evening. It is the rocks that shape the character of this land. Its granite soils determine the vegetation, and that's the deciding factor as to who will thrive here and who will merely exist.

Winter and summer, the zebra, wildebeest and giraffe

are the most robust of our animals and rarely need our help. Others, like the kudu, eland and gemsbok, quickly drop in condition and around mid-July, or even earlier in a bad year, they gather in the vlei in front of the house for their daily ration of cubes, along with others who don't really need it but won't miss a treat. There's chaos if they all feed together, so we have established a routine that almost everyone understands.

Big Fight loads up the back of the Toyota for me with bowls of cubes, puts a white sack over his shoulder like Father Christmas, and marches off whistling, followed by the eland in an orderly line, heading for a spot on the other side of the river. When they are out of sight, I quickly lay out ten bowls for the kudu milling all around me, trying to step on my feet. By this time, the gemsbok have come very close, so I drive along behind them, herding them down to their feeding spot further down the vlei. The warthogs, Thelma and Louise, with their respective litters, gallop after me, and block the road like highway robbers demanding their share, which I scatter behind a bush so the gemsbok don't notice. Except for Shashani, our oldest female, the giraffe have never been able to get their heads around a routine, but if any of them happen to pitch up at four o'clock, my last stop is at the raised feeding drum, where I stand on the back of the vehicle and pour in the cubes. And when everyone is finished, the ravens, dassies, francolins and bushpigs come in for the leftovers. There is nothing more completely satisfying than watching contented animals disappearing into the dusk with their tummies full, knowing that they will be back the same time tomorrow. If there is a tomorrow, of course.

Some of our people are from the local Kalanga tribe, others come from further afield. But over the years strong friendships have been formed across tribal boundaries, and a network has grown and taken root as friends and family members have joined us. The scouts who patrol the sanctuary every day have a deep kinship with the land and its wildlife. They've named the sable bull with magnificent horns sweeping over his back Umkoqela – tight curl; the zebra stallion with the wonky front foot is Gide Gide, and Mawavemsila, another stallion, is the one who is always swishing his tail. Khanye called one zebra Banye-Mulenge, after the rebel leader in the Congo. 'For four years,' he wrote in his report, 'he persistently tried to take over groups of females, but he lost all his battles until the year 2000 when he ousted Knob Nose, our most respected stallion, who is tame, good-looking and thought to be the strongest of them all.'

Old age had caught up with him, and the defeated Knob Nose was forced to look elsewhere for love. He finally managed to abduct a young female but, said Khanye, 'he had problems settling in with her and we observed him restlessly trying to stamp his authority. He would run at her, mouth wide open, showing off his yellow teeth, and she would obey for a while. But then we saw that she had lost a bit of her tail and there was no doubt that Knob Nose had done it. After this, she was so submissive that he could finally boast of a good wife. There was no more running around for them, and we are waiting to see their offspring if nature allows.'

Animals and humans alike, we know and accept each other as individuals. When we are out walking, I have to call Nandi away from the giraffe as she sometimes trots through their legs while in pursuit of an exciting smell, and we are always on the alert for Shashani, who can spot us from miles away and comes thundering over on the off-chance that we might have a pocketful of cubes. But let a strange dog come on to the place, and the animals panic and flee. One afternoon, I wore a new hat and the group of zebra who live around the house stopped eating and stared at me suspiciously.

At least three troops of baboons live on Stone Hills. They're a bawdy lot, and when they gather on the top of Dibe at dusk, they trade noisy insults with the gang on the other side of the river. Like a bunch of old drunks in the pub on a Friday evening, you can hear them telling each other dirty jokes and hooting with laughter. I wave every time I pass them by, and I'm quite sure that one day someone will forget himself and wave back.

If they live in close proximity to humans who leave their food and waste around, baboons can become very bold and even dangerous. This was the case at Victoria Falls and Parks staff decided that they would have to shoot a few to drive them away. But they couldn't get near them: the baboons knew perfectly well what they were up to and disappeared the moment anyone in a khaki uniform came anywhere close. Only when the rangers dressed up in their wives' clothes and hid their weapons under their skirts did they have any success, and the baboons soon caught on to that trick too.

Body and soul, we belong to this land, and in return we have given it our love and respect. We don't need to see all its creatures – it's enough to know that they are there, quietly living out their lives, somewhere among these enchanted hills.

As W.H. Auden wrote in his *Address to the Beasts*:

For us who, from the moment
We first are worlded,
Lapse into disarray,

Who seldom know exactly
What we are up to,
And, as a rule, don't want to,

What a joy to know
Even when we can't see or hear you,
That you are around...

In 1989, when the first land grabs began, I made a bargain with the god of Stone Hills. I promise I'll be good if you give us ten years, that's all, just ten years – believing that somehow it would be enough. After all, it sounded like a lifetime after my years on the move. Ten years later, David and I were on our way to Australia, knowing that we might never see Stone Hills again. With his Leppie tucked tightly under one arm, David sobbed uncontrollably at Johannesburg airport and I could give him no comfort for I, too, was aching with misery. No more godly bargains for me. He's far too inflexible.

Chapter Seven

So I'm sitting at Johannesburg airport with my son weeping on my lap, and I'm wondering what we are doing here. The boys from Scotch College who played *Chanson du Matin* so beautifully for us two weeks ago gather around to talk – they are going home on the same plane. I tell them the whole story, how we have left the farm, the murders and the threat of more. How Rich was going back regularly alone but only for the day, while David, Nandi and I sat in our room or wandered aimlessly around the garden in town. We weren't achieving anything, so it was a good time for us to visit my parents, especially since David is on school holidays. This is a perfectly sensible explanation but I'm feeling uncomfortable, as if I need to justify myself. A little voice whispers in my head – what nonsense! Admit it, you're running away. But that's not true. I would have stayed had it not been for David, but I do know that having made the difficult decision to leave, I subconsciously began to look for reasons to strengthen my resolve. Although there was no sign of trouble in Bulawayo, suddenly I could feel the tension; people looked different, threatening, even sinister. One morning, the whole town seemed to be filled with soldiers in red berets, marching along the pavements in groups of three or four. I drove back to the house too fast, in a panic. 'There's army all over the place,' I told Sue, 'something is going on and I don't like it.' I could see the concern in her face. But two days later I discovered that they were only a bunch of new recruits waiting to be transferred to another barracks, and I felt ashamed for having rattled her for nothing.

I love Australia, the laid-back land of sunshine and barbies on the beach. But being here now is even harder than being at home. I hang around the TV, shouting 'Quiet! Quiet!' every time Zimbabwe is mentioned, and it often is – more murders, more land grabs, huge political unrest. People drop around to the house with cuttings from the newspapers: every one contains more bad news. The phone calls to Rich don't help because even when he says that he is all right, I don't believe him. 'Are you sure?' I ask. 'Are you hiding something from me?'

After two weeks, he can't stand town any more, so he moves back to the farm. No one can look after himself better than Rich: his years in National Parks have trained him to be completely self-reliant. He is prepared, alert and armed – and on familiar ground. But that is cold comfort for me. Nandi sleeps by his side every night. Poombi and her triplets have been seen by the scouts and lately she's been accompanied by a boar. It's that time of the year again, of course, as it is for the pair of black eagles who have two eggs in their eyrie at the White Hills. While life continues on Stone Hills as peacefully as ever, I am lying awake at night on the other side of the world sick with worry about what might happen, dragging my depression around like a dead cat chained to my leg.

The Lucky Country is the very antithesis of the daily dramas, the grubbiness, the constant anxiety of living in the third world. Here happiness and convenience are a right (at least for its human inhabitants), and I get a nostalgic pang from watching the spider spinning her web nightly across the garden path. She simply Is and will continue inconveniently to Be, no matter how many times my father arrives back in the house with the morning paper under his arm and his hair full of sticky web. So much of the first world is dazzlingly superficial – in contrast to Africa, which is sultry, multi-layered and never predictable.

But no matter how miserable I feel, I must pretend to be cheerful for David's sake, and for my poor parents whose neat little house has been invaded. After a week or so of sitting around, I decide to send David to school, anticipating all sorts of obstacles. In Zimbabwe, we book our children into schools at birth, and I wondered how long we would be waiting for a place at Chancellor Park, the government school at the foot of Buderim mountain. David told me he was quite happy about going, but when we went to make the arrangements, he kept clasping his hands on top of his head, a sure sign of nerves. For a Zimbabwean used to interminable bureaucratic hang-ups, it was an uplifting experience. Within half an hour, I'd signed the forms and bought the uniform. And at nine o'clock on the very next day, I left my son with the teacher of his new class, looking pale but very smart in his new blue shorts and teeshirt. In my opinion, every minute at school is ghastly, let alone your first day in a strange country for which you have been utterly unprepared. I worried all day, but quite unnecessarily. When I went to pick him up at three o'clock that afternoon, I found him on the lawn behind the hedge in a clinch with a much larger boy who was 'teaching him how to wrestle'. He put on his brave face, but later the teacher showed me a story he had written that ended with the words 'please pray for my poor country, Zimbabwe'.

I spent my spare time walking round and round the houses, trying to get a glimpse of the old Buderim, the ginger mountain, as it was twenty years ago when my parents first moved there. I looked in vain – gone were the fields and the remaining patches of rainforest that had once covered its slopes. Now the new Woolworths has the most spectacular view on the mountain, right across the Pacific Ocean to Moreton Island lying shrouded in sea mist. A few years before, possums played nightly havoc in my parents' roof, and a pair of boo-book owls called from across the street, but now all I could hear was the distant hum of traffic from the main road.

I remember one well-known South African author writing about his 'exile' to Europe. He used the word lightly and in a romantic sense, in order to convey not banishment, but the pain of being away from the place he loved. He was free to return, freer than we were, but that fear that we might not gave me the smallest inkling of the desolation that refugees the world over must feel when they are driven away forever from their countries and their homes.

Rich told us that all four bushbuck were back in Buckingham Palace after their little jaunt, having miraculously avoided the local leopards. And that the morning after the gate was shut behind them, Diana had given birth to Harry. If they had returned to their enclosure a day later, we might have separated mother and baby without ever knowing what we had done. Then Cleo gave birth to Frederick – another son for our royal family. And while all this was happening, David and I were languishing in the land of lawnmowers. I begged Rich to let us come home but he wouldn't hear of it. More farmers had been killed and now the violence had spread to their workers, who were being driven away from the land, leaving their houses and all their possessions in flames behind them. For many it was the only home and security they had, and thousands camped on the roadsides, refugees in their own country. We'll come back after the elections, I told Rich, but he wouldn't be drawn. Depending on which way it went, the violence might spin out of control, then Rich, too, would be on the run. I sat in the loo with my head in my hands and wept.

After two months, I could bear it no longer. Stone Hills and the surrounding district were peaceful; if we saw that things were changing, we could make alternative plans. But we had to get home. The arrival form for South Africa that I filled out on the plane requested our permanent residential address. My pen hovered over that one; I wished I could have been more certain of the answer.

At Johannesburg airport, David rushes into his father's arms and Rich envelops us in a bear hug, all holding on tight to each other as if we will never let go. I bury my face in his neck. His beard tickles my cheeks and I shut my eyes and breathe in the familiar smell of him, the warmth of the body I have been yearning for. Home is still 700 kilometres away and Jo'burg is just another big city, but today I love it, because it is Africa. The next morning we wake to a raucous noise: not kookaburras this time but a flock of rowdy hadeda ibises, braying off key. They never sounded so sweet. We are all packed up and ready to go the following evening when Rich gets a phone call to say that fighting has broken out at Marula, the small settlement on the main road, five kilometres from our gate. Perhaps we should delay a few days in case it gets worse. 'We can't wait any more!' I shout. 'We've come this far, we *must* get back tomorrow.' I am about to cry and Rich puts his arm around my shoulders. 'I'll make a few more phone calls. It could be just a rumour.'

This is my childhood nightmare all over again. I am a weekly boarder and it is Friday afternoon. From the dormitory window, I can see my parents waiting in the car. I'm trying to pack but something is holding me back; as hard as I try, I can't move properly. It's as if I am paralysed. And I can't even shout at them through the window, 'I'm coming, wait for me!' Finally, I watch them drive away.

But Rich is smiling – 'It's OK. I've checked with the neighbours and they haven't heard about any problems.'

We have been gone for almost three months, I wrote in my diary that evening, *I am terrified that we will not be able to return – 'they' will find a way to stop me from reclaiming that part of me that I left on Stone Hills. Somehow I have to analyse my passion for the land that has overwhelmed me in the last few years. I am empty without it: it is the sanctuary for my soul. I can't believe it's possible that tomorrow I may drive through the gate again, put my arms around the dog, call Mary from the bushes and go searching for the pig. Perhaps I should never have let it become an obsession, but what would I have missed if I had experienced it any less intensely?*

We leave before dawn the following morning and at 4 pm we arrive at the Plumtree border post between Botswana and Zimbabwe. We are crushed in the queue between dozens of jostling bus passengers, inching our way to the immigration desk. It is overcrowded, filthy and inefficient, but it's the last hurdle before home, forty kilometres away, and I hardly notice the discomfort. Then at last we are waved through the exit gate that hangs cockeyed on its hinges, and we give a whoop of joy. We have left the stony barrenness of Botswana for the rolling woodland and koppies of home. No one can take that pleasure away.

We pass Ronald on the Mangwe road and he falls off his bike waving. David jumps out of the car and runs up the hill in front of us. We find him at the garden gate hugging Mafira, while Nandi the dog turns herself inside out with joy. Mafira holds out his hand to me for the traditional handshake – first clasping the whole hand, then the thumb, and the whole hand again.

'So,' he says, with a wide grin. 'You've come back to this shit!'

First there was a Going Out, and then there was a Coming In, and no, I won't use the word 'home' because it's not quite that any more. It's like being in the transit lounge of an airport waiting for a disembodied voice to announce that we are leaving again.

So many emotions, so hard to analyse. It's like believing that someone you loved has died and after three months of mourning, he is suddenly standing in front of you – that's the sort of adjustment I think I was making yesterday. I had pictured the scene so often, driving back on to the farm, doing it in reverse, playing the film backwards. As we drove out, we now drive in, but it doesn't seem quite real; it's as if the film is being played for me but I'm not actually participating in it. It's a memory, a technicolor dream, and like one's reaction to the reappearance of the dead, there's a feeling of remoteness and disbelief. This is made even more complicated because one cannot respond to it whole-heartedly, you cannot say 'here I am, I'm back, it's home and here I'll stay', because it may be a week, a month, a year and all we know for certain is that it must be temporary. I've been holding back on my emotions for so long now, ever since we drove out that day, refusing to accept anything until the moment when it is certain there is no return. It's not like the normal homecoming, back to the familiar, the continuity of one's life – I've returned to find everything even more fragmented than before and equally as disturbing. Our neighbours are scattered around, some have still not come home. The weeds must be growing in Betty's magnificent garden, her roses will need pruning. It's July with its predictable filthy weather, darkening my mood and putting a shiver in the wind.

There is half a life in the house. Bits of sticky stuff adorn the cupboards where David's pictures used to be, the walls are bare and the bookshelves empty. Rich has two bags packed for a speedy departure and he wants me to do the same. But I can't do it yet, it's so important to unpack and feel that we really are home, for however long.

On the veranda, I am amazed to find that my lanky pot plants have hung grimly on to life. I don't think they've been watered for months, and their leaves are burned by the sun. Toughened by years of neglect, they've only survived to spite me.

Suddenly I notice my old pair of walking shoes exactly where I left them under the window. They have holes in the toes and the laces are broken, but they've been waiting for me like a faithful old dog. From the bedroom, I can hear my child's laughter, the sweetest sound in the world. I'm beginning to feel better.

Chapter Eight

We hadn't been back more than ten minutes when I heard Rich calling me from the garage. 'Bookey! Guess who's here?'

I didn't have to guess, I knew – our pig had arrived to welcome us home. I tore through the house, flung open the garden gate, and knelt in the driveway ready for the moment I'd been dreaming of. Poombi was walking purposefully towards me, looking fat and fit, ears pricked, followed by a line of piglets. Sophie was immediately behind her mother, then Charlie and Danny, our three Dahlings, and Poombi's third litter. Eight months old and all present and correct.

I stretched out my hand, ready to stroke her nose as she lifted it for a first, loving sniff into mine. I was whispering endearments to her as she came up close, fixed her gaze to my right – and then brushed roughly past me as if I were invisible.

'Hey!' I called to her. 'Poombi, it's me!' But for all she cared, I could have been a pile of wildebeest droppings. I couldn't believe it; even a stranger would have warranted more interest from this haughty porcine personage who was once my treasured pig. With her children trotting dutifully behind, she barged through the gate, sniffed loudly under the kitchen door, and stalked off to the front of the house where she began grazing. It was nothing less than 100 per cent rejection by the heartless Queen of Pigs, the light of my life, and I felt as if I'd been pricked with a fork.

A radio call from Scout Frank Ncube a couple of days later saw me haring up to the dam vlei where I found the family grazing by the side of the road. Now it was my turn to play it cool. I sat a few yards away with my back towards them and waited. The piglets came straight up; Danny took a pull at my fingers, while Sophie nibbled at my knee. *They* certainly hadn't forgotten who I was. I peered over my shoulder to see if Poombi was any closer, whereupon she rather ostentatiously swung around, presented me with her backside and strolled off.

That really hurt. 'Vindictive bitch!' I shouted after her but she didn't twitch an ear.

I wasn't going to humiliate myself again. I left it for a few days, inwardly seething, until I heard that she was at the vegetable garden. Suddenly remembering that we needed some carrots, I drove up, and got out whistling. A warthog and three piglets were grazing by the fence – I didn't give them a second look. As far as I was concerned, they could be any old hogs, they didn't interest me at all. It worked: as I reached the gate of the garden, I felt something pushing at the back of my leg. The pendulum had swung and there she was, grunting softly, full of sniffs and kisses. So, hey ho, I was whole again but I had got the message – never, never again go away for so long.

When Poombi came to deliver her crushing rejection on our arrival, it was the first time she had visited the house since we had left the farm. I knew she would come, though, because the same thing happened every time we went away. Without fail, she would arrive to welcome us either on the day before or on the day of our return. It happened too often to be a coincidence. I was quite sure that she tuned into my thoughts, and when I began to focus on home, she got the message. If she turned up a day earlier, it was perhaps because I'd been in a plane, and I couldn't expect even a pig of such brilliance to understand air travel and the complexities of Greenwich Mean Time. Many pet owners will corroborate this theory, and I was fascinated to discover that Elsa the lioness, of *Born Free* fame, behaved in exactly the same way when Joy Adamson had been away.

Fortunately, neither bushbuck nor Labradors appear to harbour grudges. Nandi followed David around all day and lay by his bed at night, right up close so that he could put his hand out of the blankets and stroke her head. No one had handled Mary since we left, as Rich is allergic to her fur, but after a little initial nervousness she relaxed, and while David tickled her ears and scratched her neck, she closed her eyes and her breath caught in little bubbles in her throat. I noticed that she was a little greyer on the temples, and there were a few more white lashes mixed with the brown over those luminous blue-black eyes.

Now, even more than ever, it is crucial to live every experience as if it were our last, whether it is making love in the afternoon or taking Nandi for her evening walks where the aloes blaze crimson among the wintry koppies. I can feel the farm seeping into me again, like the sap that rises in the tree, and the roots that suddenly take hold and push their way down into the soil after a good season.

Before we left, I used to read every bulletin on the email with details of the latest attacks on farmers and their workers, the slaughter or maiming of their stock and their pets, and the destruction of wildlife. I didn't do that any more because it drove me insane. Just when I thought I was beginning to recover my equilibrium after a good day, I'd open up the emails and be plunged back into depression.

Jowel Ncube came to the house and told us for the first time that his wife was 'serious sick' at Marula. She was borne off to Plumtree hospital, coughing and unable to stand, and a few days later she was dead. AIDS had struck again, leaving Jowel alone to raise a baby of six weeks and a two-year-old.

In happier times, the pavement outside the Bulawayo City Hall was overflowing with flowers. You couldn't walk by without a dozen vendors thrusting a bunch of roses or carnations under your nose: 'mine are the freshest, Madam. Cheap price for you!' Now they were selling funeral wreaths.

For the first time, David was thrilled to be putting on his grey uniform and black shoes. 'I didn't *really* like those other boys,' he confided in me. 'You can only trust your old friends.' When I dropped him off at school, I watched him fly off to meet them, his red hair aflame and his whole body alight with excitement. There is a pure joy in being back where you belong, and yet our experience had shown me that David is the sort of person who will be happy anywhere, for he carries it with him.

Watching him with one arm around Kevin Marillier and the other around Tafadzwa Zvishumba made me think about this country and what it means to us. White Zimbabweans have always maintained that you can 'feel the difference' when you cross over the border from South Africa, and this is as true today as it was fifty years ago. South Africa is a complex country, first-world and fast-paced, whereas little Zimbabwe, tucked between the Limpopo and the Zambezi, felt (until very recently) utterly comfortable and comprehensible. Any of our borders can be reached in a day's drive. Our scenery is magnificent but somehow gentle; it never overwhelms, rather it speaks to you and makes you feel a part of it. And oh yes, we remember the snooty remarks the white East Africans used to make: 'After the war, of course, the *officers* came here while the *men* went to Rhodesia.' But while they were mixing martinis and making white mischief in the highlands, that little country to their south was building the foundations of what became one of the strongest economies in Africa.

Workaday old Zimbabwe, nothing pretentious or showy about it, but a country for which we all felt enormous affection and an equally sizeable sense of privilege for being able to belong to such a special place. Of course, I was strictly speaking an immigrant, having arrived from England as a little girl, but how I always wished that my passport gave my place of birth as Bulalimamangwe rather than Norwich, England. Sick of being the Pommy outsider at school, I tried desperately to clip my vowels and say 'yah' instead of 'yes', and I knew I had succeeded when my frustrated parents sent me off to elocution lessons. I always envied Rich his birthright, but then, in 1990, we created a third-generation Zimbabwean in David, and that, I feel, gives me a valid stake in my adopted home.

Since the beginning of the year, farm invasions had spread all over the country, spearheaded by the veterans of the bush war who maintained that land they had been promised at independence had never materialised. As we drove to town, I turned away from the plastic bags impaled on the wire fences, flapping like injured birds.

These were the symbols of the new order: between them, shanties had sprung up, tacked together with corrugated iron, sacking and plastic. Their owners squatted in the dust, watching their mealies wilt and die. As winter gave way to blistering heat, it seemed as if the rains would never come. And how would we feed ourselves if commercial farmers were not allowed to plant their crops?

Much worse was on its way, but still, black and white, we kept the faith. It will come right, we told each other, we just have to hang on. And there was always reason for hope....

An elderly white woman was stranded on a country road when her car broke down. At last, a motorcycle ridden by a black man chugged around the corner.

'May I help you, madam?' he asked, raising his hat. 'It's not safe for you to be here alone.'

The lady eyed the dilapidated bike dubiously but could think of no alternative. While the driver stared ahead, she clambered on to the back, wrapped her arms around his waist and off they went.

Half an hour later, flustered and windblown, the old lady was deposited at her farm. When she had recovered, she spoke to the cook.

'I feel terrible,' she said. 'I should have asked that kind man in for a drink.'

'Ai, no!' exclaimed the cook. 'That one is too dangerous. He's the chief wovvet [war vet] here and a very bad man!'

Every day the threats crept closer, but as soon as we drove through the farm gates after a day in town, I automatically dropped my guard. As always, the doors and windows of the house stayed open until we went to bed, and I never thought of closing the curtains. Nothing could touch us here; this was home, our little sovereign kingdom, and I felt quite secure. Rich, on the other hand, had his pistol strapped on his belt or by his side twenty-four hours a day, and he tried to make me carry one on my walks. I refused, on the basis that since I didn't know how to use it, I would be more of a danger to myself than to any would-be attacker. My excuses ran out when two local marksmen offered to give a 'Practical Pistol' course to the Marula womenfolk over a period of two days. I was quite keen on the idea, principally because I thought it would enhance my image as a rugged safari guide. I'd earned very high marks on firearms in my guide's exams, with Rich as my tutor, but once again, it was all theory. Now I'd have an opportunity to prove my practical ability. I'd seen enough movies to know that male heroes had surrendered their roles to gorgeous, black-clad, gun-toting females. Well, black didn't suit me and I was old enough to be Angelina Jolie's mother, but I felt I could probably carry it off. After two hectic days, I got the certificate but it's still in my drawer. I won't put it on the wall yet: not till I've had a bit more practice. For no matter how I took aim at the cardboard cutout man on the firing range, a bit to the left, a bit to the right, one eye closed or sometimes both – I invariably hit him in the groin. I suppose you could say I was consistent. Naturally, I blamed the weapon, but even with the new Glock (just like the ones the cops carry in the movies), my bullets are drawn as if by a magnet to a spot precisely between the legs. Rich mutters about my subconscious desire to castrate, but I've come to the conclusion that I am just a lousy shot with consistently good groupings.

A couple of months later, we were invited to attend a

course, together this time, on Ambush and Hijacking. I tried waving my Practical Pistol certificate under Rich's nose, but he insisted that we both should go. Dressed in black and fresh from the OK Corral, our local expert stood at the door of the Farmers' Hall, with his arms held chimpanzee-style in order to avoid contact with the huge array of weaponry dangling from his waist. In contrast, the South African instructor was as sleek as a seal with a palpable aura of controlled power. Nothing bulky or obvious there; his pistol was neatly down the front of his pants, his knife clipped on to his belt. He was gorgeous. For a couple of days, I was the female Rambo, on full red alert, diving out of vehicles under ambush and returning fire (or pretending to) from behind a wheel.

Most harrowing, though, were the simulated hijackings. Although we knew exactly what was going to happen, it was terrifying when a man in a black beanie suddenly shoved a plastic pistol through the window and began screaming in Rich's face: 'Get out! Get out! Or I'll kill you!' Any fumbling could be fatal, so we immediately put our hands in the air. 'Take the vehicle,' Rich told him, without conviction, 'we're going, just leave us alone.' It was crucial *not* to do what came naturally: on no account were we to take our personal belongings or look at the hijacker, for if we did he would almost certainly kill us. To protect ourselves from being beaten, we put our hands on top of our heads and started scrambling out of the vehicle, trying to keep low. We had ten seconds. This wasn't too hard for Rich on the driver's side, but it took me that long to untangle myself from the gear-stick. Finally, I landed with a thump on top of Rich and we scurried off, full of bruises and bullet holes.

I don't think I would argue with a hijacker, but the whole exercise was the complete antithesis of what Rich and most other men would instinctively do. Rich would have gone for his weapon and faced a shoot-out rather than hand over his vehicle. 'Forget it,' the instructor kept drumming into us, 'it's your vehicle or your life. What is more important? Let it go.'

We found humour wherever we could to lighten the encroaching darkness. Wonderful stories were doing the rounds, testimony that even in the toughest times, people could find something to laugh about.

War veterans had taken over Ron MacTavish's farm in the Marondera area, and confined him to his house, where he spent his days at the window, watching his tobacco crop die. He was having breakfast when there was a loud knocking on the door. Five war vets stood there, demanding that he help them to plough 'their lands'.

'Oh, I'd be very happy to,' said Ron, 'but unfortunately I can't do it without a grundig to attach to the back of my plough.'

The war vets looked puzzled and a bit uncomfortable.

'You know, of course, what a grundig is?' asked Ron.

'Of course we do,' retorted the chief war vet, squaring his shoulders. ' We are professional farmers.'

'Well, you'll know then,' said Ron, 'how important it is.'

They all nodded sagely. 'Don't worry,' they said, 'we'll find one for you. Leave it to us.'

A month later, they were back. They'd been all over Harare, looking for a grundig, they told him, but they couldn't find a single one.

Ron MacTavish picked up the phone and dialled a number.

'Hello,' he said to the non-existent person on the other end. 'What's happening with my grundig? I'm desperate for one so I can help some new settlers plough their lands.'

A pause. 'Six months, you say? That's ridiculous. Can't you get it any sooner?'

The farmer put down the receiver, shaking his head.

'Sorry, fellows, you'll just have to wait.'

The war vets never returned, and Ron still looks with affection at the ancient gramophone in his lounge that first gave him his brilliant idea.

I called Poombi my *raison d'être* because whenever I was down, a session with her and the piglets would immediately raise my spirits. Some people go to church to put their world to rights, I spent time communing with my pig, for, unlike us, Poombi lived serenely in the moment. One afternoon in late October, I joined her family on siesta and lay with my head against her belly, which wasn't as comfortable as usual because it felt as if her new brood were having a kick-boxing competition.

Yes, it was that time again, and little did the three Dahlings know that their childhood was nearly at an end. The moment Poombi started preparing herself for her confinement, she would banish them from her side forever. It was the same every time, Poombi would tell them to buzz off in the nastiest possible way, and the incredulous piglets couldn't believe their ears. Having discussed it among themselves, they clearly thought that this was just another of the old queen's hormonal hiccups, and they would come back to their mother again and again until finally she rammed the message home for good. It was a heartbreaking sight. Naturally, she was at her most protective for the couple of weeks after she had given birth, and we were always careful to keep our distance until introductions were appropriate. When the Dahlings were about a month old, I had taken David up to the eland boma and found the family there. Poombi was on the bank lined with barbed wire that had served as our unloading ramp when we first brought animals on to the farm. Snuffling loudly, she was rootling up old marula nuts half buried in the soil. Meanwhile, the little pigs, plump as cocktail sausages, squeezed their way one by one under the wire and joined their mother.

I was standing at the base of the ramp chatting to Scout Frank Ncube when David called out: 'Is it OK if I talk to them?'

'It'll be fine now,' I told him. 'Just sit here at the edge of the ramp and wait for them to come to you.'

My back was turned when I heard a gruff grunt and a cry from David as he tumbled off the edge of the ramp and on to his back. Poombi was looking down at him, bristling with anger.

How could I have been so stupid? I'd always been so careful in the past to monitor these introductions, making sure that the time was right and never, ever putting David in a compromising position. I should have realised that if he sat at the edge of the ramp, with its two enclosed sides, Poombi would feel that her piglets were hemmed in and immediately become defensive. She had rushed at David and flipped him off the end with her nose.

He wasn't physically hurt but he was devastated.

'How could she do that to me,' he was crying. 'I hate her, I hate her!'

I bundled him in the car and took him home. And when he felt a bit better, I tried to explain Poombi's behaviour.

'She sees you as one of her piglets,' I explained. 'She and you have always had a different relationship to the rest of us and it's been a very special one. At the moment, she wants to keep you away from her new piglets but she'll come round, she always has. And, think about it, she didn't hurt you. If she had wanted to she could have ripped into you with her tusks.'

I dried David's tears and left him in the bedroom. And half an hour later, he came out, red-eyed but smiling wanly.

'I know you're right,' he said. 'And I know she still loves me. I don't hate her any more but I'm very, very cross!'

We were collecting vegetables in the garden about ten days later, and David was sitting in the sandpit, when Poombi suddenly appeared from out of the trees followed by the piglets. 'Mum!' David called to me urgently. 'She's here, I'm scared she's going to do something.' I tried to sound calm. 'She'll be fine, David. Just sit tight and let her come.'

I slipped out of the garden and went to head her off. Poombi greeted me but wouldn't be deflected. She kept walking, straight towards David, and I was right behind her when she reached him. She was grunting very softly. Then she put her nose out to his, sniffed gently and laid her head in his lap. For ten minutes, he groomed her until she was sure that all was forgiven. She wandered back to her piglets, but when David was digging in the sand she came back twice to help him, putting her snout down the same hole and shovelling it out with her nose. Pigs may not be able to fly but they certainly can talk.

Chapter Nine

The tale of the elephant and the warthog.

Long, long ago, the warthog had a pair of tusks so large that he could barely lift them off the ground. The elephant was very envious because he, poor fellow, had only two pairs of tiny tusks that weren't any use at all.

One day, the aardvark came to tell the warthog that the elephant was planning to play a trick on him. But the warthog was friends with everybody, and he didn't believe a word of it. Then the elephant came to the warthog and said: 'You have such wonderful tusks, dear warthog, would you consider lending them to me for just a day? You can use mine, if you like.'

'Of course, my friend,' said the warthog. 'But you will give them back, won't you?'

The elephant promised that he would, but the minute he had the tusks, he turned on the warthog.

'Stupid, ugly pig!' he laughed. 'What do you need a fine pair of tusks for? They look so much better on me. I'll never give them back to you!'

The warthog ran to find the aardvark. 'Look at these

tiny things!' he sobbed, 'Now I'll never be handsome again.'

'Listen to me, dear friend,' said the aardvark. 'The elephant doesn't know it, but he has done you a favour. From now on, man will hunt him mercilessly for those beautiful tusks of his, and he will have nowhere to hide. But you, little warthog, can always use my burrow as your home.'

And so it came to be, best beloved (as Rudyard Kipling would have said), that the elephant has a fine pair of tusks, and the warthog lives in the aardvark's burrow.

We don't read our children the *Just So* stories any more, but animal-centred folklore like this is still very much a part of the lives of rural Africans. All our people on Stone Hills have their favourite stories. Mabhena knows why the slender mongoose is the true king of the jungle, and Mafira loves to relate how the tortoise and the lion outwitted the clever hare. Although they are fables, many are based on the close observations of people whose lives are entwined with the creatures that still live around them.

The hammerkop, for example, makes an extraordinary nest that can be up to two metres high and weigh as much as fifty kilograms. His untidy mansion may not be the last word in good taste, but he is an avid collector of treasures that he uses to decorate its roof. Dung, grass, rags, plastic bags and bones are commonplace, but it was the six bicycle tyres on the top of one nest that were the strangest choice. The Africans believe that the bird is a wizard, and that ill fortune will befall them should it be seen collecting nesting material from near their homes. And woe betide anyone who disturbs the nest, or takes the money that the hammerkop is reputed to hoard inside it, for he will surely go mad.

Some of these stories work to the animals' benefit. Ground hornbills' nests are left alone because if they are robbed of their eggs, a flock of them will come to sing and dance around the home of the thief and forever bring him bad luck. But the ravens and crows are not so fortunate: they are believed to drive away the rain, so their nests are destroyed and their chicks are killed.

Omens and messages from the spirits may be relayed through particular animals, like the python.

'It is a most respected reptile,' Khanye told me, 'and no one must harm it. It will almost always keep still if it hears you coming, but if it moves, there's a bad story awaiting you.'

Although it has no spiritual connections, even the humble wall spider who scuttles out from behind the pictures on our wall at the start of summer may be an omen. If it falls on your head, a stranger is on his way to see you.

Snakes play a major part in African belief, for when the head of the house dies he is transformed into an *idlozi*, or *izinyoka*, a spiritual snake, who will protect and bless his family. Green mambas, sand and house snakes are all considered lucky by certain clans, and may not be killed. And if a girl dreams of snakes, she will soon be pregnant.

When families grew and formed themselves into clans, each chose a different animal totem. Sibanda is the predator; Mpofu, the eland; Ncube, the baboon; Dube, the zebra and many more. As patrons of the clan, these animals must be respected. Or else. If our resident herbalist, Kephas Dube, for instance, were to ignore the taboo and eat the meat of a zebra, he'd be sorry because his teeth would fall out. And if a pregnant woman were to make the same mistake, her unborn child might well be deformed or suffer from a mental illness.

But the rare pangolin, poor soul, is no one's totem. Highly prized for their meat, their medicinal uses, and as bringers of good luck, they have traditionally been presented to the chief (and previously the king), who would reward the finder with cattle or even a wife. But should anyone else dare to eat the pangolin, he would be punished and, in the old days, even killed for his crime.

The little Bushmen had an extraordinary rapport with animals. We have found dozens of their paintings on the rocks of Stone Hills, and many more hidden among the koppies still await discovery. They date back at least 1,500 years, and in these ancient works of art you can truly appreciate the artists' astounding powers of observation and recollection. In one, the head of an antelope is all that is now visible, but from the shape of the ears, you know immediately that it is a female kudu. And below her trots a Burchell's zebra, typically plump and alert. Mostly they are a rusty red drawn from crushed rocks of ferric oxide, and by mixing this with the blood of animals, the Bushman believed that the power of those creatures would be captured and forever contained in his paintings.

One particularly fascinating scene appears to depict aspects of the trance/dance that lies at the heart of the Bushmen's religious experience. While the women sit clapping and singing by the fire, the dancers stamp the earth in a circle around them. The firelight flickers on their faces as they become caught up in the hypnotic rhythms of their pounding feet, the drums and the women's music. Power begins to boil in the bodies of the healers or shamans. Tension is rising, and as their stomach muscles contract in spasm, they bend sharply at the waist. Potency travels up the spine like a vapour, finally exploding in the head, from where the spirit of the trancer may escape through a small hole on its journey to the spirit world.

Now the restraints of his earthly body have gone, he may be transformed into a lion, an eland, a jackal – and their powers will become his own. And in the paintings, men have tails, antelope heads or the body of a predator, as man and beast are united in their spiritual potency.

Sadly, there are few Bushmen, if any, who are still able to follow their traditional way of life, and none in Zimbabwe. Above all others, they have an instinctive empathy with animals. In the very beginning, they say, animals were people and all were equal in the sight of God. The Bushman sought neither to change nor to dominate his environment; as a hunter/gatherer, he lived simply and frugally, using his formidable knowledge and skills to adapt himself to the natural order around him. He killed for food, not for pleasure, and skill in hunting was regarded as the very essence of manhood. He believed, too, that if the hunter were to succeed, he had to show respect for his quarry.

When he woke in the morning, the information he found at the entrance to his cave was as vital to his livelihood as the *Financial Times* is to a London stockbroker. But for the Bushman, the facts are written in the sand, and can be read at many different levels.

You and I, with a bit of tuition, can learn to recognise the spoor of a leopard. Like any true cat (except the cheetah), it moves with sheathed claws that leave no mark in the sand, and at the back of the pads there are typically feline double indentations. But to the experienced tracker, and there is none more skilled than the Bushman, this is only the beginning of the story. The crisp edges of the print will tell him that the animal strolled by just a couple of hours ago; and the size, shape and even the cracks on the pad may reveal that this is a known individual, perhaps the old male who regularly patrols this part of his territory.

In his Parks days, Rich sometimes worked with a half-Bushman tracker called Ben while translocating black rhino from trouble spots to what were then believed to be safe areas. For most people, tracking is a serious business, demanding every ounce of their concentration. But Ben seemed to take it very lightly. He'd be strolling along, stoking the pipe that was always in his mouth, and looking straight ahead, when someone would ask worriedly: 'So where's the spoor, Ben?' whereupon he would frown at them from under his wide-brimmed hat and point to an invisible track about three metres away. 'Over there,' he'd say. 'It's all right, I know where it's going.'

Rich remembers one time when Ben put up his hand and brought everyone else to a halt. 'You stay here,' he said, 'or the rhino will get our scent.'

With that, he strolled off in a wide circle, returning after half an hour. From the tracks and the signs around him, and a lifetime of experience, Ben knew that the rhino was on its way to rest, and that it would now be facing into the wind, alert to danger. He led the others right around it, taking them in from downwind, so when the immobilising dart whistled through the air, the rhino hadn't the slightest idea where it was coming from.

We've travelled a long way since General Smuts, voicing popular opinion, declared that the Bushmen were 'mentally stunted ... animals of the desert.'

'He is a soul debased...,' lamented one missionary in 1856, frustrated by his lack of converts, 'completely bound down and clogged by his animal nature.' In the past few decades, there has been an ever-growing interest in the Bushman, in the interpretation of his paintings, his spirituality, and the way of life of these enigmatic little hunter/gatherers.

Why do we love to hear their stories? Perhaps it is because they stir in us a subconscious longing for an age when we, too, found our way by the stars and understood the voices of the wind.

Although we tend to romanticise them, I don't believe the Bushman was essentially any different from ourselves – like us, he was a product of his environment. He had to obey its rules or perish: he was a conservationist, not out of sentiment, but from necessity. He knew too well that this year's plenty can so easily become next year's famine, when the rains fail and turn a fragile ecosystem into a wasteland. The animals were the Bushmen's moveable assets and they protected them, as they did the annual harvest of marula nuts that they gathered and stored in the caves of the Matobo Hills.

For over three million years, we were all nomadic hunter/gatherers, our lives dominated by the need to find food. Then, around 10,000 years ago, we learned to grow crops and husband our animals, a momentous step enabling large numbers of us to gather in productive areas that gradually grew into villages, towns and cities. Farmers took care of agriculture, leaving others free to develop different skills, to the point that we are now so separated from the source of our food that we have lost our sacred link with the natural world. Having silenced it under tonnes of concrete, we take solace in a dog, a cat and a potted plant, believing that these are enough to feed our barren souls.

The Grade 6s and 7s at Marula school can recite

Chief Seattle's words by heart:

'If all the beasts and trees were gone,' they chant, 'man would die of a great loneliness.'

Many of them live in mud huts with no running water. They have no toys, no books, and they are often hungry. Much of the wildlife that was once around them has been killed or driven away since the start of the land invasions, but the children still pick the velvet bridelia berries that grow in the veld, and splash in the puddles with their bare feet on the way to school.

Could it be that our children are the loneliest of them all?

In September 1968, when Ranger Richard Peek was twenty years old, he was transferred to Mabalauta, the southern headquarters of the Gonarezhou National Park. He brought with him a steel trunk full of books, a .303 rifle, a camera and a wooden box that he had made for his camping kit, and a battery-operated gramophone. And when he had laid out his possessions in his hut and stepped out of his front door, just twenty yards from the banks of the Mwenezi River, he reckoned that he was the luckiest young man alive.

Around him lay some of the least developed country in the land: 1,950 square miles of low-lying, malaria-ridden wilderness traversed by a few dusty tracks and cursed by frequent droughts, its life blood the waters of the three rivers that run through it, the Runde, the Save and the Mwenezi.

Sensible Europeans clustered in the healthful climes of the high country where the summers are mild and the winters just cold enough for a log fire in the evenings. Gona, harsh and remote, swelters in a corner of the south-eastern lowveld, pressed up hard against the border with Mozambique.

It is the ancestral home of the Shangaan people, those great storytellers and hunters, who saw no earthly reason why they should give up their traditional hunting grounds simply because the white man had declared them to be a 'national park'.

In the old days, trypanosomiasis (or sleeping sickness) was endemic in the lowveld, so cattle weren't an option for the Shangaans. As hunters, though, their tracking abilities, bushcraft, and their skill with bow, arrow and spear are legendary, as is their fierce pride in their heritage.

But the white man had the guns and he forbade the Shangaans to hunt. Instead they turned to snaring, and as 'poachers' they became criminals. Sergeant Machivana was one of those poachers whose abilities had been turned to good use by National Parks. When Rich worked with him, Mac was a tall, thickset man in his late fifties, with a strong, angular face. Mafira, our head scout, who knew him for twelve years, said he was totally fearless. Mac was a thrower of the bones, his *ti-Hlolo*: fashioned from the knuckles of lion and leopard, the scutes of a croc and the shiny nuts of the balsa wood into which he had burned patterns. He kept them in a beautifully woven bag of ilala palm. He wasn't exactly a *nyanga*, a witch-doctor, but he had the respect and awe of everyone around him.

In those days, one of the rangers' chief duties was to shoot 'problem animals' – particularly crop-raiding elephants. The night before the hunt Mac would throw his bones, and from the way they fell he could predict the events of the following day. 'Ah,' he would say, 'I see legs in the air! We will be lucky.'

But sometimes the bones would give a warning and then Mac would refuse to go. And if he were forced to, he would purposely lose the spoor or lag behind, affecting a sore leg.

Even if they disagreed with him, the other trackers would never dare to contradict Mac's predictions, but with the breezy confidence of youth, Rich decided to test them out.

A crop-raiding elephant was in the area, but Mac had refused to go out after it the following day, saying that the bones had fallen wrongly.

Rich went to see him. 'I know what the bones say,' he told him, 'but I'm going anyway, Mac. Are you sure you don't want to come?'

Mac gave him a dark look. 'You'll be sorry, *umfana*!' he said. 'My bones don't lie.'

Rich called in two game scouts, Gumala and Tom, and told them to get ready for the hunt.

They both looked very uncomfortable. 'But what about the bones?' they said. 'Something bad is going to happen.'

'Listen to me,' Rich told them. 'I have very strong *ti-Hlolo* and they tell me that everything will be all right!'

Together, the two scouts made an impressive, but slightly comical, team. Tom, who wasn't much higher than Gumula's kneecaps, went first, head down following the spoor. Towering over him, Gumula followed right behind, looking into the distance with a pair of incredibly far-seeing eyes that rivalled Rich's binoculars. It was a bit like the Shangaan version of Peter Cook and Dudley Moore.

The pair were apprehensive at first, but once they were on the elephant's tracks, they forgot their reservations. They found it, Rich dispatched it, and everybody went home – all without a single hitch.

Mac was smiling when Rich met him the next day.

'*Hele*!' he exclaimed in his deep voice, 'you must have very strong *mhuri*, *umfana*. Maybe you want to throw the bones with me sometime?'

This was an honour indeed. While they were sitting around the campfire, Mac would throw his *ti-Hlolo* on to a mat and explain to Rich what they meant.

'See this one here?' he would say, 'see how it's fallen? It's down and all the others are up. That's a bad sign.'

Then sometimes Rich would have a go and perhaps only to humour him, Mac would say, 'Yes, that's good, they fell well. You have the power!'

Mac was quite a drinker and suffered badly from gout. And Rich was quite sure that sometimes he made the bones an excuse not to go out the following day.

'Your bones aren't as strong as my powers,' he would tease the old man, 'and I say it's going to be a lucky day!' And he'd call Mac's bluff and go out anyway, much to the discomfiture of all the other scouts.

The reputation of the Gona elephants for aggression and unpredictability is not surprising when you consider the persecution they have suffered over the years. The Shangaans are renowned elephant-hunters and after they were deprived of their weapons, they collected old muzzle loaders and made their own projectiles from nuts and bolts, bits of lead and even stones. For gunpowder, they used sulphur, charcoal and saltpetre extracted from dassie urine, and the net result was an awful lot of wounded animals. Then there has always been cross-border poaching from Mozambique and South Africa, and the added pressure of tsetse fly operations in the 1950s and 60s when animals suspected of harbouring the parasite, including elephants, were shot in their thousands.

Even when Gona was declared a national park and the elephants could live in relative peace, their defensive behaviour was passed down through the generations, and became so ingrained that it's now a part of their identity. In any case, elephants never forget – and nor should they. Since the land invasions began in 2000, there's once again been uncontrolled poaching in the park.

Taking all that into account, Parks made a risky decision in 1969 when they ordered the field staff at Mabalauta to capture some elephant calves in order that the veterinary department could use them for tsetse research purposes. They needed to be young, around eighteen months, so they'd been weaned from their mothers but could still be tamed.

Sixty yards away from Rich's house, the workers constructed a strong stockade of mopane poles with sides around eight feet high. When everything was ready, Warden Ron Thompson, Rich, and eight other men climbed into a Land Rover and drove into the park looking for a suitable herd. They found one about forty kilometres away, a group of ten cows with a couple of babies, already weaned, with their tusks just beginning to protrude from the lip.

Leaving the vehicle nearby, Ron and Rich sneaked up to within thirty metres of the young elephant and, with Rich backing him up, Ron fired off a dart from a converted single cartridge rifle. It hit home, injecting the elephant with a knock-down dose of M99. Then started the agonising countdown before the drug began to take effect. Five minutes passed, ten minutes, then the calf began to stagger as his legs started to give way. The herd had to be driven off, so while Rich and Ron fired shots into the air, everyone began shouting and running at them, waving their arms. They stampeded, but as the youngster fell back and began to collapse, his mother returned. More shots and more noise, and while the herd was milling about, squealing, trumpeting and kicking up the dust about fifty metres away, Rich managed to manoeuvre the Land Rover between mother and baby, so the youngster could be manhandled into the back. The minute he was loaded, Rich dropped the clutch and roared off, while the men behind rearranged 200 kilos of baby elephant into a crouching position on his sternum and blindfolded him. Rich tore through the rough mopane scrub, expecting any minute to hit a rock or smash into a donga, while behind them, ten infuriated elephants gave chase. Even a few seconds' delay could be fatal. Finally, they lost them in the dust, while the now tranquillised calf slept soundly in the back.

All was peaceful, until he was safely in the stockade and the antidote was administered. Then the young elephant decided to live up to the reputation of his clan. He threw himself at the sides of the boma, squealing his rage at his captors. Taming him was going to be more difficult than they thought. They gave him a pile of leaves and lucerne, hoping that if they left him alone he would begin to settle down.

Later in the afternoon, Rich instructed Poliani, one of the Shangaan labourers, to stay on night guard in case there were problems with the calf. But as darkness fell, he stopped his squealing and the only noise around the camp later that night was the crackling of the enormous fire that Poli had built in front of the workshop and close to the boma.

Rich went out to see him before he went to bed. 'Why

the big fire?' he asked the Shangaan. 'What are you frightened of?'

'Those elephants,' he replied, 'they're coming to get their baby!'

Rich laughed. 'Of course they won't! We left them forty kilometres down the track. Now, if there are any problems with the calf, come and wake me up. OK?'

Rich had a last check of the spotlight he had set up on his Land Rover next to the boma. If there were any disturbance, he could shine it straight on to the calf.

An hour or so later, he was woken from a dead sleep by a frantic hammering on the door. He grabbed his rifle and ran outside, almost colliding with Poli. 'I can hear them,' he babbled, 'they're on their way!' Rich stumbled out of the hut and stood in the darkness, listening.

Apart from the chorus of frogs in the river, he couldn't hear a sound either from the calf or any other living creature.

God, these guys had an imagination.

He tried to keep his temper. 'I am tired, old man,' he said. 'We had a lot of *hlupa* catching that elephant today and I need to sleep. Don't bother me unless something happens!'

Rich slept – but two hours later, he was woken once again by knocking on the door.

'Quick,' Poli was shouting, 'they're getting close!'

Rich rolled out of bed, and fumbled for his shoes, ready to kill.

He threw the door open and strode into the dark. He listened, and listened, and still there was nothing. The man was mad.

'For Christ's sake, Poli,' he shouted, 'you're hearing spooks. Go back and sit by your fire and let me sleep!'

But the Shangaan was more frightened of his spooks than he was of the young ranger. At around two o'clock in the morning, he was back at the door.

'They're here! They're here!' he was yelling.

Rich shone a spotlight out of the window. 'What do you mean, they're here? I can't see them, I can't hear them. Now bugger off!'

He slammed the window, crawled back into bed and put the blankets over his head.

Five minutes later, he was woken by an explosion of screams, shouts, bangs – and trumpeting. In the torchlight, he could see an elephant cow pummelling the front of the Land Rover that he had left in 4WD with the handbrake on. With her tusks shoved into the radiator, she pushed it backwards twenty yards in a half circle, right to the edge of the riverbank.

Then she spiked the left fender and nearly ripped it off. Her point made, she turned her attention to the boma. But Rich was running towards her, rifle in hand, shining the torch into her eyes; so she veered away and made off towards the chalet where the mechanic, his wife and young daughter were living. She could easily break it down.

'Poliani!' Rich screamed. 'Take the spotlight and stand on the back of the Land Rover (or what was left of it). Keep the light on the *nzou*!'

As he tore up towards the chalets, he could hear the mechanic yelling for help.

'Don't worry, stay where you are!' Rich shouted back, in his most reassuring voice. 'I'm right here!'

The elephant heard that, and came blazing back along the path towards him. Now he would have to shoot her. He raised his rifle, levelled it and prepared to fire. Then the light went out. Poliani had jumped off the back of the Land Rover and was running for his life. Pitch black, no spotlight, enraged elephant just a few yards away, intent on revenge. Rich bolted, leaped over the flames of the fire and flung himself through the open port of the workshop. And she was right on his tail. She ran through the middle of the fire, pushed her massive head into the workshop, and gave an ear-splitting scream that reverberated under the tin roof – blowing Rich clean out the other side.

A few moments later, there was a loud crash as the stockade collapsed, and the sound of vegetation being flattened as two triumphant elephants, one large and one very small, ran off together into the darkness.

This is the best kind of animal story. Ten clever humans equipped with machinery, guns and expertise take on one elephant with two ears, four feet, a formidable brain and a burning resolve to get her own back, in every sense. And, for once, the elephant triumphs. Not only does she find her calf, but she comes straight after it as if she knows exactly where it is.

A few years ago, we wouldn't have believed it possible. Now we know that elephants produce infrasound: extremely low noises inaudible to the human ear, that may be heard by others of their kind over long distances. And it's quite possible, too, that they may pick up information through vibrations in their feet.

In this case, telepathy could well have been at work, something that, in any species, must surely be at its strongest between mother and child. Or was it simply that the mother elephant used her commonsense and headed for human territory where she knew her calf was most likely to be?

It all makes us feel rather uncomfortable. Whatever

scientific research may come up with, we realise that there is more, probably much more, that we don't understand. Could elephants really feel like us, and if so, what do they think of the way we have treated them? It doesn't bear thinking about.

Equally as mysterious is Poliani's insistence that the elephants were coming. It wasn't just an educated guess – he knew, hours before the event, even when he couldn't possibly have heard them.

From a rational point of view, we find it incredible. But of course, Poli wasn't trying to be rational – he was using an intuitive understanding that comes naturally to those who depend on their environment for their survival. Like all the other wild animals around him, elephants had always been a part of Poli's life. In some mysterious fashion, he could think himself into their heads, an ability that comes from the knowledge that we belong, as much as they do, to the natural world.

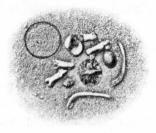

Chapter Ten

Some of our game scouts on Stone Hills are also deeply intuitive. Most of them came to us on recommendation; others relied on fancy and the power of the written word. We'd never heard of Mr Innocent Mapurisa until we received a reference from the manager of a safari camp in the Masvingo area: 'His knowledge of carrying out his duties was better than most and he maintained good rapport among the staff and was a stronghold in our workers. We still feel the amnesia of his departure at this institute. He was tireless, responsible, innovative, mature and a socially acceptable member. As a guide he was always enthusiastic and informative when dealing with Tourists.... His knowledge of animals, birds, reptiles, trees and medicinal plants etc in this area was very knowledgeable.'

Contrary to what Mr Mapurisa said, however, his erstwhile boss remembered his resourceful but light-fingered ex-employee only too well.

The second outstanding reference came from a Mr Trinos Gwarimbo, applying for the post of handyman and scout. 'He is a very competent man, of very sober habits, who has delinquently done his duties particularly mechanically and anti-poaching very well,' wrote a 'Mr Button' from Hwange. I bumped into John Burton in town the following morning, who was quick to confirm Mr Gwarimbo's more dubious qualities. Talk about shooting yourself in the foot.

Some of our scouts on Stone Hills came to us with little or no experience, and others like Mafira, Khanye and Mabhena had been in National Parks all their working lives. But they all had one thing in common – an innate patience – and the ability to see, really see, rather than merely to look. Both are invaluable qualities for any naturalist.

I'm a good one to talk. I used to keep a sign on my office desk that read 'Carpe Diem', seize the day. I believed that the faster I moved, the more I could do, and I was determined to experience every last drop of life before my time ran out. To me, the best part of the river was not where I was standing, but the most distant bend that would lead me on to somewhere else. Having charged around the world for ten years, bouncing from one experience to the next, I rushed into a career as a lawyer, only to discover six years later that other than running an abattoir or breeding minks for the fur trade, it was probably the least suitable profession I could have chosen.

I have had to cultivate the art of stillness, making a conscious decision to live in the moment. Stop walking, stop talking, stop planning. Merely be, as an observer rather than a participant, without expectations or trying to impose myself on what is around me. And I have learned that wherever I am on Stone Hills, something will be happening right under my nose (provided my glasses are on the end of it). Perhaps a damselfly, laying its eggs inside the stem of an underwater plant, or the tiny white flowers of the *lippea javanica* that seem unremarkable until I notice an even tinier crab spider, also cunningly attired in white, waiting in ambush for a fly or a mantid. I keep hoping that if I move slowly, time will follow suit.

In Africa, time means different things to different people. As Pathisa Nyati writes in his book *Zimbabwe's Cultural Heritage*: 'Time has to be experienced to become real, to make sense…. Africans concern themselves with the present, the immediate future and an unlimited past' – whereas for most Europeans, the past is forgotten and much of the present is devoted to planning for the future. This is nowhere better reflected than in our respective religions. Christianity looks forward to the promise of a better life after death; African religion teaches that we experience heaven and hell only on this earth, and that we must look back to our immediate ancestors to intercede with God on our behalf.

Frank Ncube had time, more than anyone I have ever known. With a slow and stately step, he would stalk past the bedroom window in the early mornings at the start of his patrol, hands clasped behind his back, as ponderous as a marabou stork hunting frogs along the river. Frank had little formal education, but he was a natural scholar. Rich gave him the science and Frank soaked it up and applied it to his own observations. He was born on Stone Hills, and he knew every stick and stone of it. But he wasn't willing to share its secrets all at once. Instead, he handed them to us, one by one, like sweets to a hungry child. Frank 'found' the cave with nineteen grain bins in it and the nearby Bushman painting of a hunter ambushing an impala. He took us to the legendary Dead Man's tree, and discovered the *Adenia fructosa*, unrecorded (as far as we knew) at this altitude: a thickly twisted climber that could have been more than a century old. He always had something up his sleeve.

I remember a day at the start of summer, one of those mornings when the earth is turning like a puppy in its sleep, presenting its warm, soft belly to the sun, and the ground wears a shimmer of green after the first rains. There's been a mass emergence of leopard butterflies – they are everywhere, dipping and dancing ahead of me as I walk through the grass. A light breeze among the crotons stirs the underside of the leaves, making them shine silver in the sun. Above me, a pair of Wahlberg's eagles are chasing a young hawk eagle away from their nest. They hound him until he flies higher and higher, and then goes wheeling away into the clear, polished blue of the morning sky. While I am sitting watching a red emperor dragonfly cruising up and down the river, I hear an unfamiliar call, 'Birdee, birdee', and see what appears to be a small bird of prey displaying low over the grass on fluttering wings.

I didn't know anyone else was around, but as I am driving home I meet Frank at one of my favourite places along the Pundamuka river, where the grass is soft and crushed under the sweethorn trees. We are both smiling with the shared pleasure of being alive on this perfect day. Frank tells me to back up the vehicle to a dead tree stump standing right next to the track. We climb on to the back and look down into a black flycatcher's nest with two chicks, warm and protected, who are just beginning to get their feathers.

When I get home and talk it over with Rich, it turns

out that the 'Birdee' caller is the first thick-billed cuckoo ever recorded on Stone Hills.

When an interesting nest is located, Rich will spend hours sitting in a hide close by and waiting for the perfect photograph. And when he realised the extent of Frank's powers of observation, he encouraged him to do the same.

Finding a nest is rarely a matter of luck. You might spy a hornbill heading for a tree with its mouth full of food, or happen to catch sight of a drongo speeding back to its cup-shaped nest in a fork at the end of a bare branch; but usually it's a matter of long, patient hours in one spot, plus the ability to play the bird at its own game.

'Look at the way that lourie flew out of the tree,' Frank would tell the young scouts. 'It jumped out very carefully, keeping its wings folded before it started to flap. It has a nest and it's being careful not to damage its eggs.'

Then he'll tell them about the brainless black-headed oriole who lets the world know what she's up to by calling all the way back to the nest with food for her chicks.

Frank would have been a fine detective. If he saw a lark or a pipit scampering along the road in front of him for any distance, he would pretend to leave the area, but instead go and hide where he first disturbed the bird. Chances were that it would come flying or running back to its nest a few minutes later.

'And look out for francolins with broken wings,' he told the younger men, 'they're trying to lure you away from their chicks by pretending to be injured.'

I've seen them do it, too, hobbling through the grass dragging one wing and squawking hysterically.

I was out with Frank one day when we were accosted

by two little croaking cisticolas.

'Ah', said he, with a knowing smile, 'they are insulting us, hoping we'll go away. We'll hide in the long grass and see what they are up to.'

A few minutes later, when she thought we had gone, the female scooted straight back to her nest in the reeds.

Locating a nest is one thing, but then Frank would spend hours watching it, taking notes about the time of hatching, what and when the chicks were fed and how soon they left the nest, if they were lucky enough to survive that long. Although we rarely see them, the common egg-eater is their principal predator, a snake that resembles the venomous night-adder but is harmless to man. In order to protect itself, it strikes out without making contact, and rubs its coils together to create a loud hissing sound, but that's the limit of its defensive repertoire. The snake swallows the egg and, using the bony projections in the vertebrae of its neck, slices through it and squeezes out the contents, finally regurgitating the neatly compressed shell in an unmistakable calling card.

Frank took Mafira's son, Mapfumo, under his wing. He came to us fresh from school at the age of nineteen, a strapping young man who could have ripped the bull bar off the front of our Toyota with his bare hands. I often used to take him to town with me for the day because I knew no one would dare to approach the car with him sitting in it. He had no idea of his own strength. Gently, Mapfumo, I would plead, as he'd wrench open the back doors to load the shopping.

When he left us seven years later, I asked him to write an account of what he had learned on Stone Hills.

'As a young boy,' he wrote, 'I viewed wild animals as

a source of meat. Although my father, who was working for National Parks, made frantic efforts to reverse my mind, I kept on arguing that all the land that was used for wildlife would be better off if diverted to other profitable uses, like cattle ranching and growing crops. At first (when he began work as a scout) I was shy because I still had the childish belief that animals are dangerous to humans. However, all this waned within a short period of time after I had been convinced by my workmates who played a splendid role in transforming me and my attitude towards animals and natural resources. I couldn't believe how fascinating it was getting to know all the animals and being in a position to get as close as I wished to them.

'Discovering nests and participating in the ongoing research on bird nesting behaviour was one of the most fascinating tasks that I will always miss, and even where I am going, I will not stop checking any bird that I come across. I gathered information from Frank Ncube who I consider an expert. I was over-excited on one occasion when I managed to bump into an African Rail nest (the first to be found on Stone Hills) while I was actually looking for a croaking cisticola nest, for I had seen one loitering over the place. My joy was that the African rail is such a secretive bird that it's very difficult to locate its nest but anyway, by chance in my lifetime, I had managed to find one. I will never forget the incident.

Life in the bundu is so fascinating if one is interested in it. It's amazing how some creatures that some people say are no use can be the darling of others depending on the way one eyes their importance.'

Mapfumo's father Mafira, our head scout, has made sure that each one of his seven kids has been properly educated. 'I need my children to learn more than I did', he says. In 1958, when his own father went blind as a result of an encounter with a spitting cobra, and could no longer work as a policeman, Mafira was nine years old. He caddied at the Great Zimbabwe golf course, earning the equivalent of ten or twenty cents a round, with which he bought his school books and took care of his mother and his nine siblings.

Twenty-four years in National Parks have given him some amazing stories, like the time he was carrying the mailbag on his bicycle from one camp to another in Gonarezhou. He was speeding down the hill towards the Mamonyo river when he came face to face with a group of twelve lions: a male, a couple of females and ten cubs. The adults ran away, but the cubs were curious and came trotting towards him. Suddenly, the adults leaped back on to the road, and Mafira threw down his bike and climbed the nearest tree, which happened to be rather small. Two metres up, he could go no further, and there he crouched, with the lions jumping all over his bike just below him.

'I can't remember feeling scared,' he says, 'I just sat there and yelled my head off, hoping the sound would reach Simuwini rest camp some kilometres down the road. While the lions were busy killing my bike, they sometimes looked up and snarled at me.' Luckily his bellows were heard at the camp and help eventually came – a couple of hours later.

Lions often feature in his stories. In 1981, one of the donkey herdsmen, called Cobra, went missing. Mafira and a group of other scouts went looking for him and bumped into a large male, which charged towards them. 'The lion caught Fanuel Mbebe on the thigh,' Mafira recalls, 'he then for safety forced one of his hands into the lion's mouth and caught the tongue. Then one of our scouts shot the animal and when we took it to our camp, we found that this was the one who had eaten Cobra. The next day, we found half his leg in the bush.'

Zimbabwe's bush war officially ended with independence in 1980. When the ceasefire was declared, Mafira and another scout, Nicholas, were sent into the communal lands to chase away marauding elephants. Looking for information, they stopped at a village shop, and noticed that there was an empty bus parked outside. As they came through the door, a man pushed his way out of the crowd of passengers, holding a stick grenade. 'What are you doing here with your rifles?' he shouted, 'Put them down or I'll kill you!'

The shop emptied in seconds as people started running back to their bus. Even the owner vanished, leaving his money on the counter. When the bus had driven off, the man shut and bolted the shop door. He turned to the trembling scouts. 'I am a freedom fighter trained in Yugoslavia,' he told them, waving his grenade in their faces, 'and I have escaped from the holding camp at Chipinda Pools. I am not going back with you!'

He had the wild, staring eyes of a madman. One wrong word and he would blow all three of them into bloody little pieces all over the shop.

'Wait, my friend,' Mafira said. 'Government has sent us here to protect the people from elephants. If you don't believe me, then go ahead and kill us!'

The man kept threatening them – while Mafira kept staring at the hand grenade and repeating his story until finally, he opened the doors of the shop and let them go.

When the scouts reached home, they were welcomed as if they had returned from the dead. The bus had driven straight from the shop to the camp to report that they had been blown up by an *uhlanya* with a hand grenade. The man was mad all right; not long before, he had murdered his own father, believing him to be a wizard.

And speaking of lunatics – I'll always remember 20 June, not only as the day before the shortest day of the year, but as definitely the longest night.

Rich is away, picking David up from boarding school for his holidays. I feel quite safe because, as usual, Mafira is sleeping in the spare room next to the workshop, not far from the house, and Khanye is at the lodge compound. It's around two o'clock in the morning and I'm dreaming that a baboon is being chased by a leopard outside the bedroom window. I can hear its hoarse yells; it sounds as though the leopard has caught it. Now I'm fully awake, I can hear that the noise is somewhere near the serval cats' boma, around a hundred yards from our bedroom window. And it's not a leopard: I can make out some mumbling interspersed with the yells, it's probably that crazy fellow who sometimes comes through our fence and out again – he never harms anyone, so we don't fuss about it. It must be him. I get out of my warm bed and peer through the window. The world is still and flooded with light. It's the night of the full moon: perfect for lunatics. He shouts, almost roars, and begins to gabble, but I can't make out a word of it. I wish I could see him, but the trees and garden fence obscure my view; at least he isn't coming any closer. There hasn't been a sound from Mafira, and we are not in radio contact. He's probably doing as I am, lying low to see what the fellow does next. There's no point in enraging him further. It would be a mistake to alert him by switching on the solar light, so, taking the Glock pistol from next to the bed, I creep out of the bedroom to the cell phone, which is working, thank God. First, I try the Mangwe police but there's no reply (no surprises there), then I call up Rob Rosenfels, our neighbour, and luckily he answers.

'I think he might be rabid,' I tell Rob. 'He certainly sounds it.'

'Don't use the Glock,' he advises, 'rather get a shotgun. If you have to kill him, there'll only be problems. Do you want me to come over?'

'No,' I say, 'not yet. I'll call you again if I need you, but please stand by on the radio.'

I pad barefoot into the safe and take the little .410, as Rich affectionately calls it, off its hook: the one I used to shoot the nine-foot black mamba at the garage (all right, *eight*). David still shows off about it to his friends and I try to look modest, but the truth is that I fired off the first round by accident, giving myself a terrible fright, and the mamba was kind enough to stick around long enough for me to pepper him with the second. There are two rounds in the barrel. I put the shotgun on one sofa and sit on the other one, looking at it. Oh well, at least I'm accurate. If I shoot for the head, I'll definitely get him in the groin. Perhaps I should get more ammo. I creep back into the safe and all the while the yelling, gabbling and mumbling continues, though it's not getting any closer. Nandi barks, so I shut her in the bedroom. We don't want to drive him any madder. There's a frost tonight, it's perishing outside, but for some reason, I'm not feeling the cold at all.

God, we are going to have to listen to this for hours before it gets light.

I wonder what Rich would be doing if he were here.

Certainly not sitting inside gazing at the shotgun. He'd go out and tackle the man, while Nandi and I sat safely inside. Still no sound from Mafira; if he's not doing anything, I'm sitting tight. I just wish this fellow would die of cold, or at least curl up and go to sleep; it doesn't seem humanly possible to keep up this incredible row for much longer. He's getting hoarser and hoarser but not letting up; then suddenly, I think I hear the word 'Peek' – my God, he really is after us. I hear it again and again, it sounds like he's coming for Rich. I listen more carefully, though I don't dare to open the window. No, it's not just 'Peek', it's 'Mrs Peek', so not only does he know where he is, he also knows that Rich is away and, for some reason, he's after me. There's so much gabbling, it sounds as though there are two people.

It seems silly to be sitting, staring at the shotgun. I should have it next to me. I wish I could contact Mafira and ask him what he thinks we should do. It's at times like these that you realise just how alone you are in this country. Faced with a frightening situation, you'll never raise the police and you are very lucky if you contact the neighbours. Perhaps I should let the bushbuck out, they must be panicking.

Christ, it's finally happening. The garden gate squeaks (this is why we never oil it), and I rush into the office with the shotgun, and stand in the doorway, so when the creature puts his head through the window, foaming at the mouth, I'll blow it off, or something like that. Actually, I'm feeling rather pleased with myself, although I haven't really got a clue what to do, I'm not in a panic. Footsteps come pounding across the grass – ready, aim... 'Mrs Peek!' Thank God, it's Mafira! But he is in a terrible state. 'Why didn't you come?' he yells.

'What do you mean, Mafira?'

'I had him – I was holding him for nearly two hours, calling for you, but then I couldn't keep him down any longer. He's gone!'

So, while I have been cringing in the house, ignoring his cries for help, Mafira has been battling with a thief only a hundred yards away. He had heard a noise from the adjacent tool room, given chase and tripped him up near the servals' boma. Then he got him by the throat and nearly throttled him, punched him on the nose and held him down for nearly two hours.

Mafira marches me outside to run me through the scene. He shows me where the thief had tampered with the door, where he had chased him and pulled him down into the grass. The man had stabbed him in the neck with a screwdriver but not seriously, then bitten him on the arm, which was a lot more frightening.

'If you try that again,' Mafira snarled at him, 'I will kill you!'

He brings me his striped pajamas, which are in tatters. He has been sitting on the thief, a man at least twenty years his junior, naked and freezing, waiting for me to answer his calls. If it had been a knife rather than a screwdriver, Mafira wouldn't be telling me the story.

But it had never occurred to me that Mafira might be involved.

Over and over, I explain to him why I didn't come.

'I thought you were the madman, Mafira, I couldn't hear what you were saying.'

'Why didn't you open the window?'

'I didn't want to, in case I got his attention and he started coming to the house.'

When Rich got back, Mafira handed him a crime

report: 'For two hours, I wrestled with the thief, while shouting for help from Mrs Peek who did not come out. I was so cold and tired that at last the guy managed to escape, leaving my clothes in pieces.'

I know that he didn't believe my story. He thought I'd realised what was going on, but that I was too chicken to leave the house.

Eventually, I raised the police at Mangwe. They arrived in the afternoon, when Mafira was in Bulawayo seeing the doctor about the wounds to his throat and the bite on his arm; one uniformed sergeant and another young man in plain clothes. Khanye and I took them through the sequence of events. They appeared to be listening but neither took any notes. Then the sergeant leant against his vehicle, smoking, while the younger one asked a series of inane questions. After half an hour of this, his face suddenly lit up. 'Well,' he said, 'I've got the answer.'

'And what's that?' we asked him.

'This was an inside job. Who have you fired recently?'

We gave him the name of a driver, whom we had caught stealing linen from one of the storerooms.

'There you are!' said the policeman, 'it was obviously him.'

Khanye and I looked at each other. There really wasn't any point explaining that since Mafira had been grappling with the thief for two hours in the bright moonlight, he probably would have noticed if it had been someone he knew. After the police had gone, we found two pairs of footprints. While the thief had been cutting a hole in the glass of the workshop window, his mate was busy trying to break into the manager's cottage, which stood empty five hundred yards from the house. The one spoor was a tennis shoe with a very distinctive pattern on the sole. Graham Robertson, farming further down the Mangwe Road, heard my radio call to Rob in the middle of the night and phoned me. His safari camp had been robbed two nights before and his description of the spoor matched ours exactly.

We heard nothing further from the police. The only thing that had really interested them was Mafira's performance.

'Eeh, that's a very brave man,' said the sergeant, 'not many people would have done that!' The younger one nodded in agreement.

'Do you have any lions around here?' he asked me.

I nodded.

'Just one,' I replied. 'Mafira.'

Chapter Eleven

It is five o'clock in the evening, and we are standing outside the kitchen of the Tikki Hywood Trust headquarters near Harare, Zimbabwe's capital.

'Lisa, shall I give the pavlova to Badger?' a voice calls.

Why, you might reasonably ask (as we did) was a badger – however worthy – about to eat the pudding *we* are supposed to have for dinner?

Despite how it sounds, Lisa Hywood is not some batty old lady indulging her portly pet. She is a petite blonde, founder of the Trust and one of the most toweringly inspirational people I have ever met.

And for the record, the Badger who received the burned pavlova isn't a badger at all, he is a male civet, christened by the couple who rescued him from the vendors of his mother's pelt at Chimanimani in the Eastern Highlands. They had prised open her newborn cub's eyes with matchsticks till they bled; and when they failed to sell him on the side of the road, they tried to drown him in a mud puddle. By the time he came to the Trust's property in the Mazowe Valley, Badger was hairless, traumatised, and refused to eat or drink anything but black tea. In desperation, Lisa eventually managed to feed him on Epol dog biscuits, soaked in black tea and sterimilk, and for the next fifteen months he never left her side.

Today, Badger is four years old, a father, and in superb condition. He has never recovered psychological-ly from the trauma of his early days, so Lisa will not release him back into the wild, but, like all the animals in her care, he has a huge enclosure full of interesting features and stimulating toys. And, of course, the odd treat from the kitchen to keep him sweet.

We Matabeles normally avoid Harare. We call it *Bamba Zonke* (grab it all), with justifiable bitterness. As the seat of government and the centre for industry and agriculture (or what now remains of it), the money and the power are firmly entrenched there, to the detriment of everyone else in the country. Forgetting its reputation, though, Mashonaland is at its best in September – the month of *musasas*. The Trust headquarters are a seven-hour journey from Stone Hills, and these graceful trees were clustered along the road in a gorgeous springtime flush of delicate seashell pinks, pale rusts and tender green leaves. Lightly drizzled with raindrops, they looked good enough to eat.

And there was a very good reason for this trip. We were to collect Mufara, a female pangolin, and bring her back to Stone Hills. Over the years, fifteen of these enigmatic animals have been in Lisa's care, and the majority of them have been successfully returned to the wild.

Working with wildlife has brought us into contact with some extraordinary people. An immediate sense of trust and empathy exists between those who share a passion, and what a relief it is to be able to rabbit on for hours to someone who is as single-minded as you are.

Conservationists often spring from strange places, and Lisa is no exception. When she left school at seventeen, her ambition was to become a farmer, but her parents wouldn't hear of such an unladylike profession. Instead, they packed her off to a Swiss finishing school, the same one that Princess Diana had attended some years before.

'I'm told she hated it as much as I did,' says Lisa. 'All that cooking, sewing and socialising nearly drove me demented. And those cows with bells! I felt completely claustrophobic.'

Her next move took her even further away from Africa. After doing a degree in fashion and marketing in London, she joined Percy Savage, marketing genius behind Christian Dior, where the closest she came to a civet was sniffing the expensive perfumes that contain an extract from their anal glands.

Lisa was working in *haute couture* in Paris when she received the phone call that changed her life. Her beloved father had died tragically. So she came home, flying, as she says, like a kite without a string – her security gone. Desperate for some direction, she volunteered to help move around 700 elephants from the drought-stricken Gonarezhou National Park to various wildlife conservancies. 'Sitting around a camp fire and talking to people who had dedicated their lives to wildlife opened up a whole new world for me,' she explains. 'These were real people, passionate about what they did. It didn't matter a damn if you wore khaki and no shoes, or what sort of car you drove – all that was irrelevant.'

The seed was sown, and a year later, in 1994, in memory of her father, she formed the Trust as a welfare organisation, with the aim of breeding threatened species in Zimbabwe, and increasing awareness and empathy for wildlife among local people.

Its first task was to move fourteen 'problem' bull elephants out of the Dande Valley. They were crop raiders, and if they weren't taken elsewhere, National Parks would have to destroy them. The translocation was successful, and only one bull died – of a heart attack.

Lisa then turned her attention to the little-known Lichtenstein's hartebeest, Zimbabwe's rarest antelope, of which only forty-six individuals remained in the whole country. The Trust built quarantine stations in Zambia and imported eleven: a figure that has grown to over a hundred animals. Despite its highly endangered status, very little attention had been given to the Lichtenstein's until Lisa intervened.

'Plenty of money was being give to high-profile animals like elephant and rhino, but no one was putting a cent into the hartebeest, nor into the smaller, less charismatic creatures,' says Lisa. 'The truth is that if you are small or perceived as ugly, not many people are interested. But when you work with the Lichtenstein's and get to know them, you realise that they are beautiful animals with an amazing social structure.'

It was a female hartebeest (known as Number 5) who paid Lisa an extraordinary compliment. She was in Zambia, looking after the antelope at the quarantine station before moving them down to Zimbabwe. Five days after they were captured, Number 5 began to follow her whenever she went into the pen.

'She seemed to be genuinely interested in whatever I was doing,' Lisa recalls. 'She just stood and watched me. I started offering her cubes, and she took them from my hand.'

Moving them into the trucks for transportation to Zimbabwe was a slow, stressful operation, and Lisa wished out loud that one of them would lie down, because that would encourage the others to do the same. A few moments later, she peered into the truck to see that Number 5 had done exactly that. Lisa put her hand through the slats and the female began to lick it.

'It was phenomenal,' says Lisa, 'she seemed to know that she could trust me.'

It's not only the animals who feel that way – to know Lisa Hywood even for a short time is to trust her. This lovely, vivacious girl seems to be entirely without conceit. One of the jobs she hates most is fundraising. 'People want to meet a celebrity,' she says, 'but the Trust is not about people, its focus is the animals.'

Dealings with any branch of government are notoriously difficult, but not for Lisa. She wants National Parks to be fully involved with her project, and has developed a good relationship with them that she puts down to her persistence and determination.

'I think they find me rather annoying,' she laughs. 'But they also realise that I am honestly there for the animals. I don't have a hidden agenda. They've seen what we do, and that our purpose is to give the animals back to the land, and I think they respect that.'

Lisa led us into a small thatched room and lifted a sleepy Tiggywinkle from her warm nest of grass. The Southern African hedgehog used to be a familiar sight in Matabeleland gardens and on Stone Hills, when they emerged from their winter hideouts – but no more. Ringworm, cancer and herpes kill off this inoffensive little creature, which now seems in danger of disappearing altogether.

Next, we met the servals, each in a roomy enclosure open to the others. In 2000, Lisa received a call from the

SPCA in Shamva asking her to take over two orphaned kittens. She raised Muffet and Tigger and as more servals came into the Trust, she bred from them; but although breeding is her prime objective, she believes that if it's at all possible, every animal should be returned to the wild.

'It just takes time, and each one is different,' said Lisa, as she opened the gate to an enclosure where a magnificent male was lying under a tree. 'This is Geronimo. He's four and a half and only now is ready to be released.'

She knows each one of her animals intimately and monitors them closely for any signs of illness or distress. Badger, for instance, recently started pacing up and down his fence. Lisa changed things around in his enclosure and stimulated him with different toys, and he is now settled again. 'Of all of them,' she says, 'he has touched me the most. He had such a terrible start: his eyes were infected, he had pneumonia – but he was so willing to live. And I thought: if he can do it, so can I. Badger and I developed an instant bond; he gave me a huge amount of courage to keep going and to jump my hurdles.'

Until I met Lisa, I had never really thought about animals changing, like humans, throughout their lives. But of course they do – when they reach puberty, when they breed, when they become independent, as they get older, and particularly in captivity; each stage needs a different approach, and a different level of understanding. Lisa is as concerned with her animals' psyches as she is with their physical well-being. Duchess, a three-year-old serval, is one of her greatest challenges. She was born with entropion: inverted eyelashes on both top lids. For almost two months, Lisa had to pluck out each new eyelash to prevent infection. Duchess endured this pain with incredible tolerance, and although she cried, she never once resisted Lisa's ministrations. But the serval's troubles were only just beginning. Whilst sharing an enclosure with the male, Sarabi, she somehow broke her leg. Plaster casts kept slipping off, but the vet managed to pin the ulna through her paw, removing the pin after eight weeks. The operation was a success, but after all the trauma, Duchess's relationship with humans changed. From being a friendly, outgoing cat, she shrank from everyone but Lisa. In order to rebuild her confidence, Lisa spends hours with her every day and has slowly introduced her to Shenzi and Mufasa, two playful kittens born in captivity, in the hope that they will bring Duchess out of herself and raise her spirits. And maybe one day she will be able to have kittens of her own.

Lisa has had one holiday in ten years – she booked up at a resort in Mauritius for two weeks, but flew home after six days. She just couldn't bear to be away.

Although the Trust began with fairly clear-cut aims, it has become broader and broader in scope as things deteriorate in Zimbabwe. Like us, Lisa believes that although the short term looks bleak, the key to the future lies with the children. 'I want to teach them respect for every animal, from a rhino to a chicken,' she says. And that's just where she has started, with her 'Huku (chicken) Project'. With the cooperation of the country's largest poultry producer (everyone cooperates with Lisa), and some international funding, each child in a number of rural schools will receive a young chicken, to be kept in a facility in the school grounds. As part of their daily routine, they'll spend at least half an hour cleaning out the enclosure, feeding and caring for the birds. Bonding, fortunately, is out of the question as they won't be able to tell one chick from the other; and at 38 days they will be sold as broilers to a Bulawayo supermarket. The money raised will be used for more chickens or whatever else the school needs. How clever is that?

We spent two nights with Lisa, and on Monday morning, Mufara the pangolin was placed in a wicker picnic basket for the long journey back to Stone Hills. Lisa describes them as mysterious, almost mythical creatures. 'Everything about it is odd, its long tongue, the strange smell, its hard overlapping scales; when it rolls up into a ball, it's more like an artichoke than a mammal. And yet they are highly intelligent: when you look into their eyes, they look back into your soul.'

She is not alone in her admiration for this amazing creature: apart from its many uses as *muti* (medicine) and an aphrodisiac on a par with rhino horn, no greater gift can be bestowed on a chief, and the donor can expect many favours in return. Although it is now specially protected, the practice still continues, and Negomo, the Trust's first pangolin, was confiscated by National Parks from a man in Chiredzi, who served a six-month prison sentence as a consequence.

As far as we know, Lisa is the only person ever to have kept Cape pangolins successfully in captivity. 'Somehow Negomo survived my ignorance,' she told us. 'We analysed the contents of the ants and termites they eat, and found that they were very high in protein and fat. So I fed her a combination of grated meat, mealie meal, peanut butter, milk powder and eggs, and it worked. The strange thing is that you can put a pangolin on an anthill and it won't feed. It seems that walking stimulates their digestive juices, so that's what we did with Negomo – for hours every day. I kept her for three and a half years and then released her and a male,

Hombe, into a game park on the Mazowe river, about thirty kilometres from the farm.'

Pangolins don't move very fast and it took Negomo five weeks to find her way home to Lisa. She's now been free for over three years and is still seen regularly in the area.

Far more research needs to be done on the pangolin before it can be successfully kept and bred in captivity, but through an extraordinary stroke of luck, Mudzi, Lisa's second female, gave birth three days after she was brought to the Trust.

'We watched as this tiny, pink creature appeared. Mudzi's tail was wrapped right around her as she was born, and everything happened within that safe circle. She didn't clean Dotito, the tongue isn't suited for that. The pangolin has two mammaries between her front legs, and when Dotito wasn't attached to them, she was protected by Mudzi's tail, presumably for body heat because they need very high temperatures to keep them warm.'

Because of the stress Mudzi had been through, initially she didn't lactate. Lisa left the baby with her for warmth and comfort, and although she didn't know if it would work, she fed Dotito on goat's milk. But the baby never stopped trying to suckle, and this stimulated Mudzi to begin lactating three days later.

'Although we couldn't see it happening,' Lisa recalls, 'we knew it must be when the baby's weight suddenly shot up.'

At around 2.30 each afternoon, Mudzi would emerge from her box for the daily walk with her keeper. In the wild, she would have left Dotito in the den, but Mudzi had a better plan. Picking the baby up between her paws, she would hand her over to Lisa and then trundle off happily for a few hours of uninterrupted 'me time'.

Lisa was amazed. 'She had known me only for three

days and yet she trusted me implicitly.'

One afternoon five weeks later, Mudzi stayed in her box and didn't hand the baby over as usual. When she eventually moved, she lay very still on the path leading into the bush, and Lisa was certain that she was ill. Then Dotito starting making a noise in the box, so Lisa picked her up, but instead of giving her a feed, something prompted her to put the baby by her mother's side.

Dotito crawled around to Mudzi's tail and clambered up it, using her very long, sharp claws. She fell off, made her way back and climbed up again. And when Mudzi thought she had got the hang of it, she stood up and walked off into the bush with that typically strange upright stance, front paws off the ground, 'like a little old Chinaman', as Lisa describes it.

An hour later, she stopped and rolled on to the ground. Then, wrapping her tail around Dotito, she fed her for thirty minutes, whereafter the baby climbed back on board and off they went again.

In captivity, an animal's immune system is generally lower than it is in the wild. When a female pangolin's temperature suddenly plummeted and she died, the post-mortem showed all the signs of malaria. Since then two pangolins with similar symptoms have been successfully treated with chloroquine.

Among others, the serval male Tigger was released on a wildlife ranch in Nyamandlovu south of Bulawayo; Geronimo went to the Mavuradhona Wilderness, north of Harare, and Sarabi, Nala, Muffet and Rafiki came to Stone Hills. Each animal is fitted with a radio collar, and kept in a large boma for two or three months, or until we are sure that they have settled down in their new environment. And, without exception, the moment those gates are opened, every one of them will immediately abandon comfort, regular food and security for freedom – at whatever cost. Some of them range for miles, but Scout Richard Mabhena is out all day with his radio tracking system, regularly climbing some of the taller koppies to check for the reassuring tick, tick, ticking – the signal that tells him one of them is back in the area. If we can get close enough, we sometimes manage to give them food, but not very often. There is no compromise. No matter how tame and confiding they are in the boma, once freed they are wild and we are strangers in their world.

Lisa has had more than one tragedy in her life, but her animals have helped her through. 'They have been my saviour,' she says, 'because of the compassion they have shown me, and their unconditional love. I have given to them, but I have gained far more than they have. Every moment I spend with wild animals touches my heart because of their beauty and innocence, and the sacrifice they make for man's needs and often because of his greed. Once we belonged to the world, but now we've moved ourselves away and we are destroying it. But I believe that each of us can do something to make a difference; our every positive thought and action creates a ripple effect. And that's what keeps me going.'

Chapter Twelve

A well-known parliamentarian was campaigning prior to the elections in a rural area. 'Even if we select a baboon as the candidate for your constituency,' he told the crowd, 'we are your party and you must vote for us.'

The independent newspapers pounced gleefully on that one. They produced a cartoon the following day showing the parliamentarian chatting with a group of baboons.

'No thanks,' the baboon was saying, 'I'm standing as an independent.'

We needed something to laugh about. Every Friday, lists of farms were appearing in the newspaper, earmarked for compulsory acquisition.

'When's it going to stop? ' said Mafira, frowning, as he scanned the pages of listings in small print. 'And what will happen to me if you have to go?'

'You'll come with us, of course,' I said.

'And when I die?'

I blinked. 'What do you mean? You'll want to go home, won't you?'

'No. I want to be buried here on Stone Hills, at the

top of a koppie, next to Mr Peek.'

'But Mafira, surely that's against tradition?'

'I have my reasons,' he said. 'And if you would like me to, I will tell you the whole story when I come down tomorrow.'

Apart from their economic importance as the basis of a man's wealth in African society, cattle have a deep religious significance. The head of the home goes to the cattle kraal to communicate with the spirits of the dead, and when he dies, he will normally be interred close by. Rich and I are determined to be buried on Stone Hills because it is our physical and spiritual home, and we want to be a part of it forever. But it seemed very strange that Mafira would choose to break with the traditions that mean so much to him and his family.

He was down at the house the next morning, wrapped up against the cold in his jacket and khaki longs, still in service from his National Parks days.

He sat down, settled himself comfortably, and began:

'Now, I'm going deep into my life. In 1992, I was a scout at Robbins camp in Hwange National Park, and one night in June, at around 2.30 in the morning, when we were on patrol at the Deka River, I dreamed of a man with a big beard. I didn't recognise him but then, suddenly, behind my head, a voice spoke to me. "Mafira, pray hard. We are moving you away from here, to the Matobo Hills." It didn't make any sense; I woke up and checked, but there was no one around. At last, I went back to sleep, but at 4 o'clock the voice came again, with the same message. I got up at first light to look for spoor, but there was nothing. "Please pray for me," I told the other scouts. "I'm afraid. I don't know what's happening."

'At the end of the patrol, I was called into the warden's office at Robbins Camp. He showed me my name written on a list. "I'm sorry, Mafira," he said, "but because of ESAP (a disastrous economic restructuring programme put in place by the World Bank), you must leave your job at the end of this month."

'I was very upset. I had been with National Parks for twenty-four years; I was happy there and I didn't want to go.'

'But what did ESAP have to do with it?' I asked.

'Nothing!' said Mafira bitterly. 'They wanted to give our jobs to war veterans, that was all. I left my job and my friends, and went home to Masvingo at the end of June where, once again, the dream came to me. Soon afterwards I received a letter from Mr Erwee, who often used to visit Robbins for game viewing. "I might be able to help you," he wrote, "Richard Peek is starting up a wildlife sanctuary in the Matopos. Come to Bulawayo and I will take you to meet him."

'I remembered Mr Peek well. I had worked with him in the 1960s at the Gonarezhou soon after he joined Parks. I came to Stone Hills on 20 August 1992, and there he was, *Mandevu*, the man with the big beard. That night, after we had talked, I went to bed and again I had the dream; but this time, a turtle dove flew down from the sky and right into my mouth. It settled in my heart. It was Stone Hills in my dreams and my heart is here.'

Three years ago, we scattered Rich's mother's ashes at the very top of Dibe, and as they lifted into the wind and over the farm, we hoped that her spirit would guard us and keep Stone Hills safe. But what was merely a wish for us would have been a certainty for Mafira. Like us, he will mourn the loss of a loved one, but he is not faced with that unbridgeable chasm of silence that brings such a sense of loneliness and loss to our bereaved.

Africans believe that after burial, the spirit of the deceased wanders in the wilderness – *use'gangeni* – until, a year or so later, it is called home by the ceremony of *umbuyiso*, conducted by his or her relatives. If the grave is close to the kraal, a branch of the *umphafa*, or buffalo thorn, may be dragged from there to the family hut, symbolising the return of the deceased to his loved ones. Beer may be poured on to the grave, after which the family will walk back to their hut, singing, *Woz 'ekhaye, woz 'ekhaye*, come home, come home! From now on, the spirit of the deceased will play an active part in their lives by guiding and advising them through their dreams or by way of omens. But only those who have borne children may be brought home in this way. Although the childless will be taken care of by the spirits, they can have no influence on the affairs of the family.

After the ceremony, the official period of mourning is over. The widow is free to discard her black clothes and begin a new life.

Where Christians approach God through Jesus Christ, Africans believe that they may communicate with him only through the intercession of the recently dead, or the known ancestors. This may be a father, perhaps, who in turn may consult the grandfather (a spirit unknown to the family) and so on, up through the spiritual hierarchy to the most senior of them all, God himself, or He who Dwells in the Clouds.

I was interested to know what happens to a bad person. 'He has been taken over by the spirit of an evil ancestor,' Scout Richard Mabhena told me. 'He will suffer during his life because he may be bewitched or go mad. And if, say, he steals a goat, he may start to behave like one.'

Mabhena is married to a Christian woman but they join in each other's ceremonies, and although his children have had a Christian upbringing, Mabhena is teaching them the old traditions. He is a proud and private man. 'The Mabhenas came from Lesotho in Mzilikazi's time,' he told me. 'It is the name that keeps our family together. My grandmother Mabhena was called Sivolvolo,' he laughed, 'I don't know why – it means Revolver! She threw python bones to find out the cause of an illness. And she taught me much about the medicinal properties of plants. In our culture, you never forget what you are told by your family, but if it is told to you by someone else, you forget it tomorrow.'

I asked him what was the most important tradition he taught his children. '*Inhlonipho*, respect,' he said without hesitation. 'They must honour other people, particularly their elders.'

The African belief in the influence of spirits has some very positive consequences for the living. Old people are treated with the utmost respect, as once they die and join the spirit world, they will have a powerful effect on the lives of their families.

27 July 2000. Rich was away guiding in Botswana. Mafira came down to the house, his face twisted in grief. 'Frank is dead,' he told me. He had died at home in the night and his relatives had come asking for our help.

It's a bleak winter's day and now it feels as if we are cursed, not just on Stone Hills but everyone. All over Zimbabwe, good people, and in Frank's case, talented, extraordinary people are dying from AIDS, and yet there are those still living, who are trying to finish the job by wantonly destroying their country.

But I was jumping to conclusions.

Our manager, Anthony, drove Frank's brother back to his kraal at Nyabani, some sixty kilometres away, from where they transported the body to the Plumtree mortuary. Two days later, Anthony and Mafira met the family there, and Mafira helped them to wash the body in preparation for burial. Although there was now suspicion about the cause of death, the police would investigate no further, as Frank's medical records showed that he was often unwell. But we knew he hadn't been that sick, and he certainly wasn't close to death. Something much more sinister had been going on. Frank had been married and divorced. He had then been pursued by another woman, MaSibanda, who was determined to move in with him, and had badgered him until he relented. But he was never happy with her, and recently he had told her that she must leave. The night he died, Frank had been drinking beer in his hut with a neighbour until around 10 pm. By midnight he was dead, having suffered severe pain and vomiting. Only the next morning did MaSibanda inform the family, who were sleeping a few yards away.

At 5.15 on the morning of the 29th, Mafira and I left in the dark for Plumtree. It was bitterly cold. Shorty, petrol attendant and resident comedian, sang as he filled containers on the back of the truck at 6 o'clock, just as Plumtree was preparing to greet the new morning. A drunk staggered out of the doorway of the bottle store. He lurched into the road in his socks, swaying backwards and forwards, then suddenly there was a bang as he hit the side of our truck and collapsed by the petrol pump. 'Heh, heh, heh!' Shorty giggled in mid-verse, and called out a greeting to a group of smartly dressed ladies wearing felt hats shaped like upside-down flower pots that sparkled expensively under the street lamps. Each took a broom and began sweeping the filth off the patch of pavement that would serve as her office for the day's dealings in foreign exchange. For all its potholes and rusty car wrecks, there are definitely some economic advantages in living ten kilometres from the Botswana border. I kept glancing over at a man in an expensive coat who was waiting in his Mercedes Benz to see the manager of the garage. He looked like a member of the CIO, one of those shadowy figures from the President's office, particularly in his dark glasses, which seemed a bit over the top in the pitch dark.

We reached Frank's kraal deep in the communal lands at 7 o'clock after a bumpy ride along a track that was more suited to donkey carts than cars, and Khanye arrived with everyone else from the farm half an hour later, bringing provisions for the wake. The grave by the goat kraal was still being dug, and a group of men stood by the pile of earth, talking softly. The women in their bright sarongs and duks sat silently in a field of broken, brown maize stalks, their legs stretched out straight in front of them. It looks uncomfortable to us, but in African culture sitting cross-legged is considered immodest in a woman.

Reggie, Frank's younger son, led me to his father's thatched hut where another group of men were gathered around an enormous fire behind a newly erected fence of branches in green leaf, effectively isolating the hut from the rest of the kraal. They had been there, on guard, since

Frank had died, in case a witch should try to snatch the corpse away. Traditionally, death is believed to defile all who come into contact with it, and even the ancestral spirits withdraw their protection of the family at this time.

The men were staring into the flames and they didn't look up or greet us. Reggie pushed aside a tattered yellow curtain in the doorway of the hut. I could hardly see them in the gloom but there were four or five women sitting on the floor, and MaSibanda at the foot of the coffin, a blanket pulled over her head. 'Would you like to see my father?' Reggie asked me.

It may have been impolite, but I really didn't want to. I shook MaSibanda's hand and ducked out of the hut.

The grave was almost ready, but the funeral would have to wait until Frank's eldest son, Rabson, had arrived from South Africa. He had left by car the previous day and should have been there by now. Reggie brought me a chair in the middle of the maize field but I felt awkward, sitting on my own, staring at everyone from a distance, so I walked over to the men at the graveside.

'Good morning!' I said, in English.

A couple of them muttered in response. Then I heard one of the women behind me say something in Sindebele that sounded like: 'Why can't she greet us properly?'

I should have done, of course, but I tend to shy away from displaying my limited command of the language. Now I gave them my best rendering of the traditional greeting, and the atmosphere changed immediately to one of warmth and acceptance.

A white goat wandered up to the women and the awful thought crossed my mind that they might want to cut its throat. But someone flung a rock at it, and it limped away, bleating.

Mafira introduced me to Frank's sister and I tried to tell her how much we had respected and admired her brother.

'As he did you,' she smiled. 'He spoke often of you and your family.'

I took a photograph of her with her two small children, Ignatius and Thandile, peeping out from behind their mother's skirts and grinning at the camera; and another one of the mourners. Then Frank's workmates carried the coffin out of the hut and into the sunlight, and I took one of them standing around their old friend for the last time. I had been there two hours and still there was no sign of Rabson. David was at home, and I had to get back to him. I said my goodbyes and drove away, as a sharp wind blew through the kraal and whipped up the dust in the maize field.

All I could think of was these decent people, for there was no better word for them, unfailingly courteous and caring, good citizens in their traditional way, despite the poverty and despair visited upon them by those who cared neither whether they lived nor died.

Frank was our Pied Piper of Stone Hills, I wrote in my diary that night, *but now he has taken away the sunlight and the secrets and I can feel the hills closing up behind him. Will we ever really understand them again? I feel a truly dreadful sense of loss.*

Very early on the Monday morning, I sat on the veranda with a cup of tea, and watched and listened to Stone Hills – alone with my intolerable thoughts.

A general strike had been called for three days that week and the army was very likely to be called in. 'They' were crawling in their thousands all over the Chiredzi area; large numbers were expected to invade Gonarezhou National Park. There were huts and fires everywhere. And miles of snare lines.

Shashani, our oldest female giraffe, came in to drink at the waterhole, then sashayed off with her baby behind her, his horn tufts as unruffled as a new paintbrush.

Later that day, Rabson arrived at the house with Reggie. His car had burst into flames near the South African border, and destroyed everything inside including his cell phone. He had resorted to hitching lifts and arrived home mid-afternoon.

At the funeral, as the new head of the family, he stood at the grave holding his father's spear and knobkerrie. As is the custom, Frank's body faced east; women are buried facing to the west. His clothes and other items that he would need in the next life were placed on top of the coffin. Rabson spoke about his father and then directly to him, explaining why he had been delayed. Mafira made a speech on behalf of all at Stone Hills, and both the chief of the area and the headman spoke, asking Frank to be the shadow of his home. A member of Frank's father's family put a stone at the head of the grave, and someone from his mother's side placed another at its foot.

Rabson threw a handful of soil on to the coffin with the words *Hamba kuhle: usikhonzele* – go in peace and plead for us. Then each of the relatives and the mourners followed suit. The man who had been drinking with Frank on the night of his death had left home the following morning and did not attend the funeral.

After the ceremony, everyone lined up at the gate of Frank's yard where they washed their hands in one of two dishes of water – plain for Christians, and infused with the leaves of either the buffalo thorn or the *lippea javanica* for those with traditional beliefs. Thus purified, they began to eat and drink. As is customary, Rabson told me, a goat had been sacrificed for the occasion. A white goat.

Rabson worked for us briefly in 1989 as a general labourer and before he left, he brought his father in to join the workforce. I hadn't seen him for eleven years but I recognised Frank's quiet dignity in this tall young man.

'My father always taught me to be gentle and not to fight,' he told me, 'and I've tried to be like him.'

I wanted to know if he was going to press for a further investigation into Frank's death.

'I have discussed it with the family and we have decided to let my father rest peacefully,' he said. 'Even if we conduct a witch hunt, we will never learn the truth.'

Rabson had travelled far from his days as a labourer. Now resident in Johannesburg's notorious Soweto township, he was running his own little catering business and managing to send regular money home.

He handed me an old chutney bottle filled with soil from Frank's grave, as I had requested. We buried it under the young Cape fig tree we planted in his memory. 'I would like to rest under the tree which you planted in my father's name, in years to come,' Rabson wrote to me some months later.

The first Christian missionaries arrived in this country in 1854, but for decades they didn't manage to make a single convert. There is no bible or written creed on African religious philosophy; it permeates every aspect of people's lives, through their daily activities, their rituals and their fables. It is in their blood, and one hundred years or so of Christian teachings could not erase it. In these traumatic times, many people are going back to the beliefs that unite them and define their identity. Some, of course, were never influenced by Christianity. Frank was one of them. 'Pah, that's just a novel!' he would say when he caught Khanye reading his bible. 'They're fairy tales, like the promises the politicians make.'

Ruthie is a Christian but she believes that her father still speaks to her through her dreams. I asked if her church approved. 'Oh, no,' she said, 'they tell me that it's Satanism. They say my father is dead, so I must pray for him to go away.'

Where we might say, 'That's life – and there's nothing to be done about it', Africans believe that there is a reason for every misfortune and that the spirits of the ancestors can advise them how to put things right, often with the assistance of a nyanga. The bones may be thrown and the nyanga will advise how the matter can best be resolved. Perhaps a ritual may have to be carried out to honour the dead, or recompense made to a party who has been wronged.

We all need to feel pride in our history and tradition. But, even in the West, world leaders in scientific and technological progress, our confidence is failing as we look ahead with trepidation and behind us with longing for a world that once we thought we understood.

Chapter Thirteen

Wondrous things occur in secret places. Scout Billiard Mudenda is walking by a small koppie when he hears piggy noises coming from somewhere above him. Poombi disappeared three days ago to give birth, and though we have been searching all over her home range, very discreetly of course, we thought that this time she had given us the slip. Billiard runs back to the compound to alert Mafira, and soon we are all gathered at the foot of the koppie listening to the concert of squeals, twitters, squeaks and grunts coming from inside a small hole halfway up among the rocks. Every now and then, there's a long, low belching noise from Poombi, who sounds as though she is already thoroughly brassed off with her new litter. I've never heard such a row, and wonder if they have just been born.

I'm overjoyed – we are grandparents again, for the fourth time. Against all the odds, another year has passed on Stone Hills and we've reached another milestone.

After leaving her to settle down with her new family for

a few days, I walked in quietly one afternoon and sat on a rock about twenty-five metres away from the nursery. Today, apart from a few squeaks, everything was peaceful, and after half an hour Poombi shouldered her way out of the entrance and stood alone in the sunlight. When she picked up my scent, she came straight down to meet me, and as she raised her nose to mine, she released a fragrant cloud of honeyspice: her very own *eau de cochon* and part of her most loving welcome. She accepted my congratulations gracefully, but after all the exertion of the past few days, she was clearly in a hurry to get to water and food. Leaving me in charge, she trotted off towards the eland boma, her nipples swinging. For a while, all was quiet in the nursery, then one little round head popped out of the hole, and after a few false starts, two tiny piglets stood at the entrance. I hoped there would be another, for Poombi had given birth to litters of three for the past two years, and there it was, nudging its way between the other two piglets. Then suddenly, miraculously, there were *four* – and from what I could see of their tiny warts through binoculars (four for males, two for females), we had two boys and two girls. Clever, clever pig. Poombi was never one for christenings, so I named them, then and there, the Fawlty Towers quartet: Basil, Sybil, Manuel and Polly.

Anybody who has given birth to twelve children in four years is entitled to be casual, if even a trifle irritable, particularly a single mother. She had been a model parent with her precious first litter, Gruntabel and Squeak, keeping them safely in the den for most of their first two weeks. But the Fawlty brood would never know such cosseting – at four days old, Poombi returned from the boma and ordered them out of the house. Squeaking with excitement, they tumbled out, gathering around Poombi's head to sniff at the spot where tusk met lip, which seemed to be their usual greeting. After a quick feed, she marched them off, wobbly-legged, for their first walk. Their round heads seemed far too large for their skinny little bodies, and I noticed that both Sybil and Manuel had cradle cap. I hoped I was wrong, but I'm pretty sure I heard Poombi snap 'hurry up!' at Polly, who was already smaller and weaker than the other three. I followed them at a distance, making sure that I never presented a threat by getting between my pig and her brood. As always, she would bring me into the family circle when the time was right.

Every now and then, one of the piglets would give an experimental skip and a hop, but for those first few outings, they kept very close to Mama's heels. When they gathered around her demanding food, she flopped down flat in the grass with her back to me, something she would never have done if she hadn't trusted me completely.

As Poombi munched on the thick green grass and her piglets romped around her, the dassies on the surrounding koppies suddenly began to scream in alarm. She was generally very alert to warnings from other animals but today, for some reason, she ignored them. A black eagle flew low over the trees and immediately spied the piglets. Over ninety per cent of its diet consists of dassies, but a black eagle, like any predator, is an opportunist. These piglety morsels were the perfect size, and if it could only get them into the right position, one little Fawlty would be airborne. After five minutes of flying around and viewing us from every angle, the bird left, but I had no illusions about its next move. I kept scanning the sky, and ten minutes later it was back, together with its mate. On a sunny day, Poombi would have seen their great shadows sweeping over her and run for cover, but the clouds were low and grey, and eventually even the dassies went quiet, safe in their hidey-holes. The birds came cruising over our heads, trying us out from all directions and at varying heights. But every time they came close, I waved my arms and drove them off. They'd disappear for a few minutes, then come soaring up from behind the rocks, down over the trees, high and then low – until I chased them away again. They were so persistent I began to worry that even I couldn't stop them from snatching a piglet. But at last they gave up, and hightailed it home through the clouds, steadily gaining altitude like Lancaster bombers after an aborted mission. Poombi had chosen a beautiful nursery for the Fawlty four, but their overhead mobiles were of the real and deadly kind.

11 December: Brom called to tell us that Marshlands (a neighbouring game farm) has received their marching orders. Despite all the warnings, we are not prepared for this. I feel as though a chair has suddenly been pulled out from under me as I was about to sit down. Like that time we went to the top of the World Trade Centre and felt our stomachs falling to our feet as we gazed at the tiny figures hundreds of feet below. With any sort of bad news, your instinct is to reach for solutions based on experience. OK, you think, so that didn't work. So I'll try something else. But there's no solution to this one.

The first-floor apartment didn't do for long. Poombi changed houses a number of times, and when the babies were a couple of weeks old I found them at the old cattle kraal close to their new den, a deep hole under a rock that she had sometimes used for past litters. Today, the piglets were bursting with energy, trying everything at once: bronco hopping, nose flipping, sprinting off from a standstill, racing in circles – and, when their legs became completely muddled, dropping to the ground with a thump. Through half-closed eyes, I could almost see their black leather jackets, hobnailed trotters and tiny motorbikes, as they zoomed past each other on the wrong side of the track, completely out of control. An accident was inevitable. I heard a loud crack in the grass as two little road hogs collided head-on. Basil, with the blond mane and the largest of the four, sauntered away as if nothing had happened, while poor little Polly sat in the dirt for a few minutes, looking very puzzled, before tottering off after him. According to David, they all ended up having a few beers in a bar called The Wallow.

The piglets were tired that evening and well before dusk they decided that it was time for bed. They gathered around their mother and tried to chivvy her up, but her only response was to mutter something with a mouth full of grass that sounded suspiciously like 'buzz off and go and play in the traffic'. The piglets kept looking in the direction of the den and back to Poombi. They would start off quite boldly for a few yards, then lose their nerve and scurry back to her. Since holes mean safety, it isn't surprising that even tiny piglets have a very strong sense of direction. At 5 o'clock, the four had made up their minds. Mother or no mother, it was time to go. They began trotting off to the hole, slowly at first, hoping that Poombi might catch up, then at a flat-out gallop when Basil boldly took the lead. Poombi looked up and gave a

The everlasting hills.

The view from our front veranda, down into the Pundamuka valley.

Some of the animals become very tame when they come in for winter feeding.

Even when she was living wild, Poombi always looked upon our house as home.

We had a mutual understanding about our children, my pig and I. She trusted me with her piglets as I trusted her with David.

Below left: Lilac breasted roller – the favourite bird of King Mzilikazi, ruler of the Matabele.

Below right: The deep resonant tattoo of the ground hornbills often wakes us up in the morning.

Huge male leopards live on Stone Hills but are seldom seen.

Below left: Cheetahs occasionally visit to prey on young antelope.

Below right: Lisa Hywood developed a wonderful bond with her orphaned serval, Cleo.

The world according to Badge.

After such a traumatic start in life, Badger was desperate for love and security. But we worried that he would grow into his fearsome reputation.

The meanest animal in the world meets his first,
slightly poisonous snake.

This porcupine made a few holes in Badger's bottom,
but he refused to be intimidated.

Rich had worked with wild animals all his life but of all of them,
Badger impressed him the most.

Quiet reflection
– unusual for the ever-active Badger.

I'm with Mum!

loud sigh. Half an hour later she strolled off after them, checked that they were safely in bed, and went back to grazing on a patch of new grass.

1 Jan – New Year. Rich and I move the veranda table on to the lawn with a bottle of champagne under an upturned bowl of stars; we can't see a single light, nor hear a car, nor another person's voice. Just the crickets and the occasional rasping cough of a leopard as it patrols the Hape river. I take a mince pie and go to share it with the rats, who, as a potential meal for the owls, have even less than we have to celebrate. Kay and Ray, the dragonfly enthusiasts, went back to England yesterday, after their sixth visit to us in as many years. 'The Gadfly' is playing as they leave the farm and everybody has tears in their eyes. We make plans for them to return next Christmas, and we will cling to that promise like a tree in a flooded river. Life will go on.

Basil, Sybil and Manuel were as lusty as a litter of bull terriers, but not Polly. We had been very busy with guests at the lodge, and we hadn't seen much of the piglets for a couple of weeks. Always the runt, Polly had lost condition and become very unsteady on her legs. Rich loaded up his dart gun with an antibiotic, and while Poombi was busy immersing herself in the eland trough like a small hippo, Rich fired a feathered red dart straight into Polly's bottom. We could have kidnapped the whole family for all the notice their mother took. Apart from a little jump, the piglet hardly reacted but the dart, which should have dropped out immediately, was still stuck fast. Lying on my tummy by the fence, I waited for a good half hour until Polly wandered up, and as she drew level with me I shot out my hand and managed to pull it away. That little boost was all she needed. After a week or so, she began to recover and although she was always the smallest of the four, she was just as healthy as the others.

We had no qualms about helping Polly because she was a member of our family. But strictly speaking, we had interfered, and there is a very strong argument in favour of leaving nature to take its course, no matter what the circumstances. In the natural way of things, weaker animals rarely survive to breeding age, while the healthier ones live to pass on their superior genes to their offspring. As humans, we find this a very difficult concept. For those of us who care for animals, it is intolerable to watch them suffering and we feel impelled to intervene, even if it means saving a creature that would never have survived in the wild. But how far does one take this, particularly when one is regularly faced with these difficult situations, as we are? If Polly had been a truly wild animal, we wouldn't have taken any action. In any case, we would never have been able to approach her that closely. But what do you do when an animal is clearly dying? The purists would say leave it, but Rich has no qualms, he will put an end to its suffering when there is nothing to be gained by allowing the animal to linger.

The core of Poombi's home range was the eland boma where the most succulent grass grew, thanks to our herd of six tame eland who were penned there overnight. The scouts walked with them during the day, taking notes of their feeding preferences, recording over a hundred plants that they browsed on regularly. Other pigs visited the boma but rarely, as they were put off by regular human visitations, so Poombi enjoyed almost complete sovereignty. Until Squeak grew up. She, too, wanted her litters to enjoy the best grass, and I would often find Poombi and family in one pen and Squeak with hers in another; until one day I found them both in the same pen, one at either end with their piglets, four apiece, jostling behind their respective mothers, and sizing each other up like rival gangs at a kindergarten.

After a few half-hearted threats, the piglets took maternal refuge, and Squeak led her brood out of the gate, with Poombi pretending to graze but all the time glaring at them from the corner of her eye. Occasionally, the three Dahlings would turn up, also laying familial claim to the boma: after all, they had been brought up there too. All was peaceful until the Fawlty Four, led by Basil, strutted up to Charlie, who took an irritated rush at them, as an older brother was quite entitled to do. The piglets thought this was great fun, and they did it again with the same result, and for a third time, when Basil dared to take a sniff at Charlie's backside. This was enough for mother. Hackles up and mane raised, she charged like a hairy juggernaut at all three juveniles, who quickly ducked into Squeak's boma. But this was no safer. Squeak's head came up and she was off after them, even more seriously than her mother, charging round and round the boma until the piglets dived under the fence and fled. I found them later on my way back home, trotting disconsolately along the road, teenagers rejected by their whole family. It made me sad, as things should have been so different. Were it not for Poombi's dysfunctional upbringing, she would have learned from her own mother to welcome her daughters back into the family after a new litter was born. Then they could take care of each other's kids and, apparently, even feed them if this became necessary. But Poombi had chosen the hard way and, typically, she wasn't changing her mind.

Among so many memories, I remember best a November afternoon when the air was filled with the rich, loamy smell of the earth after rain and the leaves were washed clean and sparkling. As I drove to meet Poombi and her family, now ten days old, I spied the wet head of a baby tsessebe in the grass, glistening with raindrops. It was the sort of day when you feel 'full up', as David used to say, and I, too, recall as a child those intoxicating moments when happiness dances into your life, turns you upside down, and makes people around you smile, though they may not know why.

But our childhood had passed, and we were holding back on our joy. So often, on these magical days, Shakespeare's words kept popping up in my head: 'Rough winds do shake the darling buds of May, And summer's lease hath all too short a date...', and I wondered if we would ever again be able to lose ourselves in the present without a nagging sense of dread.

I sat with Poombi in a glade of dappled sunlight, watching her family and treasuring this intimate time with them. After a while, she led the Fawlty Four up close, and placed her head gently on my leg. This was their first, formal introduction to granny and they came in for a group sniff, grunting and snuffling, and enveloping me with the wonderful warm smell of pigs.

By the end of the afternoon, they had lost all fear, and they took turns at tugging the laces on my shoes. They played until the sun slipped away, leaving the sky glowing like a ripe peach, and the sounds of birdsong gave way to the melodic hum of insects. At last light, I followed them as one by one they disappeared into their den, with mother last, so plump from all that new grass that she could hardly fit. Poombi wiggled in backwards until all I could see of her was the gleam of her tusks in the darkness. And I drove home, aching with a mixture of joy and sadness, knowing that nothing could be so perfect as tucking my little family into bed where they would be safe until morning.

Chapter Fourteen

Friday, 5 July 2002. Midwinter. I picked David up from school at 12.30 pm, and despite the cold, drizzly weather he insisted on his usual ice cream before we headed home. As I listened to him chatting away about his friends, it was hard to remember that for his first seven years, he had been brought up alone, barely in contact with other children.

Since this is apparently the most impressionable time in a child's life, he might well have been a social disaster (like his parents), and I admit I felt slightly anxious when, at three, he was spending days on all fours insisting that he wasn't a boy, but a warthog. As a latter-day Romulus or Remus, he definitely would have experienced some difficulty in adjusting to a school environment; but David came up trumps, as we always knew he would. A bit of a loner, his teachers told us, but with a huge sense of humour, and a happy knack of making friends wherever he went.

We often bumped into Poombi between the main gate and the house on our way home, so it wasn't unusual to see her and the Fawlty Four grazing outside the eland boma. We stopped the car, but instead of coming up to greet us, all five warthogs ran off and stopped some yards away. It wasn't Poombi, after all, it was Sophie, her only daughter from last year's Dahlings, and this was the first time I had seen her so close to the piglets. If her mother had been there, she would never have tolerated it.

'Poombi must have gone walkabout,' said David and I agreed. She did that sometimes, now that the piglets were growing up, but she never went very far.

We drove home and by the time I had unpacked the vehicle and hauled everything inside, I found a trail of socks, tie, blazer and shoes leading to David's bedroom. He was already under the blankets with the latest Harry Potter and an enormous lump in his shirt that would remain there the whole weekend, even when he was on his bicycle or fishing at the dam. The only time David's rat Stuart was out of physical contact with him was in the bathroom, where he would be wrapped up in a towel and put in the basin. There's a strange affinity between boys and white rats. Stuart Little, all five kilograms of him (or thereabouts), had been David's most devoted companion since we picked him up as a tiny pup from the pet shop as part of our owl-feeding programme. This was always difficult, but once Stuart became a member of the family, and we realised that each one of the rats had a distinct personality, consigning them to owl fodder became almost impossible. As a tribute to Stuart when he eventually died and his ashes were placed in an old cigar box, the remaining rats were put into comfortable retirement for the rest of their days.

I was still slightly concerned about Poombi, so I radioed Mafira later on that evening and asked him to look out for her. He called the next morning to report that Ronald had seen her at the compound with the four piglets, but when I checked, I found the Fawlty Four, alone again.

Later, Lipson reported that he had seen her at the boma, then Kephas told us that he was quite sure she had been chasing her piglets away at the ruins of the old farmhouse. But that I found hard to believe. On every other occasion, Poombi had driven her piglets off only just before she gave birth.

I couldn't sit waiting for news, so I drove the four kilometres to the House at Pig Corner on the Matanje river, Poombi's first residence as a liberated pig. Cobwebs covered the entrance to her hole, and I found the little red bowl we used for her milk still wedged in a branch of the marula tree that shaded her house in the afternoons. Except for a few stagnant pools, the river was dry. I trudged through the sand to another of her favourite places, but it too was deserted.

By Monday, I could feel a cold wind blowing through the house. Scouts Mabhena and Big Boy, who knew Poombi too well to be mistaken, had last seen her on Thursday morning. That was the last confirmed sighting; we had discounted all the other reports.

I had been with her the week before. Rich was away, guiding in Botswana, and while I had been out checking the carcass of a young impala killed by a leopard and hidden between some rocks, Big Boy had radioed me to say that Poombi was at the main gate. She had come up to me with her head raised and I had stroked the length of her nose with the back of my left hand, while tilting up her chin for a kiss with my right. As I always did.

All day the scouts searched up and down the Matanje

river. I walked the path from the windmill to Bushbuck Vlei, where Poombi had introduced me to Gruntabel and Squeak, her first litter, on that unforgettable afternoon almost five years ago. There were fresh tracks of leopard and hyena in the sand. I knew Poombi wouldn't be there, but I couldn't help shining my torch into their old hideout under the rocks. Dry leaves lay deep on the floor of the little cave; no one had lived there for a long time. I climbed up above it, to the spot where I had first seen the piglets playing below me, and sat there for half an hour, looking into the hills and remembering those deeply special moments. A wild cat came out of the trees, his large ears pricked and the black tip of his tail waving. I kept very still as he strolled past and away down the track.

A thin plume of white smoke was rising in the distance, and by the time I got home, Rich was getting ready to help fight a fire on a neighbouring farm, taking all the scouts and workers with him. He needed Mafira, who was out searching for Poombi, so I went to fetch him. I found him standing next to an antbear hole in the middle of the long vlei that runs down from the source of the Mathole River at the top of the farm.

'I've seen the piglets,' he said. 'On the way back to this hole.' He pointed to fresh tracks and the dry grass that had been used to plug the entrance. 'They probably spent last night here.'

'No sign of Poombi then?'

Mafira shook his head. 'Nothing. But you'll find the piglets somewhere in the long grass on the fence line.'

That fence was right against the Mangwe road, and I knew that Poombi slipped under it sometimes to graze on the verge where there was no competition from other warthogs. It was dangerous for her, and the workers stopped up every hole they found with rocks, but if she had really wanted to, she could simply dig her way out. But why would she have done that in the middle of winter, when the grass on the side of the road was no more appetising than what she could find in the sanctuary?

And surely the piglets would have gone with her? I caught up with them in the long grass. They were alone, and when I called out, they trotted nervously away, making a wide detour back towards their hole.

I stood in that empty vlei, listening to the silence, wrapped up and remote, as though that strong and bitter wind had blown the feelings out of me, leaving me empty of emotion.

I had run through all the possibilities, hundreds of times, and none of them made any sense. I realised then that I would never see Poombi alive again. We would carry on searching because we had to find out what had happened to her. The worst thing would be never to know.

Just let it be a leopard, I prayed to the god of the stone hills, or any natural end to seven years of an incredible life. Not dogs, not a snare, not the ultimate betrayal by humans whom she had learned to trust.

By Wednesday, the whole work force was out searching. I sat on the bed at sunrise and Nandi came in, bringing me an old cabbage leaf as a present. Squirrels chased each other round and round a tree, and I could see the sun shining through the babies' pink ears.

At 10 o'clock, I was on my way up to the boma when Mafira's voice came through on the radio. He didn't have to tell me – I knew immediately that he had found her. Driving back to the long vlei, I saw Mafira, his son Mapfumo and four workers in their green overalls standing in a circle around an antbear hole, no more than two hundred yards from the piglets' den.

They didn't know for certain but something had died in there. Always the first to volunteer for any job, no matter how nasty, Mapfumo lay on his tummy and, with Mafira holding his legs, squirmed deep into the hole. He came out with a warthog's back leg that had been partially eaten, probably by jackals. Peter arrived with a pick and shovel and Rich came with some more. They dug very deep and eventually came to the body. It was so tightly wedged that it took four workers to pull it out.

She showed no signs of injury. The most likely scenario was that Poombi had been chased into the hole by a leopard or a cheetah. She must have been in a panic, because she had gone straight down, without whipping around into reverse as warthogs always try to do, so that they can defend themselves with their tusks. And once she was deep in there, she had become stuck and it had collapsed on her. Rich wrapped her up and brought her home.

That afternoon, I sat at my desk at the bedroom window looking at the pile of freshly turned earth as Obbie and Sam dug a hole next to the tree we had planted for Abel, Poombi's old friend. And we buried our precious pig there, where she would always be close to us.

There's a large, long-legged spider who lives on the curtains of the sliding doors leading on to the front veranda. She isn't interested in us, and she's not the least bit grateful that we let her stay there. She's getting on with the business of being a spider: spinning her web, laying eggs and catching her food. I, on the other hand, know exactly who she is – a nursery web spider, probably the same one who used to live in David's bathroom with her web strung between the taps in the sink. I am honoured that she has come to live with us and that she treats us so casually: just as I feel privileged that bats fly into the house from behind the curtain, ignoring the two humans in the bed; that the dormouse had her babies in our office, and the barn owls shit on the veranda every night. All my life I have sought acceptance into the other world, the one that is inhabited by creatures that are not human nor tainted by human contact. Their world is for the most part hidden, and it operates on many different levels. Man casts a quick gaze over it and believes that he sees and understands, when in fact he does neither; for this other world does not purposely exclude us, but will open its doors only when we stand and knock, humbly asking to enter. Each room has a set of keys: they are marked Love, Respect and Understanding, and any creature may let you in, a warthog in our case, but it could be a dragonfly or a bird that has chosen to nest under the eaves of your roof. Poombi was our connection to the sanctuary and to every creature on it. She had led us across the chasm between our two worlds and shown us that secret place we know so little of. But now our bond was finally broken, and like a ribbon of mist, it began to dissolve and float away.

We told David when he came back from school, and when he went to say goodbye to her, he left a red rose on her grave. The kudu ate it that night, and we knew Poombi would have approved. We had a mutual understanding about our children, my pig and I. She trusted me with hers as I trusted her with David. When she put her head into his lap or reached up nose to nose with her tusks inches from his face, I knew without a moment of doubt that she would never hurt him.

So many issues had haunted us. If we had been forced

to abandon the farm, it was unthinkable to leave her behind. But how would her life be confined to a pen after years of freedom? And even that wasn't an option if she had dependent piglets. In the end, there were no decisions to be made. She had died alone; I hadn't been there to hold her head, kiss the soft skin at the back of her ears and tell her how much I loved her. But she had died as she had been born, a wild animal, and no one could hurt her now.

I went looking for the piglets every day. At eight months old, they could take care of themselves, provided they were vigilant; but their mother was their guardian and they would have been devastated by her sudden disappearance. A week after Poombi's death, I found them, rooting in the dust close to the main gate. They looked up and almost immediately Basil, their self-appointed leader, began to move off. All four headed for a tree around fifty yards away, but after hesitating for a few minutes, Basil slowly began circling back. He lay down suddenly and gazed at me as if he was making a decision, then got up and trotted towards the vehicle with the other three behind him. As I sat in the grass, they began grazing around me. I could have stroked little Polly, but I didn't do it. The wilder they became, the more likely they would be to survive.

I had no doubt about their intentions; once they realised who I was, they wanted to make contact. In their short lives, we were the only other living creatures that Poombi would allow them to talk to. Squeak and her piglets had always been *personae non gratae*, and there were no mothers, aunts or cousins for the Fawlty Four to rely on. We represented the only security they had left.

As the days passed, and then the weeks, we could feel a hint of spring in the air: a little rain to dampen the earth, a little more warmth in the sun. I found that I was truly appreciating the moments that can so quickly pass away forever. One afternoon, I saw Trust standing outside the kitchen door throwing little balls of sadza to an elephant shrew. I took over and it sat very close to me, round and sleek, twitching its long black nose; no more the timorous beastie who used to scamper away and hide in the rocks. I had suggested months before that the kitchen staff leave a few scraps out for them, but I hadn't checked on it. Trust had been feeding them three times a day, along with a family of slender mongooses, francolins, squirrels and Henry the bushpig.

The Queen had gone, but she had left us the keys to her kingdom.

Chapter Fifteen

'It smells revolting,' I could hear a woman's voice in Mike Bromwich's office as I climbed the stairs of the local taxidermy studio.

'Well, if you don't like it, why not give it to the Peeks? Last time I was out there, they had a warthog on the sofa and God knows what else at large in the house.'

I put my head around the door.

'Ah, Bookey,' said Brom. 'I was just trying to persuade Judith to part with their honey badger.'

But Judith was already shaking her head. 'I'd be happy to get rid of it tomorrow, but for some reason, Jack likes the little stinker and won't let me. I've told him, though, if it destroys anything in my house, I'm going to stick a .22 up its arse.'

1 October 2004. There's the faintest chance that we may be getting a honey badger, if it survives. A visiting hunter in the lowveld spied its mother trotting along with the baby in her mouth and decided that she would make an interesting addition to his trophy room. I don't suppose that the cub will ever make it, but I can't get it out of my mind. Robert Ruark called them 'the meanest animals in the world', but whatever its reputation, we have to take in every orphaned animal that comes our way.

Three weeks later, we were at a motel in South Africa's Limpopo province, on our way back from David's interview at his new school in the mountains of Magoebaskloof. With knysna louries gliding through the shadows of its cool montane forests, and samango monkeys leaping through the canopy, the area is very like the Eastern Highlands of my childhood, which wasn't of course much consolation to David, who would far rather have stayed at home. But we live in the bush, and boarding school is inevitable, except perhaps if you're on a sheep station in outback Australia where lessons can be beamed through to you by satellite. But even if such technology were within our reach, neither David nor I could have stomached another round of home schooling, the trauma of which is etched on my memory as vividly as the agony of childbirth.

So there we were, having our dinner, when Richard's mobile rang. It was Brom.

'Tomorrow?' said Rich, frowning. 'We're not really prepared for it. Can't they leave it for a day or two?'

They couldn't. Judith and Jack were off on holiday and the honey badger needed a home. Ready or not, the meanest animal in the world was about to become a member of our family. And I was the last one who could object: I'd begged Judith to let us have him, just as I had pleaded for Poombi seven years before. But a warthog is a pussycat compared to the legendary honey badger: he who is reputed 'to attack big game (up to a buffalo, biting the groin and the genital organs, the animal then bleeding to death)', that 'treacherous little animal who has no natural predators and will attack without provocation'. Oh yes, we all know the stories – if badgers could jump a bit higher they'd be disembowelling giraffes.

What little sleep I had that night was punctuated by nightmares. Our poor old Nandi dog torn to ribbons in her own house, the bushbuck flying through the fence with a salivating badger on their tails – and, worst of all, my husband and son leaving home to join the Drakensberg Boys' choir. I'd really done it this time.

There was a babble of excited voices coming from Brom's office the following afternoon and my first thought was that the badger had amputated someone's finger through the bars of his cage. But as we got to the top of the stairs, we could hear them more clearly.

'Ah, sweet!' said one female voice.

'Now let *me* hold him,' demanded another.

We elbowed our way through a crush of adoring women gathered around a small cardboard box containing a black and white creature around the size of a Jack Russell puppy. And far from swinging on the chandeliers, he was whimpering while Marina Jackson tickled his head.

'He's been fed twice a day on Lactogen,' she told us. 'I've given him his bottle a few times, but he's lost interest now. Judy says he's had a lot of diarrhoea.'

Rich ran his hands over the cub's swollen belly, feeling the protruding ribs and spine. Since his mother had died, this tiny creature who still couldn't walk had spent his days alone under a tree in the garden, crawling from one patch of shade to the next. Morning and evening, a bottle of milk had been left in his mouth from which he had sucked as best he could.

We called in at the vet surgery on the way home and put our fruit box down on Dr Gerard Stevenage's table. Apart from being a notorious streaker, this blond giant with the gentle hands sports a pair of impressive cauliflower ears, testimony to his after-hours career as the most vicious rugby forward ever spawned in Matabeleland. We had named our secretary bird after him. During her second operation for a broken leg, Geraldine's daffodil-yellow eyes glazed over and she stopped breathing. Rich was at her head, watching the oxygen. 'She's going!' he cried. Then 'She's gone!' as the big bird's head drooped and her eyes closed. But Gerard never missed a beat – summoning his two partners, they injected adrenalin straight into Geraldine's heart and within moments she was back with us, full of untold stories, no doubt, of white lights and waiting relatives.

Over the years, this little team has stitched up a tsessebe calf who jumped through a plate glass window, fixed broken wings, attended to numerous orphaned antelope and amputated an eland bull's tick-infested ear. And it was the fearsome Gerard who wiped a tear from his eye when he put David's elderly rat Stuart to sleep.

He lifted the comatose little body out of the box and cupped him in his hands.

'He's certainly a bit lethargic.' Badge opened one beady black eye and attached himself to Gerard's little finger. 'But he's sucking well and that's always a good sign. I'll give him a boost with some vitamin jabs.'

Gerard handed the badger back to me and strode off to the dispensary.

'I'm still worried,' said Rich. 'He's so malnourished he can't even lift his head. Anyway, at least he won't feel the injections, their hide's as thick as a rhino's.'

We put Badger back in his box and Gerard inserted the first needle.

Badger let out a furious squeak and launched himself at Gerard's hand, gums snapping. We all leapt backwards.

'On second thoughts,' said Rich, 'I think he'll be OK.'

The orange box lay by my side of the bed for that first night and for many nights thereafter: the badger curled up on a nest of soft towels covering a hot-water bottle, with a blanket draped over the top for darkness and warmth. In a replay of David's early days, I laid all the doings out in the bathroom ready for the night feeds – the sterilised bottles, milk formula, flasks of boiling water, Nestum baby food, vitamin and mineral supplements – and when the cub stirred and squeaked I put my hands under the blanket and lifted his warm little body out of the box. But there the similarities with the infant David ended. Badger's fur was soaked in runny poo and urine, and everything had to be cleaned up before feeding could begin. And as I frantically dabbed, rubbed and dried, the squeaks turned into shrill screams of hunger and impatience. Of course, I could have done with some help, but New Age males are pretty thin on the ground in the Marula district. True to form, my old man slept through it all. At last, I retrieved the shivering Badger from the floor and plugged the bottle in.

We put him on the carpet the next day. At first he lay prone like a bit of flotsam washed up on a beach, and then with a mighty effort he paddled forward a few inches. On the third day he managed to get to his feet, where he swayed back and forth like a chameleon, growling to himself, before falling flat on his face.

On the move, he reminded us of a small, tipsy rabbi

wearing a white *yarmoulka* pulled down low over a pair of coal-black eyes. As with some other members of the mustelid family, like the European badger, polecats and zorillas, honey badgers are formally attired – pure black below with woolly legs and a short tail, and a pale grey mantle above, rimmed with pure white, that shines like a strip of neon in the darkness.

Why the black and white? The most common explanation is that it serves as a warning – don't cross me or I'll give you something you'll never forget: or more specifically, my bottom in your face squirting a stream of filthy-smelling liquid from my anal glands. But consider the penguin or the peaceable panda – no one could accuse them of such rotten behaviour. It just doesn't add up.

In the honey badger's case, the anal glands are used only as a last resort. It's what he does with his front end that must presumably have earned him his spine-chilling reputation.

I was sitting in the shade abluting the baby Badger a few days after he had arrived, while Rich was paying the staff.

'Ruthie!' I called, spotting our cook at the garden gate. 'Could you sit with him while I go inside? He's very nervous if he's left on his own.'

Moments later, I heard an escalating roar as though someone had fired up a Harley Davidson in the backyard. Hell's Badger, who could barely stand, was up on trembling legs quivering with fury. Eyes popping, pink mouth wide open, tail up and bristling like a toilet brush, he bawled his rage inches away from a grey-faced Ruthie. And there was an appalling smell around him as his anal glands kicked in for the first time. It was one of those paralysing moments when something totally unexpected happens and no one knows how to react. Banknotes blew off the veranda table as Rich sat open-mouthed, staring at what we had believed was our helpless orphan. It was a bit like tiptoeing into the nursery to visit your newborn, only to discover Dracula waiting in the cot.

Eventually, when he didn't show any sign of tiring, I squatted down next to him and very gingerly put out my hand. Only when it was right by his nose did the roars begin to subside into growls and finally into pathetic squeaks. Then suddenly Baby Badger was with us again, collapsed and shuddering in my arms. The huge surge of adrenalin was spent and so was he.

'Honey badgers don't like surprises', I read in one of our many reference books. We could vouch for that. Never again did any of us approach Badger without first calling his name and then slowly putting a reassuring hand to his nose.

The only way to understand this Jekyll and Hyde-ish behaviour is to consider what the HB lacks. As a youngster, and except at very close range, his eyesight seems pretty hopeless. He is small and far less powerful and swift than lion and leopard, his traditional enemies. And he's generally solitary: apart from females and their cubs, the badger can't rely on anyone else to look out for him. However, despite all these shortcomings, the badger trots brazenly through the bush as if he's invincible. Why? Because he's got attitude – and plenty of it.

Badgers don't run, they confront, and through sheer nerve, very often put their enemies to flight. They've even been seen squaring up to sinister-looking tree trunks that weren't there when they last looked.

Hell's Badger (Rich takes the credit for that one) was only one of his names. When the wind blew in the bushwillows, he was Basically just Badger. But 'B' is such an accommodating letter; we managed to find a suitable adjective for almost any situation.

Baby Badger inevitably became Bigger. Brave Badgers are sometimes Bad, and Bored Badgers become Bloated when they have too much Breakfast. And when they fall into the river, they become Baptised Badgers. Thank goodness he wasn't a zorilla....

Every day we saw changes as the helpless little blob wiggling his toes in the cardboard box began to wake up and grow into his reputation. Food, love and security might be enough for a puppy but clearly a far greater input was needed for someone who is described in the Guinness Book of Records as 'the most fearless animal in the world'. It appeared that badger lore was full of superlatives.

I'd been emailing and phoning all over Africa for days before I finally found someone who had been personally acquainted with a honey badger. John Posselt and his widow, Doreen, had raised dozens of different kinds of animals – lions, cheetahs, caracals and even black rhino: another creature of legendary ill temper and unpredictability.

'The rhinos were absolutely delightful,' says Doreen, 'but quite a lot of work. Tombi lived in the garden, and she hated being alone. We couldn't be there all the time, so we had to employ a chap to sit with her during the day. And if he left for a minute, she would start screaming. She loved to play, but I'd have to hide behind a tree when she got too boisterous: even when she was very young, she was built like a tank.'

Doreen's love affair with wildlife began when she was six and her parents gave her an orphaned baboon to raise. Jill, as she was called, slept in a pram next to Doreen's bed. She sucked a white dummy and liked to be spoon fed in her high-chair at mealtimes.

Ratsi (from 'ratel' [rah-tel], the Afrikaans name for a honey badger) came into the Posselts' lives when they were stationed at Mushondike National Park in the Masvingo area. Doreen was close to tears when I called her.

'Ratsi was my very favourite animal. We all adored her.'

'Where did she stay?' I inquired.

'In the house when she was a baby, and usually under the duvet, but later she had to go outside with the dogs. She was always very busy, if you know what I mean.'

'Tell me more,' I said.

'Well, once she made up her mind to do something she was unstoppable. We couldn't leave her for more than a few minutes in the house before she'd be laying waste to it. She'd raid the fridge by lying on her side and prising the door open with her claws, and wherever I hid John's chocolates, she'd always manage to find them. She was an absolute chocoholic. Oh yes, and then there was the night when she felt lonely, so she climbed our fifteen-foot roof and started tearing up the tiles over the bedroom. And when we went out to investigate, she rolled off and landed headfirst on the concrete. She did so hate being shut out of the house.'

'Good God, wasn't she hurt?'

'Not a bit. She jumped straight up with a pleased little "prrt" and trotted off with her tail in the air. I must warn you about your cars, though.'

I could see my knuckles whitening as I gripped the phone.

'Do I need to know?'

Doreen laughed. 'Well, fortunately John was a very tolerant man. We'd just had our truck re-upholstered when Ratsi managed to open the door one night and rip it all up. It's amazing what they can do with those claws. They're like knives.'

I repeated the conversation to Rich in bed that night.

'It could be a long haul,' he said thoughtfully. 'I've just been reading that a well-fed badger can live for up to 27 years. Let's see, that means we'll be in our eighties by the time his claws wear down, if they ever do. Ah well, perhaps we'll all go together.'

Once upon a time I was a lawyer, though these days I can't really remember why. I spent the night deciding which member of our family would be the most easily bamboozled into guardianship of an elderly but still sprightly BB, and mentally redrafted our wills. I could just see the article in the Law Journals: Badger Bequeathed. We would make legal history.

Chapter Sixteen

Two weeks after he arrived at Stone Hills, little HB lay on my lap swigging the last of his morning milk. After a firm pat and a massage between the shoulders, he gave an enormous belch, then wriggled on to his back for our morning session of Nip the Finger.

I looked down at him with some satisfaction. Although his past was never far away – he still roared, growled and whimpered in his sleep – he had quickly accepted us as family. He'd become stronger too, sometimes staggering a few steps before those outsized claws became entangled and tripped him up. His afternoon siesta was spent on our bed, and at night he watched television with David on the sofa, happily sucking his finger.

But today there was something wrong. I suddenly noticed that his skin was peeling and that he had a few angry red spots on his belly. And a layer of black fur was sticking to the towel in his box. Despite all our care, the cub was ailing. Naturally, my first call was to Lisa. Trying to sound calm, I described the symptoms of our

Balding Baby Badger.

'Oh, that often happens,' Lisa said airily, 'it's because he's on the wrong milk. He'll probably be completely hairless in a couple of weeks. But don't change the formula now, just try him on solids as soon as you can.'

Privately, I thought he might be a bit young for it, but I spooned some mashed-up mince on to a small tin plate and put it on the floor. HB homed in on this new but delicious smell and, having demolished the lot, he roared with fury and attacked the spoon.

'What you must do,' Lisa told me, 'is to make records of everything he eats and his daily weight. And don't forget to take his temperature every night,' which is not as easy as it sounds. To start with, I lose my glasses ten times a day and I've taken to creeping around, hoping to catch them by surprise. Then we didn't always feed Badge in the same place – so at bedtime I'd be retrieving scribbled bits of paper from all over the house, usually minus a date. And having witnessed our baby badger savaging his spoon, I couldn't envisage myself poking a thermometer up his rectum for too much longer.

As Lisa had predicted, he did lose his fur, though not quite all of it, and it took weeks to grow back. We rubbed aqueous cream on the red pus-filled spots that grew and covered his tummy, but not much could be done about his tail. Held aloft, it looked like an old bottle brush bereft of all but a few sparse bristles. Even the SPCA might have had second thoughts about taking in such a mangy cur.

David took a picture of him to his new school and was incensed when someone innocently asked if the bizarre-looking creature with the huge head, white teeth and bald skinny body was some sort of a rat.

For the first week or so, I carted Badge around in a portable dog box, so that I could be on hand to attend to his slightest squeak. 'You'll have to stop that,' said Lisa firmly, 'otherwise you'll never get away from him. Give him a room of his own as soon as possible.' Of course this made sense, we couldn't have a fully-grown HB permanently trailing around after us. Luckily David had recently moved to a larger room at the end of the passage, so we removed the bookshelves from his former bedroom and laid a green tarpaulin on the floor, with HB's box in one corner and a few toys, like an old shoe, a snail shell and a wicker basket, scattered about. Education was not forgotten: the times tables stayed tacked up in one corner, and the nursery curtains featured a line-up of dangerous animals: lions, tigers, buffalo and rhino all glaring down nightly at the sleeping Badge.

In order to mop up after him, I bought 20 kilos of old *Bulawayo Chronicle*, and since they were all the same edition, I became thoroughly conversant with its contents. It was dated 7 December 2004, a time when bread, milk, mealie meal and other basic foodstuffs were unaffordable for most Zimbabweans (we can't remember a time when this wasn't the case). Prices were increasing weekly, often daily, and not by a few dollars at a time; they doubled or trebled. People hefted sackfuls of filthy banknotes to the supermarket, until the government made things easier by printing first the $500 note, then $5,000, $10,000 and eventually $100,000 'bearer cheques' – pieces of coloured paper only slightly less hygienic than their predecessors. And when thousands turned into millions, new currency was issued with three noughts knocked off to make it all sound so much better. Twenty years ago, a double-storey five-bedroomed house on six acres of land in a good suburb of Bulawayo cost Z$45,000. I know, because it was our house. In December 2006, I could buy three and a half slices of bread for the same price – if I could find it. (In early January 2009, the Zimbabwean government issued a 50-billion-dollar note, equivalent to US $1.25. It was enough to buy three newspapers.)

But this wasn't the sort of news that our government-controlled rag wanted to give its readers. Apart from the riveting information that the body of Mr Innocent Sibanda had been found with numerous stab wounds, and that foul play was suspected, my attention was always drawn to the photographs on page 3. I knew it particularly well because it was a single page that I put under Badger's plate three times a day to keep his mess off the tarpaulin.

Headed 'Coffee Break', it featured photographs of 'Revellers dancing at the Oliver Mtukudzi show' and 'Patrons enjoying themselves at a Bulawayo night spot', showing a corpulent man, gleaming with sweat, gorging himself on what appeared to be a gigantic hamburger. It almost obliterated his face. I was wrong, though; according to the caption, this was 'A Zimbabwe National Army Officer tucking into a *bone* at an annual party', which really seemed to be more appropriate. It must have been the back leg of a cow from a plate of festive nibbles for the favoured few.

Whenever someone new comes to live with us, I always worry about how they will fit into the household and whether life will ever be the same again. The short answer is: it won't. And after a couple of weeks, when we are congratulating ourselves that things are back to normal (at least by our standards), we suddenly wake up to the fact that the new arrival hasn't had to fit in at all, because *we've* made all the adjustments.

Still, our human visitors often surprise us with their comments.

'What is a warthog doing on the sofa/sleeping in the kitchen/rooting up the garden?'

'Poombi lives here, for God's sake. Where's she supposed to be?'

Or – 'Why can't I use the loo?'

'Because our secretary bird is there. But you're welcome to share it with her if you don't mind wading through the guano', or 'the tsessebe's there for the afternoon because he's afraid of the thunder.'

'Why can't I fetch a coke from the deep freeze?'

'Leave it to me. They're buried somewhere between the packet of rats for the owls and Badger's partially eaten spitting cobra.'

People can be so insensitive.

We solved Baby Badger's accommodation problems by giving him his own nursery, where he felt safe and secure. But, as with a human infant, those early days of eating and sleeping are relatively uncomplicated. The problems begin when the youngster takes his first steps into the wide world. Poombi had to learn a great deal, but with our protection, she picked up most of it by walking and feeding in the bush. Warthogs don't need to be taught to eat grass or dig for roots – it's completely instinctive.

On the other hand, there's a special technique to raiding a beehive and a particular expertise needed for killing a black mamba, and if a young honey badger isn't educated properly, his food may kill him. It's no quirk of nature that the baby will stay with his mother for around eighteen months or more. He's got an awful lot to learn.

This was our dilemma. Badger had come to us for rehabilitation and release, he wasn't going to live in our house for the rest of his life and a cage would be only a temporary option. But how could we teach him anything important? We couldn't allow him to go blundering off on his own without knowing something about the Basics of Badgerhood.

'Easy,' said Lisa, who never seems fazed by anything. 'Get hold of a rubber snake and show Badge how to kill it. Bat it around a bit, growl, bite the back of its head – that sort of thing.'

I did look for one, but rubber snakes, along with milk and bread, were in short supply in Bulawayo. Instead, Rich appeared one afternoon holding an extremely agitated herald snake, about two feet long.

'Where's *he* from?' I asked.

'He was in our room, lurking by the bed. You fetch Badger and we'll give him some practice with the real thing.'

I plucked the sleepy cub from his afternoon snooze and while he sat on my lap Rich put The Real Thing under his nose. Badger gave a loud sniff and the snake struck out at him, hissing furiously.

This happened three times until Badge got bored and fell asleep on my lap.

'He hasn't got a clue,' said Rich, 'put him on the lawn and see what he does.'

Leaving Badge a few yards away, we called him to where the herald lay with a distinctly malevolent look in its eye. Badger came bumbling through the grass, tripped over the snake and fell into my arms.

We tried it again but this time the herald was waiting.

As the hapless Badger came into range, it lunged at him and bit him on the nose.

Poor boy. He galloped off and rubbed his bloodied nose in the grass, then, with a bewildered squeak, came straight back for more.

Thwack! After another bite on the lip for the meanest animal in the world, we decided to withdraw both contestants.

It was a nasty thing to do but it was the only way. Heralds are only mildly poisonous, and after another couple of sessions (but no more bites), the sight and smell of that horrible creature were enough to send Badge scuttling into reverse. And the lesson stuck – he had exactly the same reaction to other snakes we met on our walks in days to come.

Although the HB looks very like a bear, he is actually a member of the mustelid family, along with other occasional little stinkers like the polecat, weasel and skunk, and less malodorous creatures such as the European and North American badger and the otter. His name, *Mellivora capensis*, means the devourer of honey. Though certainly not impervious to stings (or, it appears, injections), he is to a large extent protected from angry bees by the tough skin on his back. As further protection, the badger's ears are reduced to thick ridges of skin, and he can close off his earholes altogether when he frowns.

So HB had all the right equipment, he just didn't know how to use it. Thinking we would give him a foretaste of pleasures to come, we presented him with a blob of honey on the end of a finger. Badge turned his head away. He obviously needed more encouragement. We dabbed a bit on his nose and this time he left us in no doubt about his feelings. 'Yugh!' said our honey badger, curling his lip and shaking his head in disgust. It was a strange reaction but, in retrospect, perhaps a very good thing. We could offer a bit of practice with a herald snake, but none of us would be volunteering to act *in loco parentis* when it came to raiding hives.

The only wild honey badger I'd ever seen hadn't been averse to a bit of sweetness. We had been sleeping out on the banks of the Zambezi, surrounded by a barrier of canvas chairs and tables as a token deterrent to visiting lions, hyenas and hippos. This was risky but far preferable to sharing the nearby concrete shed with hordes of rats. The hyenas had been in a hysterical scrum for hours all around the camp that night, so when we heard a commotion from the kitchen area, only a few yards away, Rich leapt up, grabbed his rifle and shone his torch into the darkness. Out trotted a satisfied honey badger, head held high, with our only bag of sunsweet sugar swinging from his jaws.

It wasn't long before we realised that the majority of the Badly Behaved Badger stories we heard (and there were many) were almost always linked to their insatiable appetites. Many such tales come from Sinamatella Camp in the Hwange National Park, where visitors like to sit under the stars, beer in hand, watching their steaks sizzle over the camp fire. Naturally, badgers find the smell equally irresistible, but where other animals will skulk about waiting for the leftovers, a group of determined badgers regularly rumble in on the scene and steal the lot. Retrieving what they can, experienced campers dash back into their chalets for safety before the badgers get too close. They are closely followed by those who were under the impression that they could get rid of these pesky varmints by chucking a stick or a rock in their direction, but had had a swift change of heart when charged by what appeared to be the devil himself, complete with a mouthful of strong white teeth and the bloodcurdling rattle of a roar that gave the animal its Afrikaans name.

You only have to say 'honey badger' and someone comes up with a story. Friends visiting the Kruger National Park slowed down when they saw a pair of badgers in the road. For no apparent reason, one suddenly laid into the back wheel of the vehicle, so the people stopped in case they ran him over. After ten minutes or so, there was silence and the couple peered out of their windows to see if they could spot their attacker. Both badgers had disappeared, so they drove off rather faster than they should to a picnic spot a couple of kilometres further down the road. But when the driver's wife went to open the boot, she met an enraged badger, covered with dust, who had been bumping along behind them, his teeth locked on to the rubber flap over one back wheel. This time the couple took no chances. Leaving the badger glaring after them, they drove to another site twenty kilometres further on, where they munched their sandwiches nervously, half expecting the rogue ratel to reappear. After a few more hours of game viewing, they turned and headed back for camp on the same road. And who should be waiting for them but HB himself, who rushed out of the grass exactly where they had left him and once again flung himself at the wheel.

Why? Within a week or two of his arrival, our Badge had taught us a couple of inviolable rules about his kind. First, badgers hate surprises and will respond to them instantly and often aggressively. Where most animals will run away, badgers are far more likely to attack. And second, never, ever try to take something away from a possessive badger, especially his food.

But what could have roused this one to such passionate fury? He might have been surprised while courting, but the assault on the wheel and the extent of his grudge were a bit over the top, even for a honey badger. Perhaps he was rabid, a disease that badgers are prone to catch from creatures like feral dogs, jackals or mongooses.

Knowing their potential, we made sure that from the start we treated Badge gently and with considerable respect. I had read that they sometimes fly into 'fury-moods of an unusually intense, blind ferocity', and we had heard similar stories about the violent mood swings of a pet otter, a close relative of the honey badger. Writing about the young badger she was raising, Sylvia Sykes describes a game where she would 'work her up' by waving a sack at her, then snatching it away again. When the badger finally caught hold of the sack, she would 'become tense with fury, her tail quivering, her voice snarling, foaming at the mouth and her jaws clenched on it like a vice. In this mood, I could swing her round and round on the sack, and even beat her roughly up and down on the ground without dislodging her'. Badger was touchy enough without this sort of teasing, so for as long as we could, we kept rough-housing to a minimum.

Never once did our cub show the slightest sign of moodiness or unpredictability; in fact, there was no side to Badger at all. He was the most amenable little fellow – provided that we followed the fundamental tenets of the code of the badgers, something that, unfortunately, we had no way of learning except by experience.

For instance, there was the time when, in a combined effort to retrieve a stolen hair clasp from his jaws, a tasteless item that any respectable puppy would have surrendered immediately, Badger locked his baby teeth around Rich's thumb, sinking a canine into the edge of his nail – an incident that vividly but painfully illustrated the golden rule: what is yours becomes mine the moment I steal it from you, and if you challenge me, I will surely bite you. We had seen signs of this possessiveness before, but this was the first time that Badger had actually followed through.

When he was very tiny – and I was still wrapping him in his blanket and saying his prayers with him at bedtime – Grant Neilson paid us a visit. As Bulawayo's foremost animal rescue man, Grant knew exactly how to behave as a newcomer. He sat down cross-legged on the floor and quietly waited for Badge to come to him. And after much sniffing and a few false starts, our cub wobbled over and climbed on to his lap. Grant stroked his back.

'Hard to believe all those nasty stories about them, isn't it?'

Suddenly, Badger stiffened and began to growl. Grant whipped his hands away and looked down, horrified, at the bristling little beast now straddling the most vulnerable part of his anatomy. Earlier, I had laughingly repeated the fantastical stories of badgers ripping into the scrotum of animals as large as buffalo and even of humans who had supposedly crossed them. How ridiculous!

'Grant, what do you have in your pocket?'

'C-c-car keys,' his voice was trembling, 'and, um, a packet of cigarettes. He's standing on them; they're in the pouch in front of my tracksuit.'

'He's after the fags, must be the smell. Right, as quick as you can, pull them out and stand up.'

Unwinding himself with the speed of a Chinese

acrobat, Grant deposited a snarling Badger on the floor, and hurled the keys and cigarettes over the half door of the bedroom. And, almost immediately, Badge forgot what all the fuss was about and clambered back into my lap for a cuddle.

A badger's strength of will and absolute determination to get what he wants (and keep it) can be likened to a two-year-old child at a sweet counter: ankle-biters, the Australians call them. Badgers are one hundred per cent focused, both physically and mentally, on the object of their desire, and nothing in the world will deter them.

From a very young age, Badge developed a foot and shoe fetish, and once his teeth were locked on to your Achilles tendon and his legs were wrapped tightly around your ankle, he was almost impossible to shift. Rich fervently hoped that our little ankle-biter wouldn't become more upwardly mobile in the months to come.

MY HOME: words by David Peek
(Grade 8)
(spelling and punctuation by his mother)

My home is a strange entity for many reasons. In many ways, I consider it to be the most weird, deformed and utterly unprecedented structure that I have ever laid eyes on. When you first enter the 'house', you find yourself in an enormous room split in half by a twelve-foot-high wall. In the middle of this first section stands a round table; around it are seven dilapidated, moth-eaten chairs. In the corner of the room next to a rapidly decomposing plant is a bar covered with herbs, spices, aromat and all sorts of garnish laid out in awful disarray.

Branching off to the left is a long corridor. At the far end is a door that remains permanently closed, and that is my domain. The second door is my 'bathroom'. Why I place 'bathroom' in inverted commas is because by modern standards it would not come close to what you would expect to find in an average everyday home, but I guess I must come to accept the fact that our house is not an average everyday home at all. I must also add that I am not responsible for the state of this bathroom. When you first open the door, a solid shock of unspeakable stench hits you like a brick wall. I don't think I will go into its physical aspects, it sickens me to think of it. Moving on to the next room, you will find the real culprit for all this mess and destruction. Pop your head around the door, being very careful not to make a sound. Glance timidly around you. A heavily stained tarpaulin covers the floor, and once again the stench is unbearable. The sound of heavy breathing will direct you to a small shape in the corner of the room: a honey badger deep in its slumbers.

Make the tiniest sound and it will leap up and make with startling speed for the nearest foot. This is the creature that has caused us so much discomfort and heartache – aka Mr Badger – the beast that has captured my parents' hearts and souls: in short, they are besotted with it.

Just a few days ago, my mother came out of the room smeared with all kinds of disgusting things that I don't think I should mention. All she said was: 'He's a bit sick today, vomiting up all this black stuff, poor little darling.' And then she drifted off to reapply her makeup.

In the lounge, you will be faced with our fireplace and its enormous seventy-foot chimney connecting with the almost impossibly high roof, and a room lined with shelves stuffed to bursting with complicated books on zoology and biology. Another door leads into my parents' office. Enter it and the first thing you will see is the figure of my father sitting at his table, his fingers tapping away at his laptop computer. Plugs line the walls and complicated charts are stuck up at crazy angles. Moving on is my mother's area, where she sits, her fingers rapping a staccato beat on the keyboard of her laptop. Her area smells of incense, and in tiny frames are picture after picture of Mr Badger in various Napoleonic poses and, if you look carefully enough, there are one or two dusty pictures of me in my childhood....

Chapter Seventeen

It was about this time that David brought home his latest essay – a highly exaggerated and somewhat Durrellesque description of our house and its occupants. Quite unfairly, he blames Badger for the state of his bathroom when the real culprit was a lesser honeyguide chick, an obnoxious little critter that had been brought in (and presumably rejected) by a cat in Muffy and Wayne Williamson's Bulawayo garden. Like cuckoos, honeyguides don't have the slightest interest in raising their offspring, choosing to leave the work to a suitable host bird like one of the barbet clan. Very cunningly, the female honeyguide skulks about until the barbet is away from the nesting hole, then sneaks in to lay her egg, sometimes even breaking or removing the bird's own eggs in the process. Then she's off, leaving no forwarding address, while the female barbet faithfully continues to brood until the chicks hatch – at which time the honeyguide will eliminate its adoptive siblings by pecking them to death with the specially adapted hooks on its bill.

The first thing I noticed about HG was the thick yellow crust around his bill and eyes, and his incessant chittering. It's always important to keep to any new animal's routine, so before Muffy left, I asked her to show me how she fed him. At the sight of the large blob of mushy yellow Cerelac on the end of a plastic spoon, the bird went wild. Still shouting, he thrust his head into the middle of it and guzzled the lot.

'Wow! He must have been pretty hungry,' I remarked.

'Actually, no,' said Muffy. 'I only fed him five minutes ago.'

Lumps of wet Cerelac covered the chick's head and body, and though his crop was full to bursting, he continued begging for more.

'How often do you suggest I feed him?'

'It's hard to say. Sort of every hour, I suppose, but just give him some when he wants it.'

Muffy handed over the cage. 'Sorry to land you with this, but my cats would have killed him.' She had the grace to look a bit embarrassed. 'He is a bit demanding.'

A *bit demanding*. The bird books euphemistically describe them as 'persistently vocal', but that's only because they've never had one living in the bathroom, as we did after the chick kept escaping through the bars of his cage. At the slightest movement outside the door, HG would throw himself at it with a frantic non-stop twittering that nearly drove me demented. I couldn't avoid it either, as the bathroom is between David's bedroom and Badger's mildly odoriferous boudoir, so every time I was in the vicinity, I'd take the saucer of Cerelac and make yet another fruitless effort to shut him up. As I opened the door, the chick would fly into my face and cling on with his sharp little claws. Then, no matter how much I gave him, he would continue to shout for more, choking through huge gobfuls of gooey cereal.

Things got a little easier when I introduced him to grasshoppers, but at first I had to dissect them and feed him small pieces at the end of a pair of tweezers, half the length of which would disappear down his throat along with the food. Only once did I manage to silence him for a full half hour, by feeding him grasshoppers until he actually gave up and began spitting them out. On my next visit to the badger, I heard nothing from the other side of the bathroom door and began to feel a bit guilty. I wondered if HG had exploded, like the fat man in the Monty Python sketch, and I'd find bits of feather and stomach contents stuck all over the bathroom walls. But no, there he was, squatting on the pelmet like an overstuffed museum specimen, with his beak firmly shut.

At that stage, my life consisted of little but cramming food into one end of Badger and the chick, and mopping up what came oozing out of the other.

'Too much *bhotsha*' (pronounced *bodger* in Sindebele), said our cook, Ruthie, sympathetically, watching me crawling around the carpeted floor of Badger's bedroom with bucket, wet cloths and newspapers. Needless to say, the noses of Rich, Nige (his 27-year-old son) and David were far too sensitive for them to offer their services. I called them the Bodger Dodgers.

HG's grasping ways were irritating but quite under-standable for a parasite. One can well imagine his foster parents becoming thoroughly fed up with the murderous little stranger in the nest and his unquenchable greed. In order to keep the mother sweet, the honeyguide begs incessantly, a noise that would make any male want to wring his neck but elicits a positive response from females, myself included, who are instinctively impelled to silence him with food. Having exterminated the competition, the honeyguide hogs everything intended for the barbet brood, and around five weeks later, he waddles up to the entrance of the hole. The barbets are aghast at the sight of this pudgy little freeloader. Not only does he look all wrong, but he won't do what he's told, refusing to return to roost with his foster parents and showing no interest in foraging for fruit along with the rest of the gang. The barbets may tolerate him for a few days, but usually they chase him off immediately, which doesn't worry the honeyguide one bit, as he hates fruit and was going anyway. At the first opportunity, he will tag along with other honeyguides in search of beeswax, attracted by the display of their white tail feathers in flight. They may not be strangers. As a final insult to his foster parents, his own parents have been spying on the nest ever since the egg was laid, and it may well be that they are waiting for him when he emerges, congratulating themselves on yet another successful scam. But it's not all plain sailing for the female honeyguide. If the barbet catches her on the nest, she'll be beaten up, so she has to be very quick and cunning about it. But from then on it's a party, and she'll never know the frustration of finding food for an insatiable offspring from dawn to dusk, the sleepless nights, the constant worry of new motherhood.

According to a wealth of anecdotal evidence, the greater honeyguide will lead the honey badger to a hive, in the hope that the badger will tear it open and let the bird get to the grubs and beeswax. There is no doubt that the honeyguide solicits humans to do the job for him – we often experience this ourselves – but the link between bird and badger has never been conclusively proved. It was going to be interesting to see if our Badge was going to shed any light on the mystery in the months to come.

Nandi, our amiable black Labrador, had learned from bitter experience to pay close attention to each new arrival in our house, no matter how small or smelly. In a matter of months, she had watched Poombi, a puny piglet, grow into a gargantuan sow equipped with daggers for teeth and a will of iron, so she wasn't taking any chances with this one. As I deposited Badge on the carpet in front of her, she rather unwisely sniffed loudly at his rear, then hurriedly reversed as the frightened cub squeaked and released a pungent smell from his anal gland. She glared at him from a distance after that, until I hit on the idea of producing a biscuit every time Badger was close by, hoping she would make the connection. She made it all right; I couldn't get rid of her until Badger, in a desperate attempt to make friends, would crawl over and sit on her foot, whereupon she would give a loud snarl and bowl him over with her nose. But to keep the biscuits coming, she was prepared to give him one last try. Head down and bum up in the play-bow, she wagged her tail and panted invitingly into Badge's face. He lifted his head and gazed at her blearily for a few seconds, then went back to sleep. Nandi turned to me in desperation and her perplexed expression said it all. 'What', she asked, 'is the use of *him*?'

Since Badge had had such a rocky start in life, we assumed that his early difficulties in walking were probably caused by malnutrition. What a relief to discover that in the wild, the mother badger keeps her cub in the den for the first three months of its life. And no wonder. Even at that age and beyond, Badge was a hopeless liability of tangled legs and constant complaining. Thinking that he should be introduced to the bush at the earliest opportunity, we began taking him on late afternoon expeditions to the Mathole river, which runs close to the house. Badge couldn't see the point of being removed from his snug bed to this rather hostile prickly place, and he spent most of the time on my lap. And when we insisted that he try and walk with us, he would waddle between our feet, desperately calling 'prt, prt, prt!' in case we left him behind. A busy mother badger, it appears, has little patience with her bungling baby, who must keep reminding her that he is there in case she trots off and forgets all about him. If he does get into a scrape, she'll grab him by the scruff of the neck, carry him along for a few yards and then dump him on his head. Luckily for him, our little ratel had found a family of real suckers, who scooped him up when he squeaked or tripped over invisible things in the road, and found every move of this strangely balding, pop-eyed and often touchy creature endlessly fascinating and quite adorable. If we put a hand on his neck, he would instinctively stop and arch it, ready to be hoicked up by the scruff, when he would become absolutely immobile and a dead weight in our arms.

Right from the start, mornings were Badge's worst time. Like a temperamental child, he had to be woken gently with soft words and always an outstretched hand so that he could smell exactly who you were. Even after that, he never leaped out of bed; he took ages to stretch and yawn and roll about on his blankets before he was ready to face the world. Although nothing much interested him before the sun was up, I loved those early walks, for where I would normally have been striding out with Nandi at my side, I was now grounded with the badger, taking endless delight in the transformation of Stone Hills from winter to a glorious summer.

There is no escape from the blistering heat of October, the world has been in waiting too long, and with the first November showers, everything springs into action, from the scarlet velvet mites dotted about in the veld, to the newly arrived red-chested cuckoo shouting 'Piet my Vrou!' from the treetops. Within hours, butterflies are on the wing and the air is alive with the sounds of buzzing, humming and chirping. And each year I wonder the same thing: where they have all come from? Where do they hide through the long months of winter, when the grass crumbles like dry toast under your feet? November is the month of miracles. Within a mere half hour of the rains, the dead leaves of the resurrection bushes on the hillsides come alive, turning before your eyes from brittle brown to a sweet-smelling green. They say that if you cut a sprig and keep it for ten years, it will flush as soon as you put it into water. The air is redolent with the scent of camphor and pine, and as I walk among the rocks I crush a few of the tiny leaves and put them in my shirt pocket; they remind me of a day in bed as a child, the warm, comforting smell of Vick's rubbed on your chest by gentle hands, the footsteps along the passage bringing boiled eggs, toast and marmite to your cosy nest, while everyone else is at school. Africans treat chest pains and asthma with the smoke from the leaves of the bush, which, dried and powdered, are also effective in the treatment of burns and wounds.

From my window, a carpet of thick couch grass covers the prickly patches of brown scarred with hundreds of termite workings that I have looked on all winter; and as Johnson pushes his mower up and down, the clean fresh smell of cut grass comes drifting through the house. And I wish, as I always do, that I could distil some of these sounds, the smells and the light into a bottle, so by opening it ever so slightly I could keep experiencing them all over again whenever I wanted.

Abel Ncube, the man who could talk to the animals and loved our pig so dearly, was murdered some years ago, and the fig tree we planted in his memory at Poombi's grave is in leaf; it's not growing fast – the kudu see to that – but it keeps battling on. Soon after Poombi died, I was given the honour of naming Mafira's first grandchild. I called him Abel, and he visits Stone Hills every August holidays and helps us feed the animals in the evenings. He specially enjoys feeding Thelma, her daughter Louise, and their families. Thelma was looking old and emaciated this year, but with a daily ration of game cubes, she was soon back in the pink, or as pink as an old grey warthog can be.

Squeak often comes to visit with her latest brood – she's easy to recognise with her broken left tusk, but we always know her anyway because of her careless confidence. Only Squeak would dare to barge into the vegetable garden to steal a cabbage, as her mother often did. The Fawlty Four stuck together for months, but then they went their own ways. They and many of Poombi's other relations still use her home range, so when warthogs show up at the vegetable garden or the eland kraal, we can be pretty sure that they are part of the family.

November beckons you out of the house, away from the pile of papers on the desk, away from the workshop with the broken tractor and the faulty borehole pump – just five minutes down to the river or ten minutes to the top of Dibe, looking right over the farm, when the rain has washed away the smoky grey that hung over the hills and left them sparkling in the sunlight.

I was sitting on the bank of the river one morning late in that magical month, watching Badge as he blew vigorously into a small hole, covering his face with dust. That's how badgers spend most of their time – sticking their noses into other people's business, inhaling the most detailed information and then exhaling with a blast that would knock a mouse off its feet. Suddenly, there was a ripple in the small pool below me and a head appeared, followed by twelve feet or so of python, glistening wet and sequined with silver in the early sunshine. Like a stream of black lava, the snake flowed soundlessly out of the water and into the long green grass. Then its head and neck came up, long black tongue flickering back and forth, eyes glittering as it searched for prey. I sat motionless, fascinated, until Badger decided that he'd had enough. He was fed up with digging, bored with being outside and wanted his bed. He lay at my feet and whined, and then when that didn't work, he attached himself to my shoe and shouted even louder, completely ruining the moment. I carted him back to the house and put him in his box, then ran back to the river, just in time to see two feet of tail disappearing into the reeds on the other side of the pool.

Without protection, Badger would have been toast, and the incident underscored just how vulnerable these animals are for much of their first year of life, as they blunder about, blissfully unaware of danger. But let the python beware. Once a badger grows up, he won't hesitate to attack any reptile, no matter how large or venomous. Years ago, the scouts found a large python half-eaten on Dibe Hill, just behind the lodge. The snake had just consumed a rock dassie when it was attacked and killed by a badger. This takes some nerve and not a little skill, but the puzzle is how a badger deals with bites from snakes like mambas, cobras and puff adders that would surely kill any other animal. Some speculate that badgers develop immunity through a process of gradual envenomation, by eating toads, for instance, that carry toxic glands under their skin, or being stung by bees. Or, perhaps more feasibly, their metabolism may be designed in such a way as to cope with the venom. But, like so much about badgers, no one really knows.

This is not to say that they are completely unaffected by toxins, as Badger proved when we came across a group of rather gnarled and nasty-looking fungi growing at the base of a rock. He patted one out of the ground, carried it around for while and then began to eat it, much to my distress. Was this part of the envenomation process, or did the fungi perhaps contain some ingredient essential to the health of a growing Badge? I wondered if his own mother would have taken any interest in what he ate, but that seemed unlikely given her generally casual attitude towards her cub. I watched him tucking into his hors d'oeuvres for a few minutes but, when I could bear it no longer, I got hold of a long stick and tried to push it away from him. Of course, he grabbed it and rattled furiously at me, so, being a coward, I sat back and watched him consume not one but two fungi as if they were the last word in gourmet fare. Finally, he got a piece of bark stuck in the roof of his mouth, so he let me pick him up and fish it out on our way home.

An hour later, he became very agitated and was clearly in pain. He vomited when I took him outside, and after a couple of hours his bedroom was ankle-deep in partially digested fungi. He climbed in and out of my lap, crying, and all I could do was to offer him sips of milk and water in the hope that this would do something to dilute the poison. But by lunchtime he was on the mend, which was fortunate as I was by that time ministering to Nandi, who had found the nauseating pile of puke outside and had gobbled it up. I don't know why I bother.

Chapter Eighteen

By 2004, tourists had effectively abandoned Zimbabwe, frightened away by reports of violence and growing instability. Some people, however, saw this as an advantage. When the current Minister of Tourism was interviewed about the situation, he declared himself delighted by all the media coverage because 'it really puts Zimbabwe on the map'.

It wasn't all bad news for us either. We had never been natural candidates for the hospitality industry and it meant that Badger's social skills (and ours) wouldn't be constantly put to the test. For all we knew, he'd be waiting in ambush at the gate for passing vehicles, and we'd have to put a sign up in the lodge warning male guests to keep their legs crossed.

We needn't have worried. Little Casanova loved the attention from our infrequent visitors, falling into the arms of any agreeable female (and they all were) to have his tummy tickled. Despite our reclusive lifestyle, we still have a few faithful friends and for some reason they all decided to arrive over the Christmas holidays. Badge wasn't bothered in the least by David and his mates as they pounded down the passage past his room, and was perfectly content to be passed from lap to lap as we sat having tea on the veranda, provided of course that he had been properly introduced. He was terrified of strangers initially and immediately defensive, so we would ask our guests to sit quietly in the lounge for their initiation. Badge would be borne in and one of us would sit on the floor in the middle of the room with him on our lap, giving him a comfort zone from which to operate. Then, when he was quite composed, he would visit each pair of feet in turn, taking a long sniff and presumably committing the details to memory. Once the ice was broken, the owners of the feet were friends for life and Badge never forgot anyone, no matter how rarely he met them.

Knowing how passionately attached he was to family, you can imagine how distressed I was to be met by bristling growls when I went to fetch him for his bedtime stroll one night. His stiff little body exuded hostility and when he wouldn't settle down, Rich took my place, whereupon he immediately reverted to the affectionate Baby Badge I thought I knew. The next day, he was back to normal but the following evening, after I had had my shower, he was up in arms again, treating me like a complete stranger. Then the penny dropped – both times he had reacted badly I had rubbed camphor cream all over my arms and legs. It was quite simple; I didn't smell like Mummy any more and for a badger, nose is everything.

On 19 December, while the meanest animal in the world was sucking his bottle, Rich surreptitiously slipped a small insulin needle filled with the rabies vaccine under his skin. The disease was on the increase, one of our neighbours had recently shot a rabid dog as it tried to attack their dogs through their garden fence, and we'd heard that a number of people had died in a remote village in Zambia through lack of treatment. Badge would be protected, and so would everyone else, for four years. After that, well, we'd make a plan.

He felt a bit off-colour for the rest of the morning, so when I began wrapping Christmas presents later that day I thought I'd cheer him up by letting him join in. I also wanted the company and some intellectual input because I happen to find sticky tape an insurmountable challenge. First, I have to spin the roll round and round my hand until my finger finally makes contact with the tiny ridge that marks the start of it. This can take five minutes. Then, with one knee holding the wrapping in place, I can either stick the bit where it belongs or bend the end over so I can find it the next time. I cannot do both things at once, so invariably, I lose it (and my temper) and start again. I've followed all sorts of advice, but I always end up with yards of mangled tape that stick quite satisfactorily to the furniture, but never to the parcel itself.

Badge solved the problem immediately by running off with the roll – and I would never have been able to retrieve it had he not spied a large red and yellow ball under the chair. He froze and growled, and when the ball didn't answer back, he waddled in for the kill. But as he took a bite at it, the thing suddenly rolled away, sending Badge into frantic reverse gear, with his lips curled and his baby teeth bared. Everything was a challenge, to be met head-on and conquered. The wooden bars under the coffee table were not merely to be climbed over, they were grasped tightly between the front legs, bitten and battered.

Because we were at home all the time, we hadn't provided Nandi with a canine companion since Lora, our yellow Labrador, had died, and anyway, she had her hands full dealing with the assortment of creatures that kept inviting themselves into our house. Badge was one weird-looking puppy with a lot of strange habits, but he was better than nothing. One evening, as we were sitting in the lounge, she strolled over to him and tried a play-bow, panting and wagging her tail. '*Now* do you understand what I'm getting at?' At last, he did, and began weaving in and out of her feet while the astonished Nandi danced joyfully around him, taking little nips at his head. Badge's response was to tuck his chin into his chest and display his neck – where he has the toughest skin – then whip around and present her with his bottom, an area packed with unspoken threats. Spurred on by our laughter, they played till they were exhausted, at which point Badge got a violent bout of hiccups and spent the rest of the evening on David's lap, sucking his finger and watching Animal Planet on our newly acquired television.

He had a special relationship with each member of the family – deeply attached to his Mum and Dad but devoted to David and Nige, both of whom he welcomed rapturously, immediately demanding to play. I mentioned this to Nige, who remarked that it wasn't surprising as parents generally were functional. This took me aback somewhat but it sounded right. After all, in the general scheme of things, parents are supposed to be sensible beings, who are always making decisions for your own good, whereas brothers should be non-stop fun. Still, for some reason, the word rankled a little and when I finally looked it up in Chambers' Dictionary I realised why. We were, apparently, 'designed with special regard to purpose and practical use, often to the detriment of decorative qualities'. I put my glasses on and peered into the mirror, always a sobering experience. Well, though I wasn't quite the joke in the Christmas cracker, I was clearly no longer the fairy at the top of the tree. But what can you expect when you live on Animal Planet?

Other than those wayward characters who hang around safari camps, badgers keep well out of sight. Most people, even those who live in the bush, have never seen one and know nothing about them – other than their reputed propensity for removing male genitalia from their rightful owners.

A conversation I heard on the Johannesburg airport bus was a good example. 'I've seen a video of a leopard killing a lion,' said a boy of around twelve. 'Yah,' said one of the older men, trying to go one better, 'but I've seen one of a honey badger killing a ratel.' 'No, no,' said the third, 'they're the same thing, you dummy. Honey badgers kill *buffaloes*.'

Most of our staff were in their houses when Badge was at large, and he became a bit of a mystical figure, known only by his tracks around the farm. If he heard strangers, he would drop into a serpentine crawl and scuttle out of sight. We didn't discourage him. Not long ago, we were surrounded by uninhabited bushland; now we could hear dogs and cattle on our boundaries and sometimes the sound of voices. As Badger matured, he would be bound to wander, and the more he feared human beings, the better would be his chances of survival.

Even those who should know better surprised us with their ignorance. The newly qualified vet, for example, who said: 'If I were you, I'd cut those claws immediately.' 'Oh no,' said I, appalled that anyone should contemplate interfering with him, 'he wouldn't last a week without them in the bush.' Honestly, *people*.

What I hadn't considered was the period before Badge went wild, which, by all accounts, could last for a couple of years. Climbing, digging, ripping and chewing were all skills that needed practice from an early age. And anyway, a badger can never keep still.

As Badge became more adventurous, he began to hate being stuck in the room, particularly when he could hear us outside. Chewing the curtains had limited appeal and there was only so much one could do with a tennis ball once it was shredded. There was some merit in pulling open the drawers of the dressing table; he could use them as a ladder and it was fun to hook everything out and demolish it. But as it could easily have fallen on his head, we removed all the remaining furniture, whereupon Badge set to work on the fitted carpet and the skirting boards.

When we were in town for the day, he somehow managed to climb out of the window and drop into the bushbucks' plastic water dish. Then he hauled himself on to the front veranda and we found him deeply asleep behind the box where we keep the fire hoses. From then on, he was allowed to stay on the veranda for a couple of hours every night, after he had finished his supper and before bed. We would go out in relays to play with him but during our dinner he was left to his own devices.

'Isn't he adorable?' David called me to the glass sliding doors to see Badge on the other side, curled up on the cushion of one of the veranda chairs. I made some clucking noises and we left him slumbering there while we finished our meal. Half an hour later we found him sitting in the middle of a mountain of white foam, much of which was already blowing around the garden.

If you really want to upset a badger (and who would?), all you have to do is to step on his toes, whereupon he will give a piercing cry, drop to the ground in slow motion, then roll on to his back with his paws held limply in the air. Recovery is swift, particularly after appropriate noises of distress and remorse have been made by the offender, but it is not all an act – for these digits, five on each hand, are as sensitive as human fingertips. When Badge delicately winkles out an insect from behind a piece of bark, it's as incongruous as watching a bricklayer playing Bach at the Carnegie Hall – but, despite their indestructible appearance, each curved claw is packed with nerve endings. With these weapons, he can prise a tortoise shell apart, dig deep holes in the hardest soil, grip when climbing and even hang off a tree or a rock face, taking his entire weight with the very tips of his nails. When Badge was older and digging for mice or snakes, he would often push his arm into the hole up to the shoulder and feel gently around for its occupant with his claws, which always reminded me of James Herriot doing an internal examination of a pregnant cow.

There is nothing more dangerous than a Bored Badger who should be Busy, so we had to keep thinking up new ways of keeping him amused. We floated corks in his bowl, so he could bat them up and down and finally swish them on to the ground, along with the water. Then he would flip the empty bowl on to his head and march around, quite blind, like a Nazi paratrooper in an outsized helmet.

The succession of cardboard boxes he used as a bed were much more fun when they were modified and up-ended to make a proper house. Badge would creep in at one end and I'd twiddle my fingers at the other, snatching them away just before he could grab one. Out would come a little black arm to see if it could hook me and, when that tactic failed, he'd put both arms out and turn into a mobile tortoise. Tortoises meant a lot to little HB, but I never realised quite how attached he was to the shell in his room until I saw him clasping it to his belly and giving it a good badgering, madly huffing and puffing with his mouth open. Although I did feel slightly embarrassed, I felt that I should watch this unique performance for research purposes, my conclusion being that this was the reptilian equivalent of Cindy the blow-up doll, minus the red lipstick and the frilly apron.

According to Jonathan Kingdon the HB develops 'exceptionally large testes in proportion to their size, implying a superproduction of sperm'. Another superlative for our little Badge, and a good reason to start practising early. Kingdon went on to state that for its size, the badger has the largest brain of any carnivore – a fact that is obvious to anyone who spends more than five minutes with Badge and no doubt (to a lesser degree of course) with any other member of his extended family.

When Badgie tired of playing by himself, he would curl up between the bars of the veranda table where the legs made a convenient little cage. And from in there, he would try to reach out and hook his toys back into his den.

Once he gave up the bottle for a diet of meat, eggs and chicken, his coat began to shine, and he quickly gained weight. I began monitoring his calorie intake when he developed fat folds in the back of his neck, like our local member of parliament. But he was the ultimate shape shifter; even when you thought he could never fit through the bars of the table again, he somehow snaked his way in, until one day his fat little tummy did get stuck, and we had to squeeze him out like a sausage.

At Christmas, we discovered what Badgers like Best – like the rest of his human family and the Posselts' Ratsi, he was addicted to chocolate, or at least to the smell of it. Even an empty wrapping would drive him wild, and send David leaping to his feet in order to dislodge the snarling cub attached to the pocket of his shorts.

Christmas, too, brings the insects, and I found Johnson at the lodge one morning, collecting *inhlabusi*, or 'butterbums', shiny black ants with yellow abdomens, as they were emerging from the nest for their mating flight. The name means 'to taste good', so I gave him a jam jar and asked him to fill it for us. Fried in their own oil, they looked like a plate of raisins (at least without my glasses), but they smelled awful and tasted worse, so I gave mine to Rich, who shared them with an appreciative Badge. On the other hand, mopane worms, or *amancimbi*, first boiled, then fried, aren't bad at all, provided you don't examine them too closely; and crispy fried grasshoppers, or *intethe*, are delicious.

One of the most exciting events of summer is the first termite emergence. For weeks preceding their wedding flight, workers have been feeding and grooming winged reproductives – the princes and princesses – in special chambers underground. At some mysterious signal, triggered by exactly the right combination of warmth and moisture, tens of thousands of these gossamer-winged insects emerge at the same time from nests spread over a huge area. All being well, the female will float to the ground after her nuptial flutter, shrug off her wings and release an inviting perfume from the tip of her abdomen that is irresistible to a passing prince. He flies down behind her, drops his wings, and together they scuttle off in tandem to dig themselves a hole where, as a new king and queen, they begin the pleasant task of creating the next generation.

If they get that far. The event creates a feeding frenzy – toads wait at the entrance to the nest, gulping the termites down as they emerge, and while some birds hop about pecking them off the ground, others swoop through the air catching them on the wing. And with a bit of encouragement, honey badgers quickly learn to pluck or swat them off the grass stems that the termites have climbed in a valiant effort to launch themselves into the air. But honey badgers suffering from sore noses and feet also quickly learn that their hunting is better done at some distance from the nest, as the reproductives are guarded by hordes of ferocious soldiers equipped with huge jaws and a gland in the head that releases a stream of irritating, noxious fluid.

The animals aren't fussy, but the Ndebele people are. They relish the larger species, the *izinhlwa*, that they catch at night by attracting them to the light of a fire and leaving bowls of water out for them to fall in. But in accordance with some ancient taboo, they won't touch the *ivimbandlebe*, the smaller variety or 'to close your ears'. It is said that if you eat them, you will go deaf.

Life with baby Badge soon fell into a pattern. I'd get his evening meal ready in advance, put it down on his bedroom floor, and open the veranda door, calling: 'suppah!', a word that galvanised him into motion, like Pavlov's dog. And after supper, Badger was all fired up for at least an hour of play in his bedroom before lights out. The daily routines were simple in his infancy – I'd wake him by singing: 'Good morning! Good morning!' at the door, very softly, wait for him to finish his three yawns and three stretches, then go in and cuddle him for a while before giving him his bottle. And at night, after the Teddy Bears' Picnic and a few prayers – 'God bless my family and all kind friends and make Badger a good boy' sort of thing – I'd tuck him up in his blankets and creep to the door. Nauseating, I know, but unavoidably apt for our dear little bundle of bear. A few months later he'd be waiting for us on the other side of the half door with his mouth open in readiness to attach himself to your shoe or, worse, to your Achilles tendon, into which he would sink his sharp little teeth. And once you were on the ground, he would wrap all four legs tightly around your arm like a hug-a-bug and chew on your funny-bone. Dislodging him was like trying to unwrap an octopus – as soon as you prised one leg off, another one would grab hold of you. 'Don't let him dominate you!' Lisa had warned. 'If he tries, pin his head on the ground with your finger and growl.'

But Badger wasn't trying to be top dog (he knew he was), this was play, and as honorary HBs we had to learn the rules, with some modifications. Whenever he got too rough, we would say 'No!' quite sharply and he did learn to loosen his grip on this command. But as he got larger and more boisterous, he would sometimes lose sight of everything but the game and we would have to run for the door and climb over it, a set of little shark's teeth snapping behind us.

For a while I used a towel as a matador's cloak, which fixed him, until he realised that all he had to do was to barge straight through it in order to attach himself yet again to the nearest piece of my exposed flesh, usually an arm or ankle. For months, I looked as though I had been fighting my way out of an acacia thicket, but once he got his pearly white adult gnashers, which didn't draw blood quite so satisfactorily, Badge became more Bouncy but thankfully less Bitey.

Mostly, he would only play a game or fiddle with a toy once before he got bored, but there were a few exceptions. The round basket with the narrow top really fired his imagination. He explored it with every part of his body, both hands inside, lying on his back juggling it between his paws, pushing it away with his back or his nose, somersaulting over it, grasping it tightly under his belly, throwing it into the air, or just dribbling it along the carpet with his nose – all manoeuvres that he would need when he began hunting in earnest.

When it came to domination, Nandi had no compunction in asserting herself right from the start, and for the few weeks that she was in control, she was even keener on their games than Badge. He would bait her by approaching with his tail up and mouth open, making a breathy heh-heh-heh noise, then zip around and present her with his bottom. But just as Nandi lunged forward to give it a good bite, he would do a quick flip and dive between her legs to nip her feet, one of the most vulnerable parts of the body. When she did manage to catch him, Nandi would give a tremendous shove with her nose, sending him tumbling across the grass, or pick him up by the scruff of the neck and drag him around the garden, covering him with slobber. Nothing put Badge off for long. He'd break into his 'hippety hoppety' routine, a rocking gait that he would use when he was feeling particularly cheeky. He'd do a big circle around Nandi like a dressage pony before going in for the kill again, swift and low.

Re-reading this chapter, I realise that it is littered with

similes and metaphors; I have used everything from an octopus to a sausage to describe our Badger. I make no apology for this because each one is apt, but the truth is that he is incomparable, and only the shortcomings of the English language (or, more likely, my inability to find the words) make it impossible to do him justice in any other way. After all, badgers, like roses by any other name, smell just as sweet.

Watching Nandi and Badge play, I'm aware how short a time this unique relationship can last, I wrote in my diary. I was right about the time but wrong about the uniqueness of the relationship. Wildlife artist Vic Gurr, writing in his book *The Trouble with Africa*, recounts an incident in the Luangwa Valley when his dog, Baked Beans, joined a family of wild honey badgers to play with their cubs by moonlight.

My first impulse is to run to his rescue, save him from a mauling by these two savage creatures. But instead I stand and watch the game they are playing. A badger pounces on Baked Beans and pins him to the ground. The dog wriggles out from underneath and drops into a crouch. His curly tail is erect now, his head low, ears flattened against his skull. The badger stands still and waits for the dog to catapult himself towards him. They engage for a brief moment, then the dog breaks loose and runs as if in flight. But he stops in mid-stride, spins around and launches himself like a missile at the other cub. The first cub jumps high in the air and lands on both their backs, and they roll in the dirt again in a tight knot.

Badge and Nandi had been entertaining a couple of our friends on the lawn for over an hour when Badger galloped over and tumbled into my lap.

'I hope you realise,' I told Nyasha, 'that this is the meanest animal in the world.'

'Oh?' she replied, stroking his hot little tummy. 'That's funny, I thought we were.'

Chapter Nineteen

For a long time, Badgie found it hard to believe that there was life away from Mummy's lap. He would waddle between our feet on walks, chirping constantly, as he would have done in the wild to remind his mother not to abandon him. She must have been very tempted. At five months, when a baby wildebeest is already halfway through its first thousand-mile migration, our Badge was still trying to trot, and his back quarters frequently gave way with the effort. One evening, when Nandi passed him at a gallop on her way home for supper, he launched himself after her, tripped over a small stone and landed on the side of his head.

Of all the skills Badge had to learn, I think walking was the hardest, and it wasn't made any easier by an insensitive family who roared with laughter as he trotted along, pigeon-toed and bandy-legged, bouncing from one springloaded foot to the other.

Compared to our Tanglefoot, Poombi's journey to independence had been pretty simple. We had moved her four kilometres away from her comfortable kitchen to the

House at Pig Corner, an abandoned antbear hole fenced with chicken wire near the Matanje river. Every day she patrolled the river with Abel, and every night we knew she was snug in her hole, protected from leopards and other unfriendly animals. By the time Poombi chose freedom, she was familiar with every inch of her home range; she knew where to find the best fruiting trees, the safest holes and permanent water. She was as ready as a pig can be.

Apart from the danger of predators, once a warthog is weaned at around four months, she can survive on her own. All being well, though, she has her mother's protection for her first year, after which she is booted out, sometimes permanently, to make way for the new litter.

At four months, baby badgers are barely mobile. Not only do they need constant protection, but they have everything to learn. Unlike the carefree hog, their food is a constant challenge – it hides underground, climbs trees or has a nasty bite or smell. And to make it worse, badgers insist on getting up the noses of other predators by commandeering their kills: a very risky habit indeed.

What we had no way of knowing was how much Badge would do instinctively and how much he would have to be taught. It was the old question of nature v. nurture – but if the balance were to fall on the nurture side, our motherless cub was going to be totally maladjusted to a life in the wild. Just as it had been with Poombi, we humans could offer him opportunities and protection, but no more.

When Badge was six months old, his life, and ours, had settled down nicely: two walks, morning and evening, up and down the Mathole river that runs close by the house, and the day snoozing on a lap or laying waste to his bedroom.

Nandi enjoyed the outings but became fed up at having to sit for hours while Badge bumbled about in the grass and scrabbled at the water's edge. Although he was brave enough to walk through a puddle, he would back away suspiciously from the deeper pools. So Nandi would wait until he was at the water's edge and leap in next to him with a huge splash, sending a waterlogged Badge scuttling for my lap while she swam to the other side with a garland of water lilies on her head. His favourite game was ambushing our feet, particularly if they were bare or in sandals, because they would respond with an agonised 'ow!', a sound that gave Badge great satisfaction. He became particularly attached to my pair of relatively indestructible Nike sandals. I'd float one off in a shallow pool and he'd wade in to fetch it, only giving up the chase when he was out of his depth. Once he had it, and if we valued our fingers, we learned to respect the fine line between possession and play. He would of course refuse to give it up, and if we tried to distract him with something else, he would tuck the sandal under his belly and hunch over it, growling furiously, making it almost impossible to snatch it away. He spent hours investigating logs, under bushes and of course digging compulsively. Once, when Nandi came over to help him, he rushed at her with his head full of cobwebs and promptly fell into his own hole.

In the days when all Badgie required was his bottle and regular trips outside on to the lawn, Ruthie could take over when we both had to go to town for the day. But she couldn't do the twice-daily walks, and we realised that we would have to bring in someone else to fill the inevitable gaps when we weren't around. Since Khanye had already expressed an interest in getting to know Badge (and for some reason there were no other volunteers), he was the obvious choice, and on our first walk together, he tailed us at a distance, making sure that Badge didn't pick up his scent. Very gradually, he started appearing for a few minutes at first, then for longer, till Badge finally accepted him, and one night even initiated a game. It was almost dark when he began to chase Khanye around the garden, fluffing himself up in order to look larger and more intimidating. When Khanye stopped running and dodging him, Badge went into reverse, making his breathy heh-heh-heh sound, which showed off his sharp little teeth and very pink mouth to best advantage. We called this laughing, but I noticed it induced a rather nervous giggle in Khanye, who for ages was secretly convinced that Badger was bent on removing some crucial part of his anatomy.

Now in his thirties, Khanye has spent a lifetime in the bush; he was born at Robbins Camp in the Hwange National Park, where his grandfather had worked as a cook and his father was employed as a head scout. Neither of his parents was Zimbabwean – his mother is of the Lozi tribe from Zambia, and his father's family were Zulus from the south, which accounts for Khanye's *café au lait* complexion and the fact that there are always a few inches of extra leg showing under his overalls. His first job was in the Park, as pump and picnic site attendant at Shumba Pan, some thirty kilometres from Sinamatella, the nearest camp. Here he lived alone, doing odd jobs for visitors who sometimes spent the night, and switching the pump on at 6 am and off again at 6 pm. This meant walking out of the fenced-off area and through the bush for 700 metres with only a knobkerrie for protection: a hazardous occupation that resulted in some hair-raising encounters. Once, I asked him to record a few of his adventures for me.

'I had a very frightening moment at Shumba Picnic Site one morning,' he wrote. 'I was at the pump checking everything and just as I was trying to start the engine, a growl stopped me. I was looking directly into the eyes of a huge male lion, with a female, no more than ten metres away from me. In the blink of an eye, I was up on the roof of the pump engine shelter, facing the now roaring, angry lion. He jumped once towards me and stopped, looking at me now seven metres high on the roof. I saw one car passing by and tried to signal to it, but I don't think they saw me. My shouting and signalling helped to get the female lion to run away into the bush. The now alone male jumped a metre and gave a thunderous roar that shook the zinc on which I stood. To my relief he finally made for the bush and disappeared from sight.

I nearly punished the other animals by not pumping water for them, but then I thought since I was alive, they should live too.'

Sometimes in the mornings, he found a baby elephant stuck in the concrete trough, too small to climb out. Realising immediately that this was a friend, the little elephant would allow Khanye to lift its front legs on to the side of the trough, and then pull itself up as hard as it could while Khanye pushed it from behind, until it was finally over the side. From that moment, he was the hero, St Francis of Shumba Pan, and wherever he went that day the little elephant would follow. When dusk was falling, and Khanye could hear the herd approaching, he would lead the calf through the trees down towards the water. At the last minute, when it wouldn't have been safe to stay any longer, he would start running round and round a clump of bushes until the baby was thoroughly confused, at which point he would sprint off back to his house, leaving the calf to be reunited with its mother.

So Khanye was used to wild animals far larger than Badge, but in this case, size clearly wasn't the issue. 'We Africans,' he told me, 'would far rather meet an elephant or a lion in the bush than *mantswane* [honey badger]!'

Why then, I asked him, was he volunteering for this job?

'Because I want *mantswane* to prove to me if everything they say about him is true!' he replied.

Our staff had lived through all sorts of experiences with our wild orphans, but this one they couldn't comprehend.

'Doesn't Mrs Peek realise,' Johnson asked Khanye, 'that when *mantswane* grows up, he will bite her?'

Of course, he was already doing that, ripping my arms to shreds with his baby teeth when we played, but I was confident that Badge would never actually turn on us unless we broke the code and removed his food or something else he was particularly possessive over. Attack is almost always a result of fear and incomprehension – and Badger suffered from neither.

Our staff, however, were never convinced.

'Did you know that honey badgers can count?' Scout Richard Mabhena asked me one day.

I said that I didn't know but I wasn't at all surprised.

'If you watch while he is raiding a beehive,' he went on, 'you will see that he takes the combs and keeps hiding them close by. When the pile gets big enough, you can go in quietly and steal a couple; but you can only do this twice before you must run away. *Mantswane* will soon ask himself, why is this pile not getting any bigger? And he will count the combs and know that you have been stealing. If he finds your tracks, beware! He'll catch up with you wherever you are!'

'And then what happens, Mabhena?'

'There's war!'

Close to the base of the Dibe dam wall, Badge discovered his first retreat – a rock hollowed out into a little cave. He would peer through a peephole with one eye, and as we passed, he'd lunge out at us, take a quick bite of whatever bit of us he could grab, and then retreat into safety. He gave Nandi a nasty surprise by attaching himself to the end of her tail, which made her tear round and round the rock, ears flying in the wind, with Badge in hot pursuit. That little victory bucked him no end, and he trotted home that evening like a cocky little street fighter, clad in suede boots and black leggings, bouncing along with the bravado possessed only by those who know that mummy is not far behind. But the more he enjoyed his walks, the less he liked to be shut in his bedroom. We had to tiptoe around the house speaking in whispers, because if he knew we were close, he would whine for hours, desperate for company.

'I think I'd better start building him a cage,' muttered Rich over lunch, as Badgie battered at his bedroom door.

'He'll hate it even more than the bedroom,' I whispered back. 'But short of removing his teeth and cutting his nails, I don't suppose there's any other option. He's certainly not ready to go off by himself.'

So, a few weeks later, the clang of Johnson's spade on stone announced the start of Badgie's new home. Badge wouldn't have agreed, but it was a palace, at least compared to Poombi's rather rustic bachelor pad on the Matanje. Situated just outside our bedroom window, it featured a paddling pool, a brick bedroom clad in stone (matching the walls of our house), hollow logs, tractor tyres and an assortment of other toys. But despite its pleasant interior, it was in reality a maximum security prison with diamond mesh stretched over a wooden frame and secured a metre underground with layers of rocks.

Every day during its construction, I carried Badge across the trench at lunchtime and sat with him under the trees while he sniffed about. Of course, I reasoned, being a mere animal, he hadn't got a clue what we were up to.

One morning, when the cage was half finished and we were coming home after our morning promenade down the river, Badge suddenly veered off the path and climbed up the side of a termite mound. There he carefully cleared the dead leaves from a small hole and began excavating furiously, creating a mini landslide with piles of termite rubble. He dug, and he dug and he dug. I'd never seen him so determined, but when a badger is truly focused, nothing on earth will distract him. Nandi and I sat watching him for half an hour, until the dust settled and everything had gone quiet. I gave him a little while longer to enjoy his hidey-hole, then put my head at the entrance and called: 'Come on, Badgie, come out!' to be met with utter silence. After more calling, I could hear a very faint scrabbling that seemed to be miles away, and then nothing.

I tried again at lunchtime, assisted by Nandi, who tried to jam her head in the hole at the same time as mine, while panting and dousing my ear with slobber. Finally, Badge put a sleepy head out of the tunnel, wolfed down his chick, and wriggled back again, staying there until we fetched him at four o'clock for his evening walk. Watching the tip of his tail disappearing down that hole was like leaving David at boarding school – you hate losing them but you know that this is their first, essential step to independence. The difference was, of course, that David hadn't chosen to go to school (are you *mad*?) whereas with Badger, leaving home was an impulse that he was powerless to ignore. Interesting, though, how this kicked in at precisely the same time that he was due to be locked in his cage. He made quite sure he never spent a single day in it, but at night we lured him in with his supper, mostly for his own protection but also for ours, as he had recently begun tearing the wiring out of the bottom of the old mini-bus – and the lodge offers a great deal of other entertainment for a ratel with time on his hands.

We weren't entirely surprised by this behaviour. Doreen and John's little Ratsi dug a hole under their garden fence at about the same age and used to spend her days out in the veld. And in her book *The Wilderness Family*, Kobie Kruger writes that their badger, Buksie, did exactly the same thing. I couldn't help but think of the mental distress those cubs, or any other animal, would have suffered if they had been caged and prevented from following their natural instincts.

Although the Posselts and the Krugers had their badgers for around a year, both couples were employed by National Parks and so were not permitted to follow the cubs into the bush, as we could with Badge on private land. And we knew of no one else who could give us information. Then one day, Rich picked up the post in Bulawayo and brought back the latest issues of *Africa Geographic* and its sister magazine, *Africa Birds and Birding* – both, unbelievably, featuring a honey badger on the cover. And inside were articles and more marvellous photographs by the only two people in the world who have done a long-term study of *Mellivora capensis* in the wild: Keith and Colleen Begg.

Chapter Twenty

The abiding image I have of Col and Keith is a clip from their National Geographic documentary, *Snake Killers, Honey Badgers of the Kalahari*. It is midday in the scorching desert sands and the Beggs are lying under a bit of tarpaulin attached to the side of their Land Rover in the middle of the dunes. They are covered with wet black towels. The camera zooms in and no, the towels aren't black, it's the hundreds of moisture-seeking bees that cover every inch of them. As Col flips the pages of her book, she idly swats them away from her face.

The couple had a novel courtship – they met over an elephant carcass in the Kruger National Park while engaged in separate vulture-related research. Now in their mid-thirties, both are tall, slim and good-looking. Keith has close-cropped hair and a beard, and Colleen's shoulder-length hair frames a pair of deep brown eyes and a wonderful smile. She is as elegant as a gazelle – and as they stepped out of the gloomy airport customs house and into the sunlight, they looked as if they were models arriving for a photo shoot rather than an eccentric pair of scientists heading for their first, historic rendezvous with a smelly little badger (did *I* say that?).

They hugged us as though we were old friends, and thrust a framed photograph into our hands – a mother badger trotting along with a baby swinging from her mouth curled up in the shape of a peanut, his eyes encrusted with sand and tightly shut. When you watch their film, you realise why Baby Badger has sand in his eyes: his mother orders him to sit right behind her as she digs, and she half buries him in the process.

The shouting began the moment we got in the car – two beards in front, one brown, one grey, and the girls in the back – firing off questions and answers as though we were half an hour from the end of the world. And it's not as if we hadn't spoken to them before. As soon as we made contact, emails had been flying back and forth; and once they were back in South Africa for a few weeks, we were regularly on the phone. I'd called Colleen after Badger had gobbled up the fungus, asking what I should do, and she had laughed and said, 'Nothing. I'm afraid that's typical badger. I'm sure he'll be fine.' Which, of course, he was. The Beggs were just as fascinated by our tame badger as we were by their wild ones. After two days, we were so talked-out that we all had to take a snooze at ten o'clock in the morning in order to build up our strength for the next session.

At four o'clock on the afternoon they arrived, we trooped down to the Riverina apartment for the presentation. As usual, Nandi and I put our heads into the hole to entice Badgie out and ten minutes later, he appeared at the entrance, yawning and stretching, to the accompaniment of much whirring of videos, clicking of cameras, and muted exclamations of delight. Badge was quite at home with the paparazzi; Rich's cameras had been following his every move since he arrived in his orange box, but even Shirley Temple had her off-days, and our young protégé had already bitten a couple of chunks out of the microphone on Rich's video when it got too close.

Keith and Colleen lived in the Kalahari for four years, studying and filming the honey badgers, and co-operatively writing up a thesis on the life history of this 'atypical mustelid': atypical because he didn't fit neatly into the rest of the family. Desperate to make the badger conform, science has created a special sub-family for him, the *Mellivorinae*, which is all wrong in my view, as honey badgers are unique and shouldn't be forced to share their lineage with anyone, especially for the sake of zoological convenience.

One day, say Keith and Colleen, they will write a book; but having heard some of the extraordinary stories that are part of their daily lives, I think there will be dozens of them. From the rolling dunes of the Kalahari, they took one step further into the wilderness by basing themselves at Niassa, an area in far northern Mozambique so remote from civilisation that the Portuguese called it the end of the world, 'Fim de Mundo'. Here, for the past five years, they have camped out in two Land Rovers, still continuing with their badger research but also filming the lives of the local Cyao people, and studying the strange creatures that inhabit this part of the world, such as the tree hyrax, the yellow baboon, the palm civet, and what they believe may be a new sub-species of dwarf mongoose. And in their spare time, they collect spiders for the museum, and, because very little is known about the local lions (except for the fact that they have killed and eaten seventeen people in the last two years), they dart and fit them with radio collars in order to monitor their movements.

As I write, they are doing a survey of the Lugenda River in their kayak, a trip of around 500 kilometres. It's an idyllic life, provided you don't get sick. Both have suffered many bouts of malaria: Colleen has had it 'too many times to remember', and last year she ended up in a Cape Town hospital with a platelet count of 13, when the normal reading is around 100 to 110. They are well kitted out with medical supplies but, as Colleen says, 'if it's a black mamba, we'd just have to say goodbye and rest under a tree', because they would never be able to get help in time. Emergency evacuations can be arranged but only from Pemba, two days away by road and two hours by air, that is if they can solicit the assistance of one of the hunters in the area with a light aircraft.

Honey badgers are listed as 'Near Threatened' in the South African Red Data Book. To some extent this is due to habitat destruction, but beekeepers were known to kill as many as 200 a year in the Cape Province alone. The Beggs did a survey in the Western Cape, and in one of their magazine articles, Keith published a photograph of a honey badger, still alive, caught in the steel jaws of a gin trap with a look on its face of terror, pain and utter incomprehension. I can't bear to look at it. These monstrously cruel traps were easily purchased in South Africa, although they are outlawed in many other countries. Working with responsible beekeepers, the Beggs tested a badger-proof hive by simply securing it on a stand one metre off the ground. And these days, supermarket chains like Woolworths will only stock 'badger-friendly' honey supplied by accredited beekeepers. But the Beggs shrug off the praise for their achievements. Perhaps because they have lived for so long away from civilisation, they have a freshness and integrity about them; they are apparently untouched by the cynicism that seems to have affected us all in this new millennium.

Those first introductions over, we left the Riverina with Badge in the lead, Nandi at his side, and the five members of his entourage (including Khanye) trotting behind laden with cameras, tripods, binoculars, recorders and notebooks. A light rain had fallen the previous night, so the air was filled with enticing smells and Badge dug hole after hole in the soft soil, blowing noisily down each with as much huff and puff as a pair of bellows.

Some 'authorities' maintain that he blows out forcefully to disturb the occupants of the hole and get them moving, but after a bit of discussion among the experts, we agreed that this was only part of the answer. A short, forceful sneeze has the effect of clearing the dirt from the nostrils, but the long, gale-force blow has a different function. Like a radar system, it circulates interesting smells and tells the badger exactly who is at home. And of course, there's the tell-tale scrabbling of that little family of mice at the end of the tunnel, who are holding on to their hats and saying their last farewells.

While Badge was ripping a bracket fungus off the bark of a tree, a small spitting cobra slid out of the grass and into some nearby rocks. Fortunately, Badger didn't see it. In the Beggs' film, they show footage of a badger following a deadly Cape cobra to the top of a tree and right to the end of its thinnest branches. The terrified snake will try to keep its head well away from its pursuer, but if that's out of range, the badger will simply make a grab at the snake's body and fling it on to the ground. And so as not to waste time, he'll drop straight down after it, no matter how high in the tree he may be.

We repeated the story about our training sessions

with the herald, and we asked Colleen how the mother badger protects her baby from poisonous snakes. 'We've seen one growl at her youngster to drive him away when she was killing a cobra,' she said, 'and that's probably one of the most important things she'll teach him. But in fact, he's got so much to learn and so many techniques to master – digging, climbing, raiding beehives, flipping over rocks – a badger's game for anything if there's a meal at the end of it.'

Badge had already had two abortive attempts at tree climbing and both had ended with him falling on to his head. I had imagined that with a bit of practice he would get it right, but if we were to become his personal Outward Bound trainers, the sooner we started the better.

We hid a grasshopper in the fork of a low tree and called Badge over. He picked up its scent, hauled himself up with no trouble and ate it. Then he looked over his shoulder and began to whine. Rich sprang into action, cupping Badgie's bottom in his hands in an attempt to bring him down backwards. But Badge wasn't ready for the abseiling lesson, he gripped the bark with his claws and wouldn't be budged until Rich plucked him off and carried him down to the ground. Tree climbing lessons were one thing – David could help with that one – but what about digging? I didn't fancy coming home with a nose full of dirt and a mouthful of mouse.

'Well, he seems to know what he's doing,' I said, with some relief, as we watched Badge sticking his nose down his tenth hole of the evening.

'That's the easy bit,' said Keith. 'You should see them catching mice in a warren. They dig some holes, guard others and fill in the rest, but very quickly, or the mice will escape. They use dozens of tricks.'

I never thought anything could be worse than teaching David school by correspondence (and nor did he). But clearly there was. How could a family of humans who had left all their most basic survival techniques behind them somewhere in the Stone Age be expected to teach a wild badger how best to be himself? Admittedly, I had once eaten snake in Hong Kong, so I was more qualified than Rich in this regard. And since I loved raw herring and had sampled steak tartare, I couldn't excuse myself on the grounds of squeamishness either. But cooked or uncooked, black mamba was a delicacy that Badge would be enjoying all on his own.

The world speaks to us in different ways. If Rich has to assemble something, he throws away the written instructions, which I then pick out of the wastepaper basket and file away. Rich either works it out himself or follows the diagrams. At university, I lost myself in the glorious world of legalese: sopping up phrases like *de minimis non curat lex* – the law doesn't concern itself with trifles (not to be confused with the culinary) – and *in flagrante delicto* – caught with your pants down – and studying ancient Greek in my spare time. Meanwhile, Rich was busy drawing graphs or incredibly detailed sketches of the internal anatomy of rats and toads. And David is like me; from the moment I began to read to him, he would constantly be asking, 'What does that word mean?' and feeding his imagination rather than looking at the illustrations. For a worshipper of words, nothing beats receiving a book – being the first person to turn those crisp pages and to bury your nose in the middle of it, inhaling that very special smell of ink and new paper. On Stone Hills, Rich is never without a sketchbook or a camera, whereas

I am lost without my notebook or a recorder, as we try to capture its loveliness and fix it in our minds forever.

The trouble, though, with being seduced by the written word is that it is very much like falling for a man: you tend to lose your critical faculty. Subconsciously, you feel that somewhere out there sits an omniscient censor, appointed by God, who wouldn't allow lies to be published, particularly if they are couched in beautiful language – an illusion that would be completely destroyed if we could see the puny little journalist, desperate for a story, with nicotine-stained fingers and a boil on the end of his nose, tapping away at his computer.

My romance with words proved to be a problem when I first began to delve into Rich's huge library of books on natural history. I believed every word of them, particularly if the author was an acknowledged expert in the field.

'Don't take them as gospel, trust your own eyes!' Rich told me, and he taught the scouts the same thing.

'Books I've read and got much from them,' wrote Khanye, 'but Mr Peek encouraged to me to do my own observations because he says all is not written.'

Like love, all you need is time, and lots of it: time to sit and look with an open mind. Or, as de Maupassant said, recalling the advice he had received from his master Flaubert: 'There is a part of everything that remains unexplored, for we have fallen into the habit of remembering, whenever we use our eyes, what people before us have thought of the thing we are looking at. Even the slightest thing contains a little that is unknown. We must find it. To describe a blazing fire or a tree in a plain, we must remain before that fire or tree until they no longer resemble for us any other tree or any other fire.' And this is just as true for the study of natural history as it is for literature.

The authorities are pretty much agreed about highly visible animals like the buffalo, but it's their treatment of the lesser-known creatures that truly reveals who is who in the zoological world. The real experts, like Dr Reay Smithers (whose favourite animal, by the way, was the HB), either have personal knowledge or quote from scientific papers, and if they don't know something, they say so. Others merely rely on hearsay or quote directly from other inaccurate sources.

'Aggressive and attacks without provocation', says one book about the honey badger. 'Has webbed feet', says another. 'Swims well and hunts underwater'. 'Plays dead when wounded'. 'Tree climbing ability is poor'.

Where did these reports come from? After twelve years of study, the Beggs have seen no evidence of any of these assertions.

Most controversial of all is the statement that the honey badger is 'well known' to follow honeyguides to beehives. Stories abound about this association, and plausible as they may sound, there is as yet no scientific evidence for it. One of the Beggs' main reasons for being at the end of the world is that both badger and bird are there, and may give them the opportunity to prove or disprove the theory. And in time even our little Badger would be contributing his bit to solving the riddle.

Many of the books state that honey badgers give birth to one or two cubs (sometimes up to four) after a long gestation. In fact, there have only ever been two recorded cases of twins, both born in captivity, and on each occasion one cub died soon after birth. In all other reported cases, there has been only one cub, and for a very good reason. As we knew only too well, badgers are completely helpless for the first three months of their lives, and only at around eight months do they start killing for themselves, but not terribly successfully. Life is very hard in the Kalahari (and the Matobo Hills), and the mother badger is stretched to her limits by having to find food for both herself and her baby. Even at independence, which can be as late as two years old, the Beggs found that young badgers often die of starvation without their mother's support. And as for a 'long gestation', the average time recorded by the Beggs is 50–70 days (less than three months) – short by any yardstick. Apparently, a period of six months has been recorded in captive badgers but never in their wild counterparts.

The last programme in the BBC series *The Life of Mammals* opens with David Attenborough watching an orang-utan washing a pair of socks in the river and making a very good job of it. It's fortunate that the apes can't write, because otherwise they might compile their own Field Guide to Mammals, with some very accurate observations:

Homo horribilis
(sometimes jokingly referred to as *homo sapiens*)
– the killer ape
Like the house rat, this highly successful but destructive pest occurs in every country of the world. Bipedal, sparsely haired, omnivorous. Tends to gather in large, unsustainable numbers, mostly in an urban environment. Physically weak but has well developed tool-using abilities. Our most aggressive mammal, it will attack without provocation, and is dangerous to all other species. Well known for its destruction of the

environment and its tendency to kill large numbers of its own kind, using highly sophisticated tools. Impossible to eradicate. Classified as Vermin.

On the Beggs' last morning, Badge suddenly disappeared into Hongwe Tekwana, the phallic tower of granite that lies to the south of our house. I shook his bottle of grasshoppers and rushed after him, but in a few minutes he'd disappeared through a tangled screen of strychnos and into the rocks. We called and climbed and searched for half an hour or so until the Beggs had to leave to catch their plane, and I felt very lonely sitting on my rock, minus the star attraction, waving goodbye to the only two people in the world who didn't think we were completely mad.

Hongwe Tekwana is a maze of caves and deep holes in the rocks, and much of it is inaccessible except to gymnasts like Baby Badger. Leopards and baboons love it, so it was the last place I would have chosen for Badge's day retreat, but he had clearly made up his mind. I spent five minutes with a pair of elephant shrews I found sunning themselves on the rocks. One came towards me in jerky little hops, the tip of his nose twitching madly. When he was a few inches from my feet, he stopped for a quick wash and brush-up and it struck me that, in their short lives, they had probably never seen a human being.

That evening, I met Khanye back at the koppie and we started to search. 'There he is!' Khanye's sharp eyes had picked out movement behind a narrow gap in the rocks directly above us.

'Come on, Badge!' I couldn't get to him nor could I squeeze through the gap, but Badgie could – if he was brave enough. He wasn't, and after more calling and enticing, he appeared over the top, fell over his own feet and tumbled into my arms, where he sat for a long time recovering from the ordeal. I don't think he had intended to stay the whole day so far away from home, but something had frightened him and he'd taken shelter in the first available place.

Badge was just six months old and his bravado had increased in inverse proportion to his survival skills. Out of fifteen cubs in the Beggs' study, only eight reached independence. And after that, without their mother's help and protection, they became even more vulnerable. Three out of five young males in the study perished before they reached maturity: 'one was thought to have died of starvation, one became blind in one eye and was later found dead and the remains of a third were found in a hyena den'.

Leopard and brown hyena are almost always on the farm, gigantic pythons live along the rivers. People have moved in around us, some keep chickens that would prove very tempting to a hungry badger. And, lovely though it is, Stone Hills is a harsh place in winter, even for experienced adult animals.

What could we do to prevent our Badge from becoming another statistic?

Chapter Twenty One

Thirty years ago, a long-term study of a small, secretive, nocturnal mammal wouldn't have been remotely feasible. But today's technology has changed all that. Between 1996 and 1999, the Beggs darted and fitted radio collars on 25 badgers in the Kalahari Gemsbok National Park, enabling them to be tracked from the air or on the ground up to a distance of around five kilometres. This was the first step; their next challenge was to habituate the badgers to the vehicle, an exercise that took them over 2,000 hours of patient pursuit, until finally they were able to follow five females with their five cubs and four adult males without disturbing their natural behaviour.

At the end of their study, all the collars were removed. Ugly and unnatural they certainly are, but without the technology, the Beggs would never have been able to plead the cause of this much-maligned little creature and show the world what a charismatic fellow he is. Some, less ethical researchers would have used their information merely to earn themselves a doctorate, but the Beggs aren't like that. The words of George Schaller are their credo: 'Every biologist has an obligation and responsibility to protect and preserve the species he or she studies by going beyond the collection of data to finding solutions to problems....'

Without Keith and Colleen, there would be no such thing as a badger-proof beehive, nor badger-friendly honey – both of which have the full support of the South African beekeepers' association.

Badge would need our protection for at least a year, and probably much longer. Instead of scrabbling about at the foot of Hongwe Tekwana hopefully rattling a jar of grasshoppers as we did, his own mother would have found him immediately and carried him to safety by the scruff of the neck.

The next time he paid a visit alone to the same koppie, he climbed, or probably fell, into a deep hole between the rocks in order to help himself to a leopard kill. He couldn't get out, and we found him only because Khanye heard his squeaks for help before the leopard did. We dreaded the thought of interfering with him in any way, but having discussed it with the Beggs, there seemed to be no alternative but to fit him with some sort of tracking device. Badge became far more bonded to us as he got older, but at six months he was constantly disappearing and, to make matters worse, his curiosity was leading him into some serious scrapes with the other animals on the farm.

'We collar badgers initially and then put radio implants into the abdominal cavity, which means that he will have to have a small operation,' Colleen wrote. 'But for an animal that digs, climbs and generally gets into so much trouble, the implants are a much better idea than the collars. We have found that the badgers are up and digging within thirty minutes of the operation with no adverse effects....'

A terrible nightmare, I wrote in my diary, *we were lost in a rambling hotel in a strange city. I let Khanye and Badge out of the car and went to find parking space, telling Khanye to hold on to him tight (an impossible task at the best of times). I parked but then couldn't get out of the place. There was a ladder against the wall, but it looked very dangerous so I didn't dare to use it. I finally found a lift, but when I got in, it turned out to be a high-speed train taking me in the opposite direction. I knew then that I had lost Badger for good.*

Colleen's words, 'for an animal that generally gets into so much trouble', finally decided us. If Badger was a liability now, he was only going to get worse. We decided on an abdominal implant, but there were still plenty of narrow squeaks ahead for a bumptious badger before the equipment arrived and the deed could be done.

Apart from the thrill of exploring, Badge was always on the lookout for alternative homes. The Riverina phase lasted for a couple of weeks, after which he began to take a particular interest in a hole underneath a coral tree – a good choice as it was more stable than the warren of antbear holes by the river. The only snag was that it had subsided somewhat, so Badge had to take it at a run and tumble in head-first. He had a choice of two wings; the west was cosier, but in the east, he could fit his nose through the small window at the end of the tunnel or nip our fingers as we wiggled them through the gap. In the evenings when we fetched him, he'd struggle to pull himself out with his front legs, and though he'd eventually succeed, we often took pity on him and hauled him up by the scruff of the neck, just as his mother would have done. He made this easier for us when he was tiny, by arching his neck in readiness as soon as we touched it.

When badgers explore deep holes, they use their back feet as anchors, but this takes a certain amount of experience. I was always concerned that an over-enthusiastic Badge would drop into the bowels of a termite mound and disappear forever. Some of them are hundreds of years old or more, and as hard as concrete, so we couldn't have helped him short of chucking down a stick of dynamite.

Falling headfirst is routine for a badger, and their thickened skull seems impervious to pain. Not only do they fall on it, they lift and shove and butt with it, and balance on their heads to free up their front legs for lifting or digging. When Badge challenged Nandi he came straight in, neck bent and head down, offering her his strongest line of defence. And when a badger, even a small one, cannons into the back of your legs, it's like being hit with a brick.

Having got the knack of balancing on the branches of fallen trees, Badge decided to aim higher. I wasn't taking much notice when he pulled himself up into the first fork of a slender snot apple, but then he kept on going, up and up until he was at least fifteen feet in the air. There he met another fork and could go no further and at that point he realised what a pickle he was in. He couldn't go forward, nor back: he was stuck. He looked down at me and began to whine. I wouldn't have been too concerned if there had been grass underneath him, but he was see-sawing over a slab of solid rock. I'd have to try and catch him or at least break his fall. Badge wiggled a bit and suddenly his back end slipped off the tree and he was dangling by the tips of his claws.

Bits of bark were raining down on my face, so I closed my eyes and stretched out my arms. 'Let go, Badge!' I cried, in his general direction, 'I'll catch you!'

There was a rasping sound as his fingernails raked the tree, and a great furry lump hit me in the chest and ricocheted off. I just managed to grab at a passing leg before Badge landed head-first with a great thump on the rocks beside me.

I picked up a slightly dazed and winded cub and prepared to carry him home, but I'd taken only a few steps before he began to struggle. Once more, he fell on his head, before galloping back to the snot apple to try again.

'Poor badger,' said Khanye, laughing. 'In Sindebele we say, *Indwangu iyalukutha ugatsha kewzinye insuku*, some days even baboons can miss a branch!'

By the April of his first year, we were spending a lot of our time standing around staring into dark holes waiting for a small HB to emerge. He also took to making tunnels in the long grass, and then, unless we heard sniffing or saw the grass moving, we had lost him – again. He knew where we were all the time, of course, and he could hear us calling, but he would reappear only when he had finished being busy. Time was of no consequence to Badger: he knew we would wait – we always did.

I shouted myself hoarse, to no avail. Then I remembered that sheepdogs respond almost entirely to the whistle. I fished Rich's dog-training whistle out of the cupboard, armed myself with a jar of jumping grasshoppers and followed the young Badge into the vlei. When he was still within sight, I blew, and to my amazement, he came trotting straight back to me. Good boy, clever boy! I immediately offered him a handful of hoppers so he would associate the whistle with the reward. Off he went again, and a few minutes later, I gave another blast on the whistle. And another, till my cheeks ached with the effort. Badge ignored me.

I often feel that he is so focused on what he is doing that he genuinely doesn't register, I wrote in my diary. *The usual excuses we make when we can't control our children, as in: Simon isn't concentrating in class, I don't think his teachers are stimulating him enough. Of course, Einstein was also ADHD, you know....*

He responded quickly enough when I went outside in the evenings and called 'Suppah!' I'd grab him as he came racing through the door and haul him into my arms to stop him from hooking the books off the shelves on his way to the bedroom. After he'd finished with it, the latest Harry Potter was in tatters, to David's fury, and the holy bible was a good deal holier than it should have been. By grasping a handful of loose skin and one leg, I could just contain the struggling Badge as far as the bedroom, where, with one last squirm, he usually landed on his head or in the middle of the plate of food.

Chicken and wildebeest were his usual fare but, unless there was some substance to the rumours, neither would constitute his natural prey. So I was very pleased when Khanye announced that he and Big Fight had killed a black mamba. 'Oh, that's good,' I said. 'Badge can have it for supper.' I thought Khanye looked a bit startled. He appeared at the house an hour or so later, with three metres of snake, as thick as his wrist, swinging from a pole over his shoulders. I carved off a foot of it, and presented it to Badge; and after toying with it for a few minutes, he bit through the skin and began tearing off long white strips of flesh like ribbons of wet spaghetti.

We don't normally kill dangerous snakes unless they are close to the house, but we did make a few exceptions until Badge began hunting for himself. The same cannot be said for Johnson Sibanda, who boasts of killing at least 20 mambas in his erstwhile (we trust) career as a poacher. Once, when he was squatting down to tie three dead dassies together, an enormous mamba slithered up from behind, through his legs, and tried to steal one (the Sindebele name for mamba is *Ginyambila*, the one who eats dassies). Johnson grabbed the snake by the head, put a foot on its neck and with his free hand picked up a small stick with which he eventually killed it.

'Aren't you afraid of any snakes?' I asked him, having heard this story.

'Nope,' said he. 'Mambas only want to get away from you.'

'And what about spitting cobras?'

Johnson scratched his ear. 'We-ell, yes. Maybe those. They'll stand their ground and fight back.'

Soon after we had bought the farm, Johnson was on his way back from the borehole when he bent to pick up a piece of paper on the ground. A spitting cobra reared up from underneath it and spat in his eyes. We had no radio contact in those days, so, alone and in blinding pain, he walked the three kilometres to the cottage. Fortunately we were there. Rich flushed out his eyes with water and milk for good measure, and ran him into hospital in Bulawayo, where he completely recovered.

'And *ingwe* (leopard)?' I asked. 'Are you frightened of him?'

Johnson shook his head. When pressed, he admitted that he was a little respectful of *mantswane*, but nothing else.

Long before, when he had been hunting with his dogs and was halfway up a koppie, he watched a honey badger trotting by in pursuit of a honeyguide; and while the bird was chittering, the badger was making a shh-shh-shh sound in response. This information coincided with an account I had read – under similar circumstances, the badger had been heard to make a 'sibilant hissing noise'. Perhaps, one day, we could verify this for ourselves.

We just had to keep on following that badger – an occupation that was taking up more and more of our time, until we began to wonder how we'd kept ourselves busy before his arrival. Most Fridays, Rich took off for Bulawayo to attend the farmers' meeting, so we could keep abreast of the latest developments; but often I didn't leave Stone Hills for weeks – an arrangement that suited me perfectly. Besides provisions, there was nothing out there that we wanted. We wore our clothes until they fell apart, and we mourned them like old friends when they died, which was often a lot earlier than it should have been, thanks to Badger. Each time I went to visit the family in Australia, my mother persuaded me to buy some pretty clothes that looked quite delightful in the shop mirror but were absolutely no use to me at home, or even in town, when I would spend most of my time climbing in and out of the back of the truck loading supplies.

When the days, weeks and years don't really matter, time passes in a blur. And then I'd meet someone in the street who looked vaguely familiar and we would both stop dead and stare at each other. Then one of us would blurt out, 'Golly, I didn't recognise you!', adding quickly: 'You must have changed your hair', or 'Have you always worn glasses?' which was a lot safer but less truthful than saying: 'My God, you've aged!'

When friends did come to stay, I would interrogate them at length about the latest gossip from town, then fall asleep over the dinner table, and would have forgotten every word by the next morning. But although wife-swapping was still a hot topic in the school car parks, it seemed that most people were spending more time examining their bank balances than the attributes of other people's spouses.

Apart from political propaganda, the local newspaper could be an invaluable source of information to those of us who were a little out of touch, like the time it announced that 'According to the Government gazette, New Year's Day will be on Monday 1st January', but one couldn't rely on it for anything more informative. For that, a plan was needed, and Maggie Kriel stepped into the breach. Once a popular broadcaster on national radio, she began compiling a fortnightly information sheet called the *Morning Mirror*, which she emailed all over the country and beyond. It usually began on a light note, but as things became increasingly difficult, there were more and more messages of condolence for people who had died of heart attacks or other stress-related illnesses, and too many others in desperate need, many of them old and destitute. Then there were pages of houses for sale, plus advertisements reading 'Good homes wanted for our two dogs, owners leaving the country'.

Zoe, one of my oldest friends, was among them, the

last one to go – after years of indecision, she was finally following her mother and son and emigrating to England. Zimbabwean families are scattered all over the world, and ours is typical: some in South Africa, some in New Zealand, others in Australia.

Our network of friends and acquaintances is a protective barrier between ourselves and the rest of the world. Real security is an illusion, of course, like the emperor's new clothes, but it's one that we cherish. Your doctor, your dentist, your neighbours: no matter how little you see them, each one is a brick in the wall, and when it is removed, a chilly wind blows through the gap, until finally you are standing alone on your mountain, exposed and vulnerable, like a mouse before a mamba.

Orange Grove Drive, Harare: I'm sitting in Zoe's house surrounded by packers, and the noise of shouting and hammering as they fill dozens of boxes and carry them out to the removal van. She has discovered her long-lost wedding ring and the clay water bottle we used in '73 when we slept in the cave by the sea on the island of Samos. She says that the house becomes more and more beautiful as it is emptied of distracting clutter, and certainly it is at its best in spring: I love the soft sunlight on my body as I take an open-air shower in the ivy-covered recess; the wood and the whitewashed walls, the edible fig at the top of the steps, and the doors and windows everywhere turning the inside out and making it all feel Mediterranean.

Zoe has the eye of an artist: she has collected smooth black river stones from Nyanga, dried grasses and flowers from her garden – treasures that she cannot take with her. Along with the clay bottle, we put them all in a

hole in the garden and cover it with soil. They'll be
waiting for her when she comes back. If she ever does.

The wonderful thing about Badger, as it had been with
Poombi, was that he was far too absorbed in the present
to be worrying about the uncertainty of the future, and
to some extent, it was catching.

One day on Stone Hills is never the same as the next,
but Badger took what little routine there was in our lives
and turned it upside down. When he was little, we would
go for two walks a day, morning and evening, mostly
along the river close to the house, with frequent
excursions into the garden or games in his room (when I
wasn't swabbing the carpet). This was gradually
extended until, when he was a year old, we were
spending five hours a day walking in the bush with our
badger. And when we went to fetch him in the late
afternoon, he would be waiting for us in the same place
as we had left him at eight o'clock that morning.

He was always a mumsy little chap, and when I called
'Badgee, Badgee!' he'd come hurtling out from his hidey-
hole and throw himself at me for a cuddle, a practice that
when he was fully grown made me feel as though I was
being embraced by a sumo wrestler.

Khanye came along on every walk, but he knew far
too much about Bad Badgers to rush into a relationship
with this one, even if he was supposed to be tame. But
after a very suspicious start, they both began to relax,
particularly when we were having supper and Khanye
played nursemaid on the front lawn.

Badger gets easily bored if you play the same game every
day, so sometimes we play a chasing game with socks or

a towel, or rolling a tyre around with something making a noise in it. The tyre is also turned into a little room where he goes to hide, and there I cover him with a towel.

Badge was reasonably demure until just before sunset, known as 'badge o'clock'. He'd fluff himself up to twice the size, raise his tail, and with a hippety-hoppety he'd be after Khanye, who would very obligingly run away. When Badge managed to grab his foot, Khanye would leap sideways, and dance the knees-up like a leggy puppet on a string.

In those early days, Badge seemed to feel duty bound to give Khanye a hard time, particularly when he was walking him alone.

When it is my turn to take him on an afternoon walk, I get to his place and start to call. He stays put in his hole until he gets bored or feels sorry for me, as I try all sorts of tricks to call him out. Sometimes I imitate Mrs Peek to fool him, but he soon picks it up and stays on, probably laughing. I think when he hears me calling, he says to himself – 'oh, it's that boring old Khanye again. I'm not going'.

Hunting lessons were conducted with grasshoppers, which Badger discovered up trees, under stones and even in the river. 'Whatever will Badger teach his children?' remarked Khanye. 'Grasshoppers that swim? Snakes that live in bottles?'

One morning, when he was three months old, I saw Badge staring into the long grass by the water's edge. He stood very still – and suddenly began to wag his tail from side to side. Staring fixedly, he went into a little crouch and pounced – on to a large, yellow and presumably very dozy cricket. Both parties were equally surprised by this, particularly Badge when he felt the cricket struggling under his paw. He took tentative little munches at it, watched in fascination as it tried to escape, then pounced again. Badgie's first kill was all over in ten minutes. The tail wag was, we were to discover, reserved for very exciting prey, like mice or the occasional dassie. Apart from being an indicator of extreme emotion, it also seems to be a weapon of mass distraction, especially when it is waved over the bolt-holes of a family of mice to intimidate them into staying put while Badge is excavating at the other end.

Although badgers are game for anything, pouncing is perhaps one of those moves better left to the leopard. Badgie moved through the bush like a bulldozer, and when he tensed and leapt into the grass, I was always reminded of the song 'I feel the earth move under my feet', as almost invariably a slight scurrying ten feet away announced the rapid departure of his intended prey.

His climbing techniques developed very slowly, probably because I always felt sorry for him when he got stuck and helped him down. He'd sit in the fork of the tree or at the top of a rock, whining pathetically and holding out a front leg – a plea for help that no responsible mother could resist.

If you spend long enough with any animal, you can't help but try to put yourself into its mind. At first, it's no more than a guess, but with time and patience, the day will come when you feel that you have reached a far deeper level of understanding.

Hunter/gatherers of old, like the Bushmen, chased for hours after antelope, trying to second-guess where the animal would be likely to go and where it would hide;

reading and interpreting its spoor when this was visible, and relying on their experience when it wasn't. They used techniques that one can only develop through years of patient observation and total familiarity with the animal and its environment.

Our game scouts are trained in subtleties. They spend every day, usually alone, walking on Stone Hills. They have no appointments to keep, no set destination; their job is to watch and listen – and often to wait, their senses attuned to the slightest sound or movement.

When we found Badge sniffing around an area of flattened grass, Khanye looked at the surrounding spoor and knew that a wildebeest had been resting there, and probably a sick one, as it had defecated where it lay. Sure enough, ten minutes later we came across a scraggy old cow, who died a couple of weeks later. Badge was our catalyst for all sorts of new discoveries. If I hadn't followed him to the top of a prominent rock in the middle of a vlei on the western side of the Mathole, I wouldn't have seen the piles of droppings that identified this as a favourite cheetah look-out. In Namibia, cheetahs climb trees to get elevation, but here they use rocks, though this was the first we had found on Stone Hills.

Like all the scouts, Khanye has an excellent knowledge of birds and trees, and our lengthy badger walks gave me a chance to refresh my memory. He has a pair of binoculars but these are a relatively new acquisition. Frank was positively scornful of such unnecessary baggage. 'I don't need those things,' he said, 'I have my eyes!' And they were formidable, as one highly respected doctor of ornithology discovered when he made a snap identification of a pipit (one of those impossibly drab little brown jobs), only to hear a soft voice behind him say, quite correctly, 'No, it's not a Richard's, it's a Long-billed.'

By tradition, antbears and hyenas are regarded as evil creatures who cooperate with witches. Honey badgers aren't unlucky, Khanye told me, but they are equally as fearsome because they are so powerful and don't die easily. When a baby is born, a piece of badger skin may be wrapped around its waist to give it the badger's attributes of strength and courage.

No one outside of Stone Hills believed that Khanye would handle such a dangerous animal; until Rich photographed Badger on his lap, and Khanye took it home to his family in Victoria Falls to prove that the devil *mantswane* was actually an angel in disguise.

Chapter Twenty Two

Beware the bored Baby Badger. Now that he had demolished the chair covers, pulled the fire hose across the veranda like a gigantic white snake and got his head stuck between the bars at the base of the veranda table, he was ready for something a bit more stimulating.

We were enjoying a few badger-free moments after supper, when Khanye knocked on the glass sliding door, looking very concerned.

'He's gone after the zebra. We were playing with the tyre when he heard them and ran off into the dark. I've been calling, but he won't come back.'

Every evening, a constant flow of animals visits the waterhole in front of the house. Badge hadn't shown any interest in them, until tonight. We each grabbed a torch and ran. About a hundred metres from the house, we could hear the zebra milling about, snorting, then the sound of galloping hooves. The bachelor stallions sometimes knock off tsessebe young with a swift kick; and often kill male baby zebras the same way. What chance would little Badge have against that gang of thugs?

The light from Khanye's torch bobbed between the trees, became fainter and disappeared.

'Badgie!' I could hear my voice quavering. 'Badg-ee!'

The zebra had gone, and all I could hear was the plaintive call of the fiery-necked nightjar: 'Good Lord deliver us!' I very much doubted if He was listening.

Fifteen minutes later, Rambo was back, flag flying, all in one piece, with Khanye panting behind him. He'd done his first meet and greet, and he'd got away with it.

It's difficult to describe how it feels having your heart in your mouth, but that's where mine spent most of its time as Badger introduced himself to the other animals on the farm. He wanted to be everybody's buddy, and we wondered what his mother would have done about it. Would she have warned him off, or let him find out the hard way that not everyone was to be trusted?

Lone wildebeest bulls stake out territories and wait for the girls to come wandering in. Some get lucky, others, like old One Horn on the far side of the Mathole river, have lost the edge. For months, he hopefully hung around his little patch but no one came near – except other lonely bulls with adjacent territories, also looking for love. At the sight of an intruder, One Horn was suddenly fired with a surge of testosterone. Snorting loudly, he'd begin pawing the ground like the randy old bull he was, depositing the strong, tarry smell of the glands in his feet. Then he'd urinate, drop to his knees and horn the ground, while wiping his facial glands in the wet soil. And finally, to top off the performance, the old bull would rub his throat and beard in the whole exciting concoction. Once those necessary little preliminaries were dispensed with, off he would go at the gallop to chase his rival round and round till they both got bored and went back to their respective territories.

Today, we can see him, head down, a hundred yards away. He looks as if he is asleep. Badge gets wind of him but begins by tracking him backwards and running in the opposite direction. Nandi doesn't join in: she learned a long time ago to leave all the other animals well alone. Badge must have noticed that the smell is getting fainter, because after a while he turns around and heads straight towards his quarry, tail up and nose stuck to the ground.

We call uselessly, and follow at the run, keeping Nandi close. With Badge glued to his heels like a dwarf sheepdog, One Horn trots away, then suddenly stops and wheels around to face his pursuer. We hold our breath. Badge stops too, and slowly zig-zags towards the bull – as if he's found himself there by mistake. A sort of 'fancy meeting you here' situation. One Horn puts his head down and Badge walks straight up to him. What will it be this time, a thrust with the horn or a kick? Now they are nose to nose. One, two, three seconds. The wildebeest picks up his head, turns and walks slowly away. 'Not such a bad young fellow,' we could hear him saying. Badge comes tearing back to us and flies into my arms. He's made another friend and he can't contain his excitement.

Having dropped our little socialite at the Riverina Apartments for the day, we were strolling back to the house when I remarked to Khanye that we could be sure that we were the only two people in the world that had ever seen a honey badger making friends with a wildebeest.

'Not quite,' said he, 'two people – and a dog.'

As his curiosity took him further afield, Badge began to find lots of other interesting homes, particularly in the rocks across the river. On one, we found the remains of a clay grain bin with an aloe growing in the middle, and Grain Bin Koppie became his favourite retreat for a couple of weeks. A little further west, he disappeared into a small gap under a monolithic boulder for ten minutes or so. He was trespassing, no doubt about it, but, other than the dassie that came shooting out of the exit hole on the other side, no one else appeared to be at home. Unless you are nasty, noisy or smelly enough to deter intruders, there is no privacy in the bush. Badge went straight back there the following day, and I arrived at four o'clock to take him for his walk. And there in front of the entrance to his new home, about ten yards away, were two porcupines, back to back, quills erect, stamping their feet and turning in tight circles, like a couple of flamenco dancers.

I stood absolutely still with Nandi in front of me, quivering, as the porcupines continued their *pas-de-deux*, rattling their quills like spears – until Badgie's head suddenly popped out of the exit hole. Nandi bounced towards the porcupines, I yelled at her, they disappeared under the rock and Badgie ran after them.

Porcupines are territorial but, unlike the promiscuous wildebeest, they are monogamous. We find their needle-sharp quills all over the farm. These hardened hairs sit loosely in the porcupine's skin, and when under attack, he will rush backwards or sideways, trying to plant them somewhere in the body of his adversary, often a lion or leopard. Sometimes these are so deeply embedded or in such a position that the animal can't dislodge them, and this can be not only painful, but dangerous. If the quill breaks, what's left of it under the skin can set up a festering and often fatal infection.

Puffs of dust came blowing out of the hole. I waited for growls or squeaks, but heard nothing. In fact, when he was hunting or killing, we were to find that Badge was always completely silent. I could do nothing but wait. Ten minutes later (or was it the next day?), Badgie appeared with a quill sticking out of his head. He put his head back into the entrance hole to see if he could stir up any more excitement, then trotted up to us. I pulled the quill out from behind his ear, and he climbed into my lap, moaning. I was only being friendly, he whined. How dare those great bullies give him a jab, when he, little Badger, hardly had a prick to his name?

As Africa's largest rodent, porcupines will eat almost anything, even bulbs, which are fatal to stock. They do, however, draw the line at *Boophane disticha*, the ox-killer, a bulb containing alkaloids so toxic that they have caused a number of human deaths. The bulb, with its crown of fan-shaped leaves, grows partially out of the ground and this is what drew Badge's attention to it. He dug out what looked like an enormous onion wrapped in countless layers of papery skin and, with it, Badge devised his very own version of pass the parcel, with one player. He peeled off layer after layer, until by the fifth lot of wrapping, and still no present, he was beginning to lose his cool. He rolled the rest of the onion around, jumped on it, head-butted, ripped, bit, straddled and kicked it like a football. Bits of shredded skin were scattered everywhere as if someone had up-ended a wastepaper basket. I know he felt cheated but he enjoyed the experience so much that he destroyed every *Boophane* he found from then on, just for fun. He didn't appear to actually eat it, but he couldn't have minded the taste, which is not surprising in an animal who once ate fungus for tea.

Badge's resistance to toxins was further tested by his liking for toads. Not as individuals, you understand, but as a gastronomic delight, comparable to a Frenchman's penchant for frogs' legs. He found his first one at the water bowl in the bucks' enclosure. The toad froze when Badgie sniffed at it, which sent him flying backwards, fluffing out his fur to make himself look bigger and more frightening. The toad didn't appear to care one way or the other, but when Badge kept patting him on the back, he decided to head for home. This was a mistake. Badge pinned him down and began to rake at the toad with his claws, which released some powerful-smelling toxins from under its skin. As he ripped and raked, Badge turned his head to one side, wrinkling his nose and baring his teeth in disgust. At last he began to eat it, and judging by the crunching and smacking of lips, the poor creature eventually died. We waited to see what effect, if any, the bufotoxins would have on Badge's digestion. I found the answer the following morning in his bedroom. Mounds of stinking black poo, and a chirpy little honey badger looking forward to his next meal of toad-in-the-hole, or wherever else he could find one.

Due to the poor toad's total lack of resistance, this could hardly have been described as a hunt. If one ignores the retarded cricket, his first real kill happened in mid-May, when he was eight months old on a walk with Rich. He began to dig at the base of some small trees, and as he became increasingly worked up he started to wag his tail. More furious digging – until a small hole became a large one, then Badge stuffed his nose in it and pulled out a pouched mouse, with its very white belly and short tail. Rich thinks that he was so excited he swallowed it whole. Thanks to Badge, we have met all sorts of interesting rodents that reside on Stone Hills, but sadly our acquaintance is always abruptly curtailed by their instant decapitation.

Anything in a hole was irresistible to Badge and it was fortunate for him that Poombi was no longer around. Once she had a family, she treated even Nandi, her oldest friend, as an enemy. But Badge had a special interest in warthogs and we were fascinated to find he seemed to know instinctively that their holes could only safely be approached from behind. He'd made one slip-up, when an adult female and three babies had exploded from their den and nearly flattened both him and Rich, but he left the real drama for me.

On our way home at dusk, I saw something moving out of the corner of my eye. It disappeared down an antbear hole. Nandi was immediately alert, but instead of sniffing around carefully, she galloped over and stuck her head right in after it. I managed to drag her away, hoping that Badge, who was busy digging somewhere else, hadn't noticed. He was there in seconds, of course, but like the idiotic dog, he ran straight in without the usual careful investigation. I heard a series of loud thumps and dust came billowing out of the hole. It wasn't an antbear I had seen, I was pretty sure of that, so it must be a warthog, or two, or more. It sounded as though someone was walloping a carpet underground, only I knew that it was Badge being slammed up against the wall by a pig's massive head. Where I stood, hanging on to Nandi, who was straining to join the fray, I could feel the ground reverberating beneath me as the battle raged up and down the tunnel. Ten minutes passed. Every thump was unbearable. I knew that badgers were hard to kill, but the warthog had all the advantages of a head like a 6-kilo sledgehammer and deadly tusks. It couldn't take much longer. I'd have to peel little Badge's flattened body off the sides of the hole, like pitta bread from a Turkish oven. Then the banging suddenly stopped, and like a cannonball, a half-grown pig burst out of the hole and fled into the trees.

It was a silly thing to do, but I couldn't help it.

'Badge?' I called softly with a sob in my voice. 'Badge, can you hear me?'

I'd have to go home and call Rich. We'd bring a shovel and dig his little body out. I'd put him by the bedroom window, close to Poombi. A head appeared from the hole and Nandi leaped at it.

My God, he was still alive! Suddenly, he was standing there, covered with blood and bristling with emotion.

'Why the hell didn't you stop him!' he shouted at us (I'm quite sure of this), and then he was off at a gallop through the trees, hot on the trail of the fleeing hog.

Somehow, we got Napoleon home, trotting proudly beside us as if he had rewritten history and single-handedly won the Battle of Waterloo. There was no sign of a limp, nor a trail of blood, but I dreaded to think what I would find when I cleaned him up. After he'd finished a celebration supper of diced black mamba, I armed myself with warm water and a sponge and began trying to dab him off, while Badge did cartwheels around the room. Ten minutes later, he was as good as new, clean as a whistle. Not a single drop had been his. Somewhere, far away by now, a little warthog was nursing his wounds.

'You're just trying to compete with my mouse,' Rich complained when we got home. 'Next time it will be a giraffe, and then he'll be next door looking for a bloody elephant.'

What a boy.

Chapter Twenty Three

When old Kephas Dube was herding his cattle among the koppies near the Hape river, he encountered an enormous black mamba. Twice more he found it in the same area, and now everyone knows the spot as Enyokeni, the place of the snake. Our larger rocky features have traditional names, like Dibe, the hill that looms over the house, and Dunu – both named after local chiefs – and, further east, the imposing Mahlalayedwa, the one that stands alone. We refer to many of the smaller koppies by particular incidents that have occurred there. Badge is responsible for Lizard Koppie on the edge of the Long Vlei, a great swathe of grass that sweeps down from the lodge into the rugged hills of the Pundamuka valley. It was here that he spent fruitless hours trying to extricate a plated lizard from a narrow crevice in the rock, where it had wedged itself firmly by inflating its body.

Khanye and I were discussing place names on our way home with Badge one October evening. In the worst of the heat, we had taken to fetching him after five o'clock and staying out later and later, which of course suited Badge's nocturnal inclinations very well indeed. About a kilometre from the house, when we could hear the generator and see the lights through the trees, he suddenly ducked off the path into the long grass, braked and came scuttling backwards, finishing up wrapped around my foot. If Badge was frightened, there had to be a good reason. Having recovered his composure, he released me and went in again, but this time more cautiously. Out of the grass, a two-metre Egyptian cobra reared up directly in front of him, maybe a foot off the ground, its hood spread. Badge was dicing with death, but I didn't try to call him away. He wouldn't have come, and any loss of concentration might have been fatal. Of course, badgers may well be immune to snake venom, but our boy wasn't going to be part of an experiment if I could help it. Badge pursued him silently, slowly forcing the snake to retreat, and all we could hear was a long, rushing hiss, enough to make your blood run cold. The snake struck and Badge dodged.

'It's after him!' Khanye whispered. The cobra dropped down into the grass and while we were peering into the gloom, it suddenly came up again, close to where we stood, with Badge a couple of feet in front of it, still harassing it, not sure what to do next, but instinctively knowing that this was a meal, albeit a rather tricky one.

'Rich shouldn't be missing this,' I said to Khanye. 'We should get him here with a torch and the video.'

'I'll go!' he replied, far too quickly, I thought.

'Nope, I go, Khanye,' I said firmly. 'Remember you're the scout, you've been trained for this sort of thing. Anyway, I'm not staying here in the dark with a furious snake.'

We never got to flipping a coin, because Badge

remembered that he had a far more convenient meal waiting for him at home. He left the snake, came up for his congratulatory hug, and trotted off victoriously, his tail flying high. After his breakfast the following morning, he tore off down the Long Vlei straight to the new Enyokeni, but naturally the cobra had gone, though perhaps not far. They're most active in the early mornings and evenings and, being very territorial, tend to use favourite termite mounds as a daytime retreat.

Badge tracked the snake for a while, retracing his route exactly from the night before, then lost interest and followed me as I began to climb the small koppie nearby. I was sure that I remembered seeing some paintings there long ago, so I began skirting it, checking the overhangs. One minute Badge was with me, the next an earth-shattering growl came blasting from deep inside the rocks and sent me flying backwards and to the top of the nearest boulder, where I almost collided with Khanye. But where was Badge? We shouted, clapped our hands, 'Badgie! Come on, Badgie Boy!', inducing another bout of ferocious snarls. Dust poured out of the hole. With one accord, we both turned and looked behind us; we were about five metres up over another pile of rocks, so there was no chance of jumping without breaking a leg. Oh, the silly things, you say. I was always complaining that we didn't see enough of our leopards, and here we were, unarmed, eight metres from an infuriated cat, shouting and clapping like maniacs. But we couldn't leave without our little boy. Ten minutes passed, fifteen, thirty – more deep-throated growls and more dust billowing out of a small hole that only a cat could have squeezed itself into.

'Badge must be trapped in there,' I said to Khanye.

'She's probably got cubs.' Guinness Book of Records or no, even Badger couldn't get out of this one. Every adrenalin-filled muscle in our bodies was urging us to run, but we were rooted to the spot, as dotty as a couple of old ladies inside a lion's den trying to rescue their chihuahua.

What a way for his life to end, I reflected; nobly to be sure, but so early. And what woeful foster parents we were – his own mother would have taken him away from trouble and made him aware of the danger. I'd led him straight into it.

'There he is!' I followed Khanye's finger, and indeed there he was, out in the open at last and looking very chipper. Thank God! Another toe-curling growl rumbled out of the cave. Surely Badge would rush back to us for safety, but oh no, not him. Like a pop star making a brief appearance on his balcony, he gave us a quick wave and disappeared – straight into the gap immediately next to the leopard's hideout.

'He's crazy,' I said.

'There has to be a kill,' said Khanye. 'Remember last time he did that – when you were away? He got stuck in a deep cave and I had to rescue him.'

'Yes,' I said, 'but the difference was that the leopard wasn't there that time.'

We climbed off our rock very gingerly and began looking around, keeping our eyes on the dreaded hole. There were at least five narrow entrances, all very close together. We could see a couple of feet in, at which point they disappeared steeply down into the darkness. Bones were littered around the outside of the cave: leopards had used this hideaway for years, undetected, until today when they'd finally been sprung by a small badger with nothing better to do than to stick his nose in where it wasn't wanted. I waited at one side of the entrance, and the next time Badge popped out for air, I was right there, arms out-stretched. 'Come on, darling,' I whispered urgently, 'come to Mum.' When he got within reach, I scooped him up and started off down the koppie. But thanks to Badge's desperate struggles to free himself, I tripped, gashed my leg on a rock, and dropped him on his head. And back he went to the leopard's lair, to be greeted by another bout of growling, amplified no doubt by the walls of his cave. Somehow, Badge must have got himself into a position very close to the big cat but out of his reach.

By the time Rich arrived an hour or so later, the growls had subsided into rasps.

'It doesn't sound like a leopard to me,' said Rich.

'Why ever *not*?' I said crossly. Khanye and I had been risking our lives trying to retrieve Badge from a potentially fatal situation, and now here was Rich playing down the glory. Just because he hadn't been there. 'Of course it's a leopard, what the hell else could it be? She's probably got a sore throat after all that growling.'

Rich was not deterred. 'It's not quite right,' he insisted. 'The sound's too rhythmic.'

'We've been listening to it for ages – it couldn't be anything else!' I turned to Khanye for support. 'Could it?'

He nodded, but not very emphatically.

After emerging briefly to say hello to his dad, Badge disappeared back into the caves for the rest of the day. And when we called him out for his afternoon walk, he was perfectly composed and even cockier than usual. Now we had an *Engweni*, the place of the leopard. Leopard Rock, I called it, after my old home in the Bvumba mountains, and that will always be its name, despite the fact that Khanye let me down badly a couple of months later.

He reported that Badgie had chased a porcupine into a cave. 'And guess what?' he said. 'The porcupine was roaring at him, and it was the same sound we heard that morning at Leopard Rock.'

Despite my disappointment at the death of a good story, it was a relief that Badge's reputation for fearlessness hadn't led him to a leopard's lair, for it would have been a confrontation that he certainly would have lost. Badgers often fall prey to both lions and leopards, but not without inflicting some nasty injuries on their attackers.

Badgers, it appears, are silent hunters and killers – and very sensible, too. You don't want to draw any unwelcome attention when you are on the verge of procuring your next meal.

But at all other times, they have the knack of being able to tell you exactly how they feel at both ends. Depending on their mood, they growl, whimper, whine, chirp, rattle or roar from the front and may release a noxious pong from the rear if you upset them. Less intimidating but equally as telling, their tail is a banner, giving one an immediate clue as to the state of the nation. Flying high, he's full of his own importance; half-mast, *comme çi comme ça*; and held low when he's out in the open and vulnerable, belly to the ground, desperately trying to avoid the attentions of a larger predator.

Human beings are compulsive talkers: Rich and I have lived and worked together for nearly 25 years, but we still feel the need to keep on chatting. Of course, it's fine when *we* do it, because *we* are discussing important issues, but infuriating when you are trying to work or have a few quiet minutes with the bushbuck, and the guests at the lodge are all crowded on the veranda, yelling at each other and screaming with laughter.

And if I'm out on the farm alone, I find talking to myself is so much more companionable than merely thinking. 'It's the first sign of madness,' we told each other at school, so it was a great relief to find that I could hold a two-way conversation with Badger. He's always far too busy to be wasting his time on trivialities, and tends to ignore me when I gurgle on about beautiful mornings and gorgeous sunsets, but he constantly tells me what he is doing and how he is feeling. And though I wouldn't be able to distinguish the sounds if they were played back to me minus the Badger, when they are combined with his body language, I understand them perfectly.

As soon as his confidence grew a little, he insisted on always taking the lead on walks, and I'm quite agreeable that he should act as advance snake-spotter. When he was very young, he chirped non-stop to tell us that all was well and he was a happy Badge. The chirp, too, is a way of keeping in contact when we lose each other on dark nights, or should I say, we lose sight of Badge. 'I'm over here!' he calls, and we chirp back to let him know that we have heard.

Then there's the excited churr he makes when he's in the middle of digging up a mouse. 'Getting closer, I'm really on to it now!' And the disappointed one, when after all that work his quarry has escaped. Once he has consumed his mouse, scorpion or other unfortunate inhabitant, he often lays claim to the hole by plonking his bottom over it and widdling, or even defecating, which Khanye compares to a schoolboy spitting on his loaf of bread to stop his friends from pinching it. Only a boy would do that.

Badge has a chirp for every occasion, some low, some higher-pitched; and there's the weedy whine accompanied by a wrinkled nose: 'I want my apple *now*', at the end of the morning walk, or 'pick me up, I'm tired', or 'I don't want to go that way, it isn't time to go home yet!' Fortunately, we have rarely heard his full-throated roar since he was little, and he never growls at us except in play or if we get too close to his food.

When he was still the Carpet-Chewing Badge of the Boudoir, Nige and he invented a special bedtime game, which often got completely out of hand. Badge would disappear through a hole in the tarpaulin (that was meant to protect the carpet), and when he was tunnelling his way around the room, Nige would put his fingers through another hole and waggle them. Immediately, the lump under the tarp would shift direction, and like an orca closing in after a Patagonian seal, Badge would surge along and burst out with a loud *tjak!*, mouth wide open, to savage Nige's fingers, hand or any other bit of bare flesh that presented itself.

In fact, no task was ever so absorbing that Badge wouldn't stop midway to come over and give you a bite, probably to convey his frustration that you weren't helping him dig his hole or turn over a log.

When his tummy was full, he sometimes lost interest in hunting and picked up a stick to start a game. But before you could join in, you had to ascertain just how much value its owner put on this particular stick. If Badge trotted over and laid it at your feet, like a Labrador presenting you with a pheasant, this was your invitation to participate.

Games were normally played according to the badger, but in one game of rugby, Rich made the rules. Badge dug up a large tuft of grass, hugged it to his tummy, and rolled around, daring Rich to try and take it from him.

After a few preliminary pats to test the water, so to speak, Rich made a grab at the tuft and swung it up in the air. As Badgie danced around him, Rich threw it into the river, whereupon his opponent waded in, plucked it out of the water and ran off, with Rich in hot pursuit. When Rich caught up with him and managed to retrieve the tuft, Badge ran straight back to the water's edge, inviting him to throw it back in. They repeated this game a few times, until Badge suddenly ran to the top of the riverbank and sat there guarding his tuft.

'No, Badger,' Rich told him. 'That's out of bounds. Bring it back into play.'

And with that, he came straight back to the same spot as before and the game continued – according to the rules.

He was snuffling about underneath a fig tree one evening, while Rich sat on a low branch with his feet resting on a rock.

'After a while, he came over very sweetly to say hello and sat on my shoe, dear little chap,' Rich told me that evening. 'I was busy fiddling with my camera equipment, when I felt a claw hooked inside it. I pulled away quickly but the shoe came off – and Badger mantled over it, daring me to challenge him. I tried dragging it away with my toe but he roared, making it quite clear that I would probably lose my foot if I persisted.'

Rich grabbed a stick and tickled Badgie's bum, and as he turned, Rich snatched at the shoe.

'Well, that was a silly thing to do,' I remarked, receiving a glare from my husband. 'You know how possessive he gets.'

To a honey badger forbidden fruits are the most appealing things in the world, and though fruity is not the description *I* would give to Rich's shoes, Badge knew immediately that he was on to something really good. Grasping the shoe in his mouth, he took off at a trot into the trees, head held high.

'He kept tripping over it,' said Rich, 'and every time he stumbled, he growled, convinced that I was somehow to blame.'

Cursing at the thorns jabbing into his bare foot, Rich hobbled after Badge, who took refuge in a narrow slot between two rocks. With a long stout stick in his hand, he climbed on to the rocks immediately above Badger. After a bit of manoeuvring, he managed to insert the end of the stick into the heel of the shoe, and slowly lever it out of the crack – with Badge still attached to the other end. And just as Rich heaved them both into the air, Badge gave a quick shake of his head and tumbled to the ground, jaws still clamped around his prize.

Rich was stymied. 'He took off at a hell of a pace, with Nandi chasing him, looking very virtuous because she knew he'd done something naughty. I followed them to a koppie about 150 metres away, and he disappeared into a small hole in the rocks and didn't come out. Then I limped the two kilometres home, dragging all my camera equipment. They were my most comfortable shoes. *Bugger* Badger.' I've said it before, B is such a useful letter.

As our bond with him grew stronger, Badge felt less inclined to spend his days alone, particularly if it was me who was deserting him. He was probably starting to make unfavourable comparisons between his Spartan hideouts in the rocks and his snug little box in the spare bedroom. Rich began leaving half an apple for him as a goodbye gesture at the end of the walk, which Badge would usually accept, but if I was trying to slip away, he'd often abandon the apple and slink after me. Poor little adolescent Badge, torn between family and independence.

We had given him the freedom to go wild but he wasn't ready for that, and we wondered if he ever would be. And what would total independence mean? The Beggs had discovered that the home range of their male Kalahari badgers was an incredible 600 to 800 square kilometres. Our granite hills were more hospitable than the desert, but our resident badgers were still likely to range over huge distances, particularly when on the scent of a female. And when badgers are hungry, as in every minute of the day, they get into trouble. Big Trouble. They steal chickens, they muscle in on the baits hung by hunters to attract leopards, and the hunters shoot them. Then there are those unmentionable people who will kill a badger for fun, because they are just a pest, after all, and put them in a corner of their trophy room, so they can tell stories about their encounter with the meanest animal in the world – thanks to Robert Ruark. Or put him in a cage where he can die of loneliness and boredom while people peer at him through the wire.

And things were changing around us. Since 2000, people had been moving on to commercial farms all over the country, building their huts and planting crops. Where once we were surrounded by silence, now, on a clear night, we could sometimes hear the sound of cattle bells and barking dogs: spelling danger to a wandering badger. We may not be a desert, but survival in the Matobo hills is still a tough call. We knew that Badger would eventually go off on all sorts of adventures that would lead him far away, but if he could always be sure of a meal and a warm welcome, there was every chance he would continue to use us as his base.

We'd had a particularly miserable walk one winter's

morning when Badge was eight months old. The sky was an inky black and the wind was tearing at the trees, so Badge very sensibly amused himself by exploring the porcupine cave, and being thoroughly scolded by the dassies who were sheltering there. At around 8 am he took himself off into the rocks and when he had disappeared I began to walk home. I could almost taste that first spoonful of hot porridge topped with dark brown sugar. Five minutes later Badge was crying at my heels. He led me back to the porcupine cave and began rolling around with a stick: an invitation to play. If I'd joined in, I wouldn't get breakfast *or* lunch, so instead, I rather callously turned my back and waited for him to get bored. Half an hour later, he was still playing but less noisily. The sun suddenly appeared through a hole in the clouds, the wind dropped to a breeze, and at last I could feel my feet, as the first warmth of the day began to seep into me. When I glanced over my shoulder, Badge had turned his back. He was wriggling around as he did when he was getting comfortable, and waving his legs in the air, but less and less as he became sleepier.

Badge captivated everyone who met him; not merely because he was funny and affectionate and adored the attention, but mostly because he had all the qualities we admire in other human beings: courage, loyalty, humour, determination – and absolute honesty. How many of us can measure up to that? The word 'failure' doesn't feature in a honey badger's vocabulary; though he would sometimes fall into my lap for a bit of comfort after an abortive hunt, Badge would perk up again in minutes, ready to slip his fingers surreptitiously into the side of a shoe or trot off after an interesting smell.

And if one small, secretive creature can teach us so

much, shouldn't we treat every other animal with respect and awe, realising that we know so pitifully little about any of them? We waste so much time trying to understand ourselves, when the real miracles are all around us, if only we would open our minds.

Looking back at Badge, I felt overwhelmed with love and tenderness for this vulnerable little creature who had lost everything meaningful in his life, but given us so much. It could have been so different: *if* his mother had left him in the den on the day she met her end; *if* Mike hadn't mentioned us to the safari operator's wife, he would have died and no one would have cared or known what they had lost. Badger had enriched our lives beyond all expectations and given us an undreamed-of opportunity to see the world through his eyes. Poombi had left us with the keys to the kingdom and he had opened another door into this magical place, another connection to all who live on Stone Hills.

And so I left him, happily sucking his toes in the sunshine, and gradually falling asleep.

Epilogue

Over three years have passed since that winter's morning, and although much has changed around us, we still wake to the sun rising over the Pundamuka valley. It hasn't been easy, but we are learning not to let our anxieties overwhelm us. For when you are armed and waiting for one disaster to come galloping around the corner, something else, completely unexpected, is sure to be sliding under the back door.

Against all the odds, Zimbabwe continues to stagger from one calamity to the next. In Binga, one of the country's poorest areas, villagers are said to be surviving on a mixture of water and dry cow dung. And it is no better in the cities. The criminal neglect of water supplies and every other part of our infrastructure has led to another tragedy. Raw sewage runs through our streets, and to date there have been over 10,000 reported cases of cholera, an epidemic that is now spreading across our borders.

Cholera and people – Zimbabwe's two most unwelcome exports.

In Johannesburg, the guard in the parking mall runs

after us yelling: 'Zimbabwe? Where from?' 'Plumtree,' we tell him.

'Hey!' he shouts, 'me too!' He grabs our hands and pumps them through the open window. 'Ah, take me home!'

Millions have been forced to leave the country as economic refugees; most of them live under appalling conditions in South Africa, trying to earn something to send home to the family. And those who are better off – who migrated to Australia or New Zealand – so often keep their homes, even if they can ill afford it, because they hope they'll be back some day, 'when things come right', knowing in their hearts that this may never happen.

But there is another side to the story, the one you don't hear about on the news. That bond, for instance, that grows between people in troubled times; the courage and unfailing good humour of the ordinary Zimbabwean; and the fact that, although most schools have closed, the teachers at Marula Primary carry on doing their jobs, even though they don't earn enough in a month for their bus fare home to Bulawayo.

'What can we do?' says Mrs Dube, their stalwart headmistress. 'Nothing.' She waves her bible at me. 'But, I'm telling you, God will prevail!' (Oh, how I regret the day I admitted to being an infidel....)

And then there's the miracle that happens every year – that day, one week after the first rains, when once again we hear its heartbeat and feel Stone Hills stretching under our feet and coming to life: a resurrection more poignant this year than ever before.

A double rainbow plunged down on to the rocks in front of the house, drenching them in a brilliant light. And in the evening, its colours seemed to melt into the sky, as it turned from a pale blue to a dark, smoky pink within the rainbow's arch. I tell myself the same thing every year: if I were given only one day to live, this would be it.

A trio of wobbly-legged warthog piglets jostle and play in the emerald grass, at their mother's heels. I reckon I must be a great-grandmother many times over by now.

For the birds, the race is on. All day long, they are whizzing back and forth, beaks full of nesting material or food for their chicks. They're not weighing up whether it's safe to lay their eggs this year, wondering whether next year might be better; they're just getting on with the job.

The meaning of life, I once read, is simply – life. No more, no less. If only we understood that as well as the animals do.

For us, the only way to deal with the situation is take refuge in the positive wherever we can find it and, on Stone Hills, there is still so much that gives us joy and hope – like Poombi and Badger, and all those other wild animals who have so freely given us their trust and love.

Countless wild animals throughout Zimbabwe have been the silent victims of lawlessness, hunger and corruption. The bigger picture is beyond us; all we can do is to take care of those within our boundaries who look to us for their protection and survival.

If they are to have a future, it lies with the children of this country – like the Grade 6s and 7s at Marula School who crowd into Khanye's weekly conservation classes, and have made Boney M's 'Don't Kill the World' their theme song. This year, they entered a competition sponsored by the UK-based Marwell Trust called *Living with Cheetahs*. They wrote essays and poems, and under Rich's supervision, created a life-sized model of a cheetah, using scrap wire, dry grass, old plastic bags, papier mâché, and the seeds of the wait-a-bit thorn for its eyes. They won – of course.

Late in November, they spent an afternoon here building erosion barriers with rocks and branches. And in the evening, at our annual party, each child received a certificate to say that they had completed our conservation course. In the background was a picture of Badge, and the words *Ubenjengo Linda – Unqine – Uhlakaniphe – Ubelesibindi*: Be like the Badger – be strong, be brave, be clever.

Stone Hills often feels like an island perched on the tip of a powerful and malevolent volcano – sometimes it roars and rattles the windows of the house. But nothing disturbs the peace of the everlasting hills; for like the summer storms that sweep across their heads year after year, this, too, must pass.

Our lives may change tomorrow, but until they do, Rich will keep filming and taking his magnificent photographs, and I'll keep writing about Stone Hills: trying to fix this precious place in my mind, so I can remember all of it when one day we are no longer here.

The meaning of life – is life. Let's celebrate it where we can.

December 2008
Bookey Peek

Formidable

Contented

...and fulfilled

Baby in the house

A world of surprises

Intrepid explorer

Living on the edge

Shoe thief

Fascination

Mafira Chanyungunya

Richard Mabhena

Frank Ncube

Jabulani Khanye

Ruthie and Beatrice